Reforming Women

Composition, Literacy, and Culture

David Bartholomae and Jean Ferguson Carr, Editors

Reforming Women

The Rhetorical Tactics
of the American Female Moral Reform Society,
1834–1854

Lisa J. Shaver

University of Pittsburgh Press

Published by the University of Pittsburgh Press, Pittsburgh, Pa., 15260
Copyright © 2018, University of Pittsburgh Press
All rights reserved
Manufactured in the United States of America
Printed on acid-free paper
10 9 8 7 6 5 4 3 2 1

Cataloging-in-Publication data is available from the Library of Congress

ISBN 13: 978-0-8229-6548-0
ISBN 10: 0-8229-6548-8

Cover art: "Ohio Whiskey War." Illustration courtesy of the Ohio History Connection, AL04188
Cover design: Melissa Dias-Mandoly

For my mother, Ann Shaver, who understood the importance
of women's organizations.

Contents

Acknowledgments

Even though one name appears on the cover, a manuscript is always a group effort. I am indebted to so many people for their assistance and encouragement throughout this project. Initially, I assumed my exploration of the American Female Moral Reform Society (AFMRS) would end with a couple of articles, yet when I had the opportunity to teach graduate courses on women's rhetoric, I discovered that my students were enthralled by this group. Students had never heard about antebellum female moral reformers, and they made so many intriguing contemporary connections. Their enthusiasm encouraged me to introduce the AFMRS and its rhetorical tactics to other individuals studying women's rhetoric.

I am especially indebted to Jane Greer and Liz Tasker Davis. When I was in the early stages of writing this book, I was assigned to a writing group with these two amazing women at the Rhetoric Society of America (RSA) career retreat held in conjunction with the RSA conference in San Antonio in 2014. Since then, Jane and Liz have read much of this book in five-page increments. They have offered invaluable feedback, suggestions, encouragement, and accountability. Indeed, their fingerprints are all over this manuscript, and I am so grateful for their brilliance and especially their friendship. Additionally, I have received generative feedback from Kate Adams, Mike DePalma, Nan Johnson, Kelly Ritter, Jan Swearingen, Wendy Sharer, and anonymous reviewers, who read drafts of this manuscript and the two articles that contributed to it.

I have also benefited from tremendous institutional support, which included a summer sabbatical and a research leave from Baylor University. The Baylor University Library's Interlibrary Loan staff also helped me locate numerous materials essential to this project. I am also grateful to the American Antiquarian Society and the Oberlin College Archives for their assistance in obtaining images. Portions of chapter 2 originally appeared in "'Serpents,' 'Fiends,' and 'Libertines': Inscribing an Evangelical Rhetoric of Rage in the *Advocate of Moral Reform*," which was published in *Rhetoric Review*'s January 2011 issue (used by permission of Taylor and Francis). Portions of chapter 3 originally appeared in "'No Cross, No Crown': An Ethos of Presence in Margaret Prior's Walks of Usefulness," which was published in *College English*'s September 2012 issue (copyright 2012 by the National Council of Teachers of English. Used with permission).

I also want to thank my friends and colleagues in Baylor University's English Department. I am also grateful to my colleagues in the Rhetoric and Composition field, especially my dear friends Cristy Beemer, Suzanne Bordelon, Sarah Bowles, Jen Cellio, Abby Dubisar, Liz Mackey, and Kate Ronald. My family and friends outside of the academy are also a constant source of encouragement and support. They, along with my loyal four-legged companion, Wylie, refuse to let me take myself too seriously.

These early reforming women possessed tremendous determination and grit. I hope you find them as inspiring as I have.

Reforming Women

Introduction

Resonating Rhetoric

Resolved, That the same amount of virtue, delicacy, and refinement of behavior, that is required of woman in the social state, should also be required of man, and the same transgressions should be visited with equal severity on both man and woman.

—Declaration of Sentiments and Resolutions, 1848

This is the sixth of twelve resolutions ratified at the Seneca Falls Convention in 1848. In what would become a manifesto for the women's rights movement, the *Declaration of Sentiments and Resolutions*, presented in Seneca Falls, New York, cited men's numerous injustices against women. These included depriving women of the right to vote; denying women the facilities for obtaining a thorough education; precluding women from profitable employments and; if married, ceding complete control of a woman's property, wages, and, physical well-being to her husband. Among their list of injustices, these early women's rights advocates also included society's different code of moral conduct for men and women. Whereas premarital and extramarital sex was customarily ignored or tolerated in men, when revealed, it had devastating consequences for nineteenth-century women. So-called ruined women were often banned from respectable society. They forfeited advantageous marriage prospects and the possibility of working as a governess or teacher. Some women were even disowned by family members.

Scholars usually trace the origins of the Seneca Falls Convention and the *Declaration of Sentiments and Resolutions* to the antislavery movement, and with good reason. Women's involvement in the antislavery cause had highlighted their limited rights. When they dared to speak publicly against slavery before audiences of men and women, Angelina and Sarah Grimké faced opposition and violence. And even though they were elected delegates to the World's Anti-Slavery Convention in London in 1840, Elizabeth Cady Stanton and Lucretia Mott were prohibited from participating. So it is not surprising that eight years later Stanton and Mott collaborated with Matilda Gage, Martha Coffin Wright, and Mary Ann McClintock to write the *Declaration of Sentiments and Resolutions*. Clearly women's involvement in antislavery organizations was a strong motivation in the early women's rights efforts; however, the sixth resolution proposed and confirmed at Seneca Falls points to another movement—female moral reform—and its influence on women's rights.

Fourteen years prior to that fateful meeting in Seneca Falls, the New York Female Moral Reform Society organized in New York City in 1834. Quickly expanding to a national movement, the group changed its name to the American Female Moral Reform Society (AFMRS) in 1839.[1] In fact, the AFMRS became the first national reform movement organized, led, and comprised predominately by women. As such, it offers a portent of rhetorical moves and messages women would use to advocate for women's rights throughout the nineteenth century.

Calls for moral reform arose in response to the rapid influx of people into the country's industrializing cities and the growing visibility and seeming acceptance of prostitution, brothels, and lascivious behavior. The historian Larry Whiteaker defines moral reform as the "restoration and protection of moral purity."[2] He notes that while other activities such as gambling, drinking, swearing, attending the theater, and reading titillating novels were often characterized as sins and vices, the term *moral reform* was reserved for *sexual behavior* deemed immoral.[3] Private citizens in New York City had launched various moral reform initiatives aimed at prostitution and to uphold the seventh scriptural commandment, "Thou shalt not commit adultery." Although women had played integral roles in these earlier endeavors, they eventually became frustrated with male city and church leaders' reluctance to boldly combat rampant licentiousness. In the first issue of their periodical, the *Advocate of Moral Reform (AMR)*, the women argue that "religious editors will not bring the subject before the public in such a manner as to warrant much hope" and that they are forced to do this work because men "will not do it."[4]

With the formation of the AFMRS, women took matters into their own hands and eventually decided that they were better suited to the cause of moral reform than men. Using its periodical as the primary vehicle of reform, the

AFMRS sought to educate, warn, and galvanize women. With the scriptural passage "For there is nothing covered that shall not be revealed; neither hid that shall not be made known,"[5] prominently displayed on the *Advocate*'s masthead, the AFMRS took aim at immoral behavior, particularly the double standard that overlooked promiscuous behavior in men while harshly condemning women for the same offense. In the *Advocate*'s first issue, the AFMRS ardently reminds readers: "No effort need be made to fasten disgrace upon the licentious woman; she is disgraced already, and effectually shut out from all communication with the virtuous of the other sex: but the licentious man, as guilty and polluted as the woman is still permitted to move in respectable society."[6] Statements such as these, openly expressing women's frustration, resonated with women in and beyond New York City.

By 1840 the *Advocate* was one of the era's most widely distributed reform periodicals. And by 1841 the AFMRS had 555 auxiliary societies stretching from Maine to the Wisconsin Territory—representing more than 50,000 women.[7] The AFMRS's membership included several female reformers. Lucretia Mott—an abolitionist, Quaker preacher, and one of the organizers of the Seneca Falls Convention—belonged to an AFMRS auxiliary society in Philadelphia. Lucy Stone—an abolitionist and women's rights activist, and Antoinette Brown (Blackwell)—also an abolitionist and women's rights activist and the first American woman ordained as a minister, served as officers for the large, active AFMRS auxiliary society at Oberlin College.[8] Most members of the New England AFMRS auxiliary were also members of the Boston Female Anti-Slavery Society,[9] and even Seneca Falls, New York, had its own AFMRS auxiliary. This lineage alone indicates the AFMRS's influence on later women's reform efforts.

"Moral reform," claims the historian Patricia Cohen, "was one of the more controversial strains of social activism to arise in a decade suffused with radical movements." Daniel Wright argues that it was "a feminized movement, not only in membership, but in leadership and agenda." Carroll Smith Rosenberg also claims that female moral reformers "were among the very first American women to challenge their completely passive, home-oriented image" and "create a broad, less constricted sense of female identity."[10] Moral reformers were upset with moral and economic double standards for men and women. They were also driven by deeply held religious beliefs that were bolstered by the religious fervor of the Second Great Awakening. In churches and revivals, especially Charles Finney's crusades throughout the Northeast, predominately female crowds heard an urgent call for Christians to save their country. This call to Christian activism, which drove numerous social reform efforts, was especially evident in abolition, temperance, and moral reform. Of these three movements, moral reform remains somewhat obscure to rhetoricians. While historians, including Wright, Rosenberg, Whiteaker, Anne Boylan, and Barbara Berg, have studied the female reform movement, it has received relatively little attention from scholars in women's rhetorical history. This is likely due to the AFMRS's lack of a prominent public speaker and its reliance on gender appropriate rhetorical tactics.

Discussions of women's reform efforts often center on courageous and dynamic public speakers who are repeatedly anthologized. Indeed, scholarly examinations of women's antislavery efforts frequently center on Sarah and Angelina Grimké, Lucretia Mott, and Sojourner Truth. Likewise, much of the attention on women's temperance has focused on Frances Willard, the Women's Christian Temperance Union's (WCTU) defining leader, even though Carol Mattingly convincingly shows that the WCTU acted as an empowering rhetorical force for groups of women across the country.[11] Wendy Sharer acknowledges that histories of rhetoric tend to privilege individuals rather than collective rhetorical action.[12] For women, this tendency is particularly limiting considering that nineteenth-century women participated in countless benevolent, evangelical, social aid, and reform societies and movements. Indeed, the historian Anne Firor Scott asserts that female reformers "exhibited a strong propensity to form all-women organizations, which they could run to suit themselves."[13] In short, nineteenth-century women acted, and they usually chose to act together.

Reforming Women, which focuses on the AFMRS's rhetorical tactics, helps address this scholarly void on women's collective rhetorical action. In doing so, it adds to the valuable work by other scholars in women's rhetorical history who have examined nineteenth-century women's organizations and reform movements including Carol Mattingly, Anne Ruggles Gere, Shirley Wilson Logan, and Susan Zaeske.[14] The AFMRS had numerous strong female leaders, including longtime president Mary Anne Hawkins, who helped found the AFMRS and served as its president for more than thirty-five years; Margaret Prior, the first female city missionary for the AFMRS, who I discuss in more detail in chapter 3, and Sarah Ingraham (later Sarah Bennett), who helped organize auxiliaries, served as corresponding secretary, compiled Hawkins's and Prior's memoirs, and edited the *Advocate* for thirty-five years. Yet in the pages of the *Advocate*, these leaders subsumed their individual identities, efforts, and accomplishments within the group, which itself can be viewed as a feminine rhetorical tactic.

AFMRS leaders and members relied almost exclusively on what Lindal Buchanan refers to as "feminine delivery styles." Female moral reformers selected conventional, gender-appropriate means of influence, including written media, speaking in domestic settings, and speaking before groups of women. Buchanan notes that feminine delivery styles have garnered far less attention than those women who spoke, lectured, and debated before mixed assemblies—relying on masculine delivery styles. Moreover, she calls for scholarly recognition of feminine delivery styles and how they enabled women to participate in public discourse. As opposed to masculine delivery methods, which "initially created considerable resistance and controversy," feminine methods of delivery allowed women to "express their ideas in a nonthreatening, indirect manner."[15]

Reforming Women answers this call through an in-depth examination of rhetorical tactics employed by the AFMRS. Specifically, I examine the AFMRS's use of gender, the periodical press, anger, presence, auxiliary societies, and institutional rhetoric. Each of these tactics contributed to women's ethos and affirmed their rightful role as social reformers. In using the term *tactic*, I am drawing on some of the distinctions between strategies and tactics that French theorist Michel de Certeau describes in *The Practice of Everyday Life* to emphasize the rhetorical challenges antebellum female moral reformers faced. According to de Certeau, "a tactic is an art of the weak"; it "is determined by the absence of power just as a strategy is organized by the postulation of power." Moreover, he explains that tactics are "imposed" and "organized" by those in power.[16] Whereas strategies are the purview of those in power, tactics are adaptations by those without power—in this instance, women. "Constrained by law and custom, and denied access to most of the major institutions by which the society governed itself and created its culture," Scott notes that women "used voluntary associations to evade some of these constraints and to redefine 'woman's place.'"[17] Working collectively within this controlled environment, female moral reformers also adapted those rhetorical tactics that were available to them such as publishing periodicals, house-to-house visits, and forming auxiliary societies. Here, it is important to specify that I am referring to the rhetorical means available to white, middle-class women. While the AFMRS's membership was more diverse than women's benevolent organizations, the movement was primarily led and made up of middle-class, white women.[18]

For the AFMRS, gender-appropriate rhetorical tactics became especially important. AFMRS members not only gravitated toward these tactics, they made them their own, and women reformers repeatedly used these tactics throughout the nineteenth century. Additionally, de Certeau notes that tactics are timely, opportunistic, and agile. This type of adjustment in tactics is evident in the AFMRS's rhetoric; as they gained a more in-depth understanding of the underlying causes of prostitution and other social problems facing women and children, they shifted from moral suasion to circulating petitions and establishing an institution.

My examination of the AFMRS carefully outlines rhetorical tactics the group employed from its subjected position. I show those tactics available to women, how they acquired them, and why they were drawn to them. To examine these tactics, I rely primarily on the *Advocate*, which was produced, sold, and distributed by AFMRS members, and operated as the society's main vehicle of reform. It was in the *Advocate* that the AFMRS explained why it had to take up the fight for reform and why women were better suited to the cause. It was in the *Advocate* that women expressed a righteous anger and railed against societal double standards. It was in the *Advocate* that city missionaries described the heart-wrenching scenes they encountered in New York City's poorest neighborhoods. It was in the *Advocate* that auxiliary societies proudly announced their formation, shared their local efforts, and exchanged ideas. And when the AFMRS decided to build an institution to provide refuge to young women and children, the *Advocate* became a means of raising funds, locating respectable jobs for women, and finding foster and adoptive homes for children.[19]

During the nineteenth century, publishing periodicals was a vital rhetorical tactic for female reformers, enabling them to create a public space and control it. In her foundational study of women's reform periodicals, Bertha-Monica Stearns notes from 1830 to 1860, "a group of periodicals definitely addressed to women, and very largely edited by women, *clamored loudly for some Right, or agitated vigorously against some Abuse.*"[20] For women, periodicals were both an accessible and a socially accepted way to engage in public debates. For female reformers they provided a way to establish ethos, create awareness, promote a cause to a broad audience, and attract supporters.

My in-depth analysis of the AFMRS's periodical also reveals the feminist rhetorical practice of *social circulation*. Social circulation is one of four critical terms of engagement that Jacqueline Jones Royster and Gesa Kirsch identify in *Feminist Rhetorical Practices: New Horizons for Rhetoric, Composition, and Literacy Studies*. Royster and Kirsch explain, "The notion of social circulation invokes connections among past, present, and future." Furthermore, they note social circulation operates as a "metaphor that helps us imagine the ways in which women's rhetorical activities take on different meanings in different contexts across time and space."[21] My study of the AFMRS and the periodical it produced highlights the rich array of rhetorical tactics that female moral reformers used to communicate, connect, educate, organize, equip, and embolden women in their own movement as well as reform movements throughout the nineteenth century. I show both how female moral reformers linked their work to other religious and benevolent efforts and organizations, and how contemporary scholars can do likewise. Looking at women's rhetorical efforts before and after moral reform is important because nineteenth-century women's societies did not follow any linear progression from women promoting benevolent causes to women pursuing feminist agendas.[22] Social circulation also helps us draw connections with female moral reformers today. In their periodical, these women circulated ideas as well as their anger, frustration, and despair at inequitable social and economic systems that judged women differently than men and often consigned women and children to poverty.

These problems still exist more than 170 years later, and these women's raw emotions still resonate and circulate in classrooms. In my women's rhetoric courses, our study of the AFMRS and readings from the *Advocate* generate passionate discussions. Students point to different moral expectations for men and women that still exist today—contemporary sex trafficking, genital mutilation, so-called honor killings, sexual harassment in workplaces, the epidemic of sexual assaults on U.S. college campuses, and female rape victims who are routinely accused of inciting the violence against them. Sadly, the list goes on and on. Clearly there is powerful rhetorical force in words and actions that motivate us to critically analyze today's inequities and conclude that we are still struggling to achieve the sixth resolution presented at Seneca Falls. Ultimately, *Reforming Women* connects us to this rich rhetorical legacy.

Reforming Women concentrates on the AFMRS's first twenty years, 1835–1855, which led to the establishment of its Home for the Friendless, which remained open for 128 years. The book's chapters are organized around rhetorical tactics that were essential to the female moral reform movement and to women's reform movements throughout the nineteenth century: gendering, publishing periodicals, expressing anger, using presence, mobilizing auxiliary societies, and employing institutional rhetoric to establish and manage institutions.

Chapter 1, "Gendering Moral Reform," shows how women applied the fluid concept of gender to gain license to pursue moral reform. Defining gendering as women's strategic use of the societal gender distinctions assigned to them to garner ethos and assume power, this chapter describes the complex rhetorical situation out of which moral reform arose. Factors contributing to this included New York City's ascension as America's center of commerce, the rapid influx of workers from rural America and Europe, limited economic opportunities and low wages for women, and ineffectual laws and law enforcement. Out of these emerged a vibrant sex trade—most notably, rampant prostitution. In response, private citizens launched various rescue and moral reform initiatives. Most of these efforts were short-lived; however, the group that persevered, the AFMRS, was comprised of women. Ultimately, in claiming that moral reform was a gendered movement, this chapter explains why women were more willing and motivated to pursue moral reform and how they laid claim to this work.

Chapter 2, "Radiating Righteous Anger in the *Advocate of Moral Reform*," shows how both anger and publishing periodicals became important rhetorical tactics for female reformers. The AFMRS initially used its periodical to draw attention to immoral acts perpetrated against women and to rally supporters to their cause. Specifically this chapter shows how the AFMRS used its periodical to create a public forum for women, publicly censure male philanders, claim moral authority and agency, condemn certain social narratives while exploiting others, and to encourage education and vigilance. Through its periodical AFMRS members also did something respectable nineteenth-century women rarely did—they expressed their anger. While moral reform enabled women to enact their Christian beliefs, it also provided a cathartic release for the frustration and anger many felt. Nonetheless, to avoid being summarily dismissed as radicals, moral reformers had to maintain a tenuous balance between their anger and the social respectability that was essential to their ethos and effectiveness. In this chapter, I show how AFMRS members managed this balance by strategically using their periodical to situate their anger within an evangelical framework that disassociated this anger from themselves to their duties as God's emissaries and Christian mothers.

Chapter 3, "Being Present," examines presence as an essential rhetorical tactic used by nineteenth-century women. By examining missionary reports written by Margaret Prior, the AFMRS's first female city missionary, this chapter delineates an ethos of presence. Prior's missionary reports show the diverse ways her presence contributed to her actions, reputation, and relationships, and also demonstrated her compassion and Christian beliefs. Through her presence, which occurred during what tract and benevolent societies commonly referred to as "walks of usefulness," Prior argued that New York City's poorest neighborhoods and their residents were worthy of attention and assistance.

Chapter 4, "Igniting Auxiliary Power," describes how auxiliary societies became an essential rhetorical tactic in women's reform efforts. Women traditionally formed auxiliary societies to local religious and benevolent organizations established by their husbands or male relatives. They also formed auxiliary societies to large male-dominated, national federations such as the American Bible Society. The AFMRS similarly recognized the vital role of auxiliary organizations, and by 1841 had successfully mobilized more than five hundred auxiliaries. Drawing from auxiliary society reports published in the *Advocate*, this chapter details how auxiliaries became a means of advocacy for women, a mutually affirming network, a source of financial support, a means of geographic expansion, and a site for women's rhetorical education. Moreover, it shows how auxiliary societies gave women guidance and license to act as well as the freedom to choose their own actions.

Chapter 5, "Establishing an Institution," claims that founding institutions became a rhetorical tactic for nineteenth-century women by outlining the institutional rhetoric the AFMRS used to construct and support its Home for the Friendless. While the AFMRS's first impulse was pursuing broad social reform through moral suasion, as the movement matured, it determined that opening an institution was a more pragmatic means for exacting change. Through an analysis of the AFMRS's institutional rhetoric, this chapter shows the group's shift from moral reformers to guardians. Its examination of institutional rhetoric looks at both the strategic messages the AFMRS used in its communications about its Home for the Friendless as well as how the home operated symbolically and became an important rhetorical resource for the AFMRS. The chapter also shows that AFMRS members did not completely relinquish their roles as reformers. Instead, they turned their attention to social issues they encountered through their work as institutional managers.

In a brief epilogue, I conclude this study by returning to this sixth resolution in *Declaration of Sentiments and Resolutions*. I claim female moral reformers' demand for a single moral standard is still far from resolved—pointing to many ways that the gendered double standard in moral behavior manifests itself in society today,

Female moral reformers wrangled with methods deemed acceptable and unacceptable. While they relied exclusively on gender-appropriate means, they pushed those boundaries in progressive ways that still speak to us today. In their periodical they adopted a direct, confrontational tone that often targeted men and male-led institutions, including churches and state legislatures. Their candid, unapologetic discussions of sexual licentiousness breached longstanding social taboos. Moreover, they openly expressed their anger at male infidelity—an unseemly act for women at the time. In that sense, the early years of the AFMRS can be viewed as a turning point and precursor of nineteenth-century women's reform. And even though some of their tactics, such as publishing a periodical, circulating petitions, or even establishing a national organization, were not new for male-led reform movements, for women in the 1830s, these overt methods of social change were revolutionary.[23]

Reforming Women claims that the AFMRS has much to teach us about American women's rhetorical history by showing us the ways *most* women encountered and enacted the myriad of women-led reform efforts that were pursued throughout the nineteenth century. The AFMRS's rhetorical tactics show us how women combined rhetoric and their Christian convictions to educate, recruit, and galvanize other women to action. *Reforming Women* also speaks to us today as these nineteenth-century female moral reformers direct us to inequities that still exist in society. Altogether, this study of the AFMRS shows us the development of a distinct women's rhetoric and an early feminist consciousness.

Chapter 1

Gendering Moral Reform

No! no! this work of Moral Reform never belonged to woman; she may be in it, as in the cause of Temperance, an efficient helper, but the principal work belongs to men, and when they come up and take the mighty labour off our hand, most gladly will we retire; but if they will not do it, we *cannot* be silent: we cannot behold in the midst of us a vast whirlpool of vice, annually swallowing up thousands, and hold our peace: we must speak out or do violence to our own consciences.

—*Advocate of Moral Reform*, 1835

Using a common nineteenth-century feminine trope, female moral reformers portray themselves as reluctant reformers. In the first issue of their periodical, the *Advocate of Moral Reform* (*AMR*), published in 1835, they claimed they were being drawn out of silence and into public action by their consciences, their religious convictions, and because men would not take up the cause. The women who organized the AFMRS knew well the hazards of pursuing moral reform. They had observed minimal success achieved by efforts to reclaim prostitutes in asylums and the enmity directed at those who sought to prevent immoral behavior through broad public awareness efforts. Undeterred, they forged ahead taking up the mantle of moral reform.

During the early nineteenth century, private citizens in New York City launched various rescue and moral reform initiatives aimed at prostitution and to uphold the seventh scriptural commandment, "Thou shalt not commit adultery." Interestingly, the two groups that persevered longest in their reclamation and reform efforts—the AFMRS and the New York Female Benevolent Society—were women's groups. Antebellum moral reform efforts were both relegated and embraced as women's work. Throughout this book I explore rhetorical tactics the AFMRS used in its vehement moral reform campaign. However, the AFMRS's first initial rhetorical tactic was claiming ownership of the cause by gendering moral reform as work better suited for women.

With the formation of the AFMRS, which sought to prevent immoral behavior through awareness and education, women began to use their gender strategically to assert and defend their role as social reformers. Gender is a fluid, socially constructed, and imposed category subject to change when combined with race, class, ethnicity, region, religion, etc. Typically, gender prescriptions have resulted in the inequitable distribution of power between men and women. That said, women have embraced some perceived or prescribed gender representations, and rejected others. In that sense, Jessica Enoch explains, "the process of gendering is deeply rhetorical in that it relies on discursive, material, and embodied articulations and performances that create and disturb gendered distinctions, social categories, and asymmetrical power relationships."[1] For my examination of the AFMRS, I define *gendering* as women's strategic use of societal gender distinctions assigned to them to garner ethos and assume power.

In the last twenty-five years, scholars in rhetorical history have shown numerous ways that nineteenth-century women applied the fluid concept of gender as a rhetorical tactic to seize power and expand their boundaries of activity. Lindal Buchanan opens *Regendering Delivery: The Fifth Canon and Antebellum Women Rhetors* with a story of how Lucy Stone appeals to male chivalry and successfully "wields the rhetoric of gender to defuse" an angry mob.[2] In *Well-Tempered Women: Nineteenth-Century Temperance Rhetoric*, Carol Mattingly shows how women "deftly made use of women's prescribed role both to establish their authority and to challenge traditional limits for women."[3] Likewise, using what Nan Johnson terms the "eloquent mother trope," both Johnson and Buchanan claim that nineteenth-century women rhetors expanded the realm of motherhood to public reform efforts to broaden their spheres of influence and activity.[4] Just as the church pulpit, political platform, and judicial benches were the province of men, the home, hearth, nurseries, and church pews were the province of women. Repeatedly, women claimed their reform efforts were merely an extension of their roles as mothers and Christian guardians who promote the spiritual and moral welfare of society for their children and other vulnerable persons. In that sense, gendering also has the potential to negate women's contributions by suggesting that—women just do what women do—rather than showing how women used and expanded the limited power and methods available to them to agitate for change.

To understand women's role in moral reform, this chapter first describes the history of prostitution in New York City, highlighting the factors that contributed to New York's thriving sex trade. It also describes the distinct groups that arose to combat this immoral industry. Drawing from these two discussions, I argue that women gendered antebellum moral reform and highlight the reasons why women were more willing and motivated to pursue moral reform than men, and how they made the movement their own. Ultimately, this chapter describes the context from which this brave group of reforming women emerged.

A CITY OF INFAMY

Antebellum New York City supported a thriving sex industry. After a visit in 1848, Norwegian traveler Ole Raeder described the city as a modern Sodom and Gomorrah. "I am sure it may well be compared with Paris when it comes to opportunities for the destruction of both body and soul," bemoaned Raeder.[5] Widely dispersed from the poorest slums to the most affluent neighborhoods, conservative estimates claimed that New York City had two hundred brothels in 1820; that is in addition to saloons, gambling halls, and rented rooms, which were also common locations for commercial sex. By the end of the Civil War the number of brothels had tripled.[6] Several factors, including New York City's rapid rise as an industrial and commercial center, ineffectual laws and law enforcement, and limited economic opportunities for women, combined to create a city of infamy, the primary symbol of which became the prostitute. Prostitutes were considered the major culprits in breaking the seventh commandment, so moral reform efforts initially targeted them.

Rapid Growth

One of the factors contributing to rampant prostitution was the city's rapid growth. Early in the nineteenth century, New York was already the largest city in the United States. Benefitting from goods flowing in and out of its harbor, and later the Erie Canal, New York was a beacon of trade—attracting manufacturers, commercial houses, and every manner of business enterprise. In 1836 New York held a 62 percent share of America's import business, and this harbor and canal traffic attracted throngs of people searching for jobs in factories, in shops, on ships, on docks, as well as positions as clerks in commercial houses. By 1835 twenty-five to thirty thousand people were crowded onto every square mile of Manhattan, and the city's population quadrupled over the next thirty years. With this rapid growth came demands for cheap housing, which resulted in several city slums, including the infamous Five Points. These crowded slums became hotbeds for drinking, gambling, robbery, and prostitution; however, brothels and purveyors of prostitution could be found in every section of the city. While prostitution increased in most industrializing cities in the Northeast, New York's unparalleled growth exacerbated the problem.[7]

Prostitution, which was typically confined to a specific area, operated outside of public view. Yet, unlike large European cities where the commercial sex trade was concentrated in red-light districts, prostitution was widely dispersed throughout New York. In 1869 a concerned citizen writing under the pseudonym George Ellington asserted, "It would be more difficult to state where they [brothels] are not, than where they are."[8] In slums, scantily dressed prostitutes advertised their services from windows and doorways in addition to actively strolling streets. At night, prostitutes paraded along Broadway, and in finer neighborhoods brothel madams welcomed clientele into ornately decorated parlors where they could flirt, pay for sexual favors, or accompany one of the female residents to her bedroom.[9] Some brothels operated under the guise of boardinghouses or shops although neighbors observing a steady stream of male callers surely caught on.[10] During the day it was difficult to distinguish well-dressed, parlor-house prostitutes from respectable ladies. In an 1856 series of magazine columns titled "New York Dissected," Walt Whitman noted: "The experienced city observer may everywhere recognize, in full costume and with assured faces, even at this broad daylight time, one and another notorious courtezans taking a 'respectable' promenade. These horrible women, with quiet assurance, walk the street or sit at lunch in fashionable refreshment saloons, not recognizing their 'customers,' but not, to the unpracticed eye, in any wise distinguishable from the painted and haggard lady of fashion."[11] Notice that Whitman's reproach is directed at the prostitutes, not their customers. Despite such widespread condemnation of prostitutes, with rising rents and limited space, New Yorkers were seldom at liberty to choose their neighbors. Orderly urban development was decades away.[12] Moreover, as the demand for housing drove up rental prices, landlords, including some of the city's most respected businessmen, welcomed brothels as tenants because they were both willing and able to pay their exorbitant rent demands.

New York attracted legions of aspiring young clerks who helped fuel a vibrant male sporting culture. During the day they kept ledgers, wrote business letters, and worked in shops, but at night they enjoyed all the amusements antebellum New York had to offer. Most lived in boardinghouses or rented rooms above businesses, so they were unaccountable to family, and the anonymity of a large impersonal city seemed to encourage vice with its gaming houses, saloons, dance halls, brothels, and theaters, which often devoted the third tier to prostitutes and their patrons. If any young man had difficulty finding the pleasure he sought, he could consult a brothel guide. One such

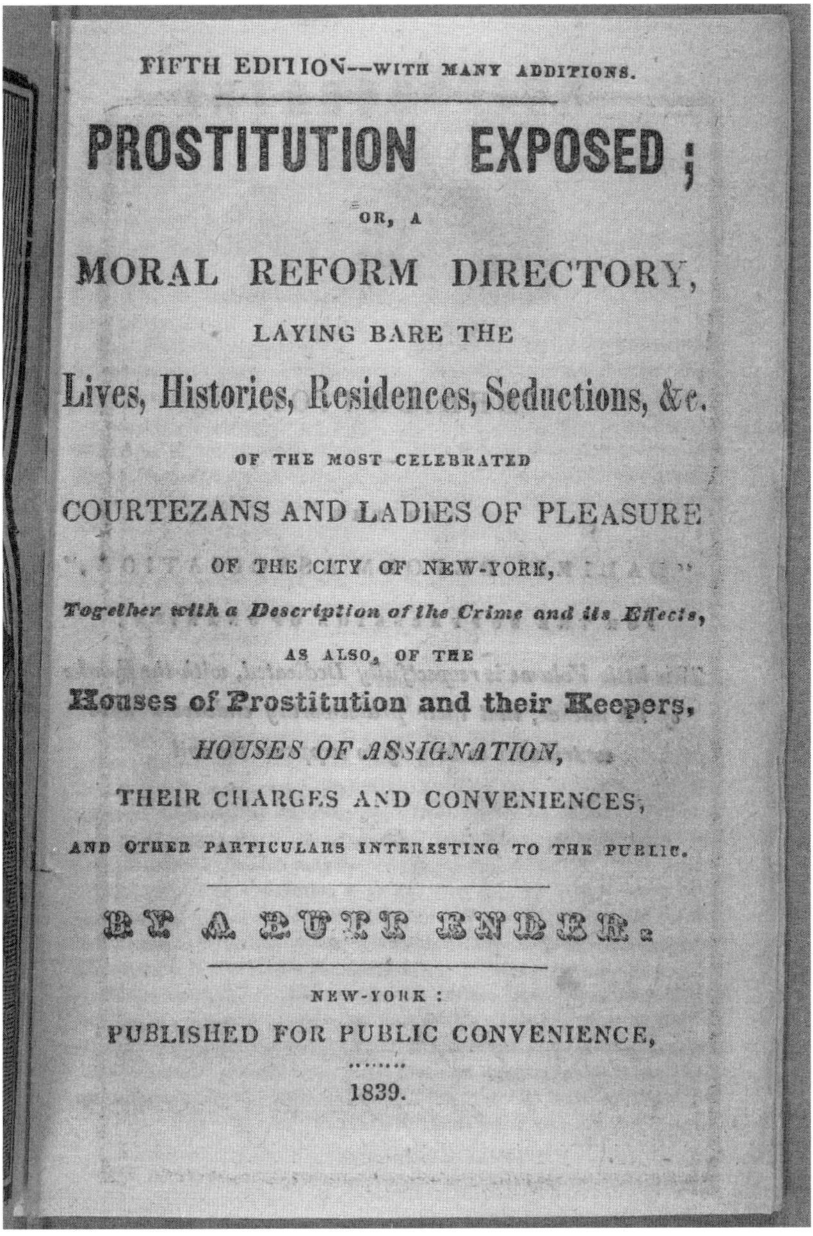

FIGURE 1. *Prostitution Exposed*, 1839. This brothel guide, which mocks moral reform efforts, highlights New York City's vibrant sex trade. Courtesy of the American Antiquarian Society.

guide, "published for public convenience" in 1839, even mocked moral reform efforts. Published under the nom de plume Butt Ender, the guide was dedicated to the Ladies' Reform Association and carried the long title *Prostitution Exposed; or, a Moral Reform Directory, Laying Bare the Lives, Histories, Residences, Seductions, &e. of the Most Celebrated Courtezans and Ladies of Pleasure of the City of New-York.*[13] In such a city, Whitman, bemused, that mothers would "feel little hope and much painful fear" if they knew how many of their beloved sons frequent brothels and keep mistresses.[14]

However, the sporting life was not simply limited to young clerks and the laboring classes. In the middle of a sermon in 1857, Reverend William Berrian, the powerful and respected rector, who had occupied the pulpit of New York City's prestigious Trinity Church for three decades, admitted that during his fifty years as a minister he had not "been in a house of ill-fame more than ten times."[15] Berrian's admission was certainly intended to shock his parishioners and draw attention to the city's brothels. Yet, amid New York's pervasive sex trade, the most surprising aspect of the confession may have been Berrian's scant number of brothel visits. Bachelors and married men, young and old, rich and poor, routinely partook of the city's sex industry. In addition to the city's rapid growth, other factors fueling these lascivious lifestyles included New York's transient male population, rigid courtship practices, economic pressures that forced men to delay or forgo marriage, and discontent with women's power or "petticoat government" within marriages. Hence, there was more at play than sexual gratification—masculine identity and pride contributed to the city's expansive sporting culture. Although few men like Berrian made public confessions, prostitution was implicitly approved of and flourished in New York City.[16]

Ineffectual Laws and Law Enforcement

Ineffectual laws and lax law enforcement was another factor that contributed to prostitution in New York City. Unless it was associated with theft, violence, or public disturbance prostitution rarely garnered police attention. However, city officials and police officers did attempt to reduce the visibility of prostitution through vagrancy and disorderly conduct laws. Vagrancy laws primarily targeted lowly streetwalkers—the prostitutes most vulnerable to police harassment. However, any woman walking unattended after dark could be arrested on suspicion of being a prostitute by an overzealous or malevolent patrolman. Vagrancy was an elastic concept that morphed into another way to control women, particularly poor, working-class women. For example, Mrs. Matilda Wade, who while walking a few blocks from her home to her husband's place of business in 1855, was arrested by a patrolman as a vagrant and common prostitute. As a result, Wade was publicly paraded as a prostitute; subject to an invasive medical exam to determine if she had a venereal disease; convicted without trial, testimony, evidence, or counsel; and incarcerated for five days before her husband and lawyer could gain her release along with twenty-nine other women who had been arrested illegally. Without money or an outside advocate fighting on her behalf, Wade might have remained in jail for six months simply for walking on the street unaccompanied after dark.[17]

Officials occasionally pursued disorderly conduct charges against brothels, but these were difficult to prove, so disorderly conduct charges were primarily used to intimidate prostitutes and brothel madams. Police officers might also raid a brothel, but such raids were usually more of a public performance than serious law enforcement. Because saloons and brothels were a revenue source, and rich, influential businessmen often held the leases, politicians were reluctant to close them.[18] Moreover, some of the politicians who railed loudly against prostitution quietly availed themselves of prostitutes' services. Ultimately, most law enforcement efforts targeted female prostitutes and ignored the male customers who financially fueled the practice. Of course, these laws were made and enforced by men whom were elected by men. According to one critic, "prostitution is really the only crime in the penal law where two people are doing a thing mutually agreed upon and yet only one, the female partner, is subject to arrest."[19]

Limited Economic Opportunities for Women

Combined with the masses coming to New York City, limited economic opportunities and low wages for women significantly contributed to prostitution. For some women prostitution was an economic necessity; for others, it was an attractive economic alternative. Indeed, part of the problem in gauging the extent of prostitution in New York was an oversimplified view of prostitutes. Nineteenth-century novels, moral reform literature, and even police accounts failed to acknowledge the wide array of women who entered prostitution, and the fact that it was an occasional or part-time occupation for many. Most of the data on antebellum prostitutes came from the lowest echelon of prostitutes—those who appeared on police registers or spent time in jail, city hospitals, almshouses, or asylums. However, women from every social class engaged in prostitution and ranged in age from girls as young as twelve to women old enough to be their grandmothers.

The historian Larry Whiteaker describes a hierarchy of prostitution that existed by the 1830s and was well-known to both prostitutes and their patrons. At the top were parlor prostitutes, who earned between $50 and $100 a week. They worked in lavishly furnished, elegant parlor houses, which resembled upscale residences. Parlor-house prostitutes were young and attractive. Most were well-educated and skilled musicians or artists who charmed and entertained their sophisticated patrons. Callers who could not afford a trip to an upstairs bedroom might spend part of the evening flirting and drinking in the downstairs parlor.[20]

Next in the hierarchy, and the largest group of prostitutes, were the genteel streetwalkers and theater prostitutes who usually resided in comfortable brothels near the theater district. Because of their fashionable dress, during the day these women often passed as respectable ladies. Yet at night, any unaccompanied woman in the theater district was assumed to be a prostitute. Theater prostitutes typically came from middle to lower socioeconomic classes. Some were former domestic servants, seamstress, or factory workers. Others, particularly streetwalkers, kept their day jobs and worked as part-time or occasional prostitutes to supplement their income.

At the bottom echelon of prostitutes were slum prostitutes. They usually worked in the city's poorest neighborhoods out of saloons, gambling halls, or ramshackle brothels. They typically catered to the lowest economic classes as well as sailors or other transients. Moral reformers often told the story of a prostitutes' fall down this hierarchy of prostitution—a path that turned beautiful young women into sickly hags, drunkards, and drug addicts. This cautionary tale was used to warn women and to generate sympathy; however, such downward spirals were exceptions rather than the rule. Most slum prostitutes came from impoverished circumstances. They were often found in hospitals and almshouses, and because they were more apt to be involved in drunken brawls and other forms of disorderly conduct, they were more likely to spend time in jail. Hence, slum prostitutes were the most visible group, and thus, became the primary target of moral reformers.[21]

One of the main sources of data on antebellum prostitutes is a study conducted in 1858 by Dr. William Sanger, the resident physician at the women's prison on Blackwell's Island. The study was based on a survey of two thousand prostitutes. Sanger developed the questionnaire and police officers administered it. Clearly, this method raises questions about the study's credibility. For instance, police officers may have coerced women's participation, some prostitutes may have provided the type of responses they believed the police officers wanted to hear, and the sample was drawn from the prostitutes that officers encountered—the lowest echelon of prostitutes, typically comprised of poor women and a high percentage of immigrants. Additionally, Sanger interpreted the survey results through a middle-class moralistic lens. Even with these caveats, Sanger's study disrupts stereotypes about the women who worked as prostitutes and the different motivations that drew them into the profession.[22]

The general profile of a New York City prostitute that emerged from Sanger's study was a young, single, white, foreign-born woman from a poor working-class family. Difficulty finding jobs and lodgings often forced immigrant women into prostitution, and with immigrants continually coming into the city, the proportion of nonnative-born prostitutes increased throughout the nineteenth century. Interestingly, black women, who were usually even lower than immigrants on the socioeconomic scale, comprised a small number of prostitutes. This was likely due to the small percentage of African Americans in the city's population as well as prejudice, which made prostitution an even more dangerous pursuit for black women.[23]

Sanger's study also shows some interesting variations from this general profile. For instance, of the 2,000 prostitutes interviewed, 490, or almost 25 percent, claimed to be married. For some women, prostitution may have offered a way out of bad marriages; many acknowledged that their husbands had abused them, deserted them, drank excessively, refused to support them, or had taken up with other women. Yet, 71 of the 490 prostitutes who were married said they still lived with their husbands.[24] Outraged by this fact, Sanger condemned their husbands as accessories to the crime, concluding that "such cohabitation implies a knowledge of the wife's degradation, and a participation in the wages of her shame."[25] This comment discloses Sanger's moral bias. In nineteenth-century New York, morals became a luxury many families could not afford. While there were cases where men maliciously prostituted their wives and daughters, there were also instances where women chose prostitution as a way to support sick, disabled, or unemployed husbands or to supplement a husband's insufficient income. Additionally, 320 of the prostitutes in Sanger's survey indicated that they were supporting children.[26]

In the nineteenth century, social safety nets did not exist, thus any woman, no matter her social class, might turn to prostitution to pay rent, buy food, or procure coal for heat. While concerned citizens established and contributed to benevolent organizations, these efforts were no match for the massive needs in New York and other large cities. Even in wealthy or middle-class families, the death of a father could result in a "complete reversal of circumstances," and in working-class families wives and daughters often needed to supplement the household's income.[27] In fact, 25 percent of the prostitutes in Sanger's study listed destitution as their reason for turning to prostitution. Vice paid far better than virtue; seventy-five of the prostitutes Sanger interviewed had previously worked—primarily in domestic service, sewing trades, factories, or as piecemeal laborers, which barely paid women subsistence wages. Nevertheless, Sanger's study showed that just as many women chose prostitution out of *inclination* (513) as those who resorted to prostitution out of *destitution* (525).

Many young women probably hoped prostitution would enable them to live in better places, work fewer hours, accumulate savings, or afford nice clothes and other luxuries out of the reach of most working women. Indeed, 124 prostitutes in Sanger's study said they became prostitutes because they perceived it as an easier life. In this sense, some of these motivations can also be interpreted as agency—a woman's desire for financial independence; freedom from the control of a father, husband, or employer; or just a different life. While a prostitute earned a living by selling her body, in many cases, she was also an independent woman who lived unattached or restrained. It was the mid-nineteenth century before pimps began to seize control of prostitutes when they turned to these middlemen for protection. Up to that point, prostitutes were by far the best paid female workers in nineteenth-century New York. In one night, a prostitute could earn what it would take a domestic servant or seamstress weeks to earn. While payment varied widely, the average income ranged somewhere between ten and fifty dollars, and less than one dollar was considered low for a New York prostitute's services.[28]

As one prostitute told her aunt, "Every young girl is sitting on her fortune if she only knew it."[29] Indeed, some women did accumulate fortunes in the sex trades. According to tax records, at least twenty-four known prostitutes amassed five thousand dollars or more in real estate and personal property in antebellum New York. Some prostitutes ascended to the role of brothel madams. Whereas men managed gambling halls and saloons, women managed brothels, which were lucrative businesses in antebellum New York.[30]

For most women, however, prostitution was a part-time or temporary profession that lasted four to seven years. When they quit, some women married or pursued another occupation. If they managed to save money, some set up businesses or migrated to another part of the country where they could hide their former profession. Moral reform literature depicted the grim deaths of prostitutes racked with disease or addiction. Sanger also believed that most prostitutes died prematurely after about four years in the profession, but he provided no evidence to support this claim.[31] Certainly, prostitution could be a dangerous profession. In addition to the degrading nature of the work, prostitutes dealt with undesirable clientele, violence, arrest, alcohol and drug addiction, and sexually transmitted diseases. Many prostitutes died during childbirth, like numerous women of the era.[32] Nevertheless, many women took these risks to support themselves or their families, to live easier lives, or to achieve some measure of independence. While their motives varied, they all underscore the limited economic opportunities available to most nineteenth-century women.

Even though this book focuses on female moral reformers, I believe prostitution and moral reform represent two sides of the same coin. On one side, female prostitutes made an embodied argument turning sex into a commercial act to survive a patriarchal economy that afforded women few economic opportunities. On the other side, female moral reformers fought inequitable social and legal systems that harshly punished women adulterers while ignoring their male companions.

These factors—New York's emergence as an industrial and economic center, the rapid influx of individuals from rural American and Europe, ineffective laws and law enforcement, and limited economic opportunities for women—combined to create conditions in which prostitution flourished. In response, several groups organized to combat the problem during the first half of the nineteenth century. Because they were facing entrenched economic, institutional, and social systems these efforts failed to eliminate or even significantly reduce prostitution, and most were short-lived. Examining these groups highlight the two main approaches to moral reform (reclamation and prevention), the challenges inherent in moral reform efforts, and the rhetorical tactics commonly used. Moreover, the two groups that persisted, the New York Female Benevolent Society and the AFMRS, highlight how moral reform efforts became gendered.

EZRA STILES ELY
AND THE MAGDALEN SOCIETY OF NEW YORK

Most complaints about prostitution in the early nineteenth century arose on the grounds that prostitution was a public nuisance, not a problem of immorality. If prostitutes operated quietly and peacefully, residents and authorities usually ignored them.[33] However, ministers, city missionaries, and church volunteers who encountered prostitutes during their outreach endeavors were often moved to try to help these women. The first organized effort, the Magdalen Society of New York, was inspired by the work and writing of the Presbyterian minister Ezra Stiles Ely. While working as chaplain for the New York City Hospital and Almshouse, Ely ministered to many prostitutes and later included several sympathetic depictions in his book *Visits of Mercy* (1811). In one entry Ely writes: "Early this morning, the woman of ill fame who yesterday requested me to pray with her, resigned her mortal life. She was rational to the last moment, and often said, after I left her, that she knew she was an exceedingly vile sinner, but could not help entertaining some feeble hope that God would pardon her sins through Jesus Christ. Her present state is known to God alone but possibly she may have entered the kingdom of heaven, while such as trust in themselves that they are righteous, shall be forever excluded."[34] As in this instance, Ely often used the accounts of the sick and destitute people he encountered to instruct the so-called righteous, but his sympathy and especially his use of a prostitute's humble plea for salvation is significant. Nineteenth-century society deemed prostitutes the lowest of sinners; while they might be welcomed by God in heaven, they were not welcomed anywhere by respectable individuals. Even conversation about prostitution was deemed inappropriate.

Nonetheless, Ely repeatedly used sympathetic portrayals to change perceptions of prostitutes and move Christians in New York to help reclaim these women from their lives of sin. Telling the story of a fifteen-year-old girl who was lured into prostitution by her sister, Ely lamented that if the girl returns to health and wishes to lead a moral life, there is no place for her to go. She cannot remain in the hospital, so she must return to her former life. Thus, Ely implores:

> It is the duty of Christians to seek the wanderer and, if possible, reclaim the most abandoned. If proper means are not used to reform those who have departed from the paths of peace, the pious ought not complain that the wicked continue in iniquity; and that persons once polluted return to their wallowing in sensuality. What has been done to restore the fallen females of this city? To which of them has any benevolent society proffered protection? What female has sought to convince one of the miserable of her own sex, that the door of mercy is unfolded.[35]

Through this series of rhetorical questions, Ely not only called on Christians to help the city's fallen females, he particularly called on women, assuming they would want to help those of their own sex. The assumption, that women would want to help other women, was later borne out by women's reclamation and moral reform efforts. Moreover, this is one reason why moral reform became gendered. In fact, after reading Ely's plea about the fifteen-year-old prostitute, two women volunteered to help this girl, who was illiterate and motherless.[36]

In another entry, Ely shared the tragic story of a widow with many children who entrusted her eldest daughter to a woman whom the widow mistook to be a "fine lady." The woman promised the mother that she would employ her daughter as a chambermaid in the city. But the woman brought the girl to the city, turned her into a prostitute, and kept her hidden from the mother who came to the city twice in search of her daughter. Four years later, Ely encountered the girl in the hospital near death, alone in the world, and inconsolable. "Such copious weeping I never saw before, in any single instance," laments Ely.[37] He also describes how a former brothel madam residing in the same hospital ward had been greatly affected by the girl. The former madam claimed, "I thank God that I never stole away and ruined such an innocent child as that. That's all my consolation!"[38] Ely's sympathetic accounts helped draw distinctions between prostitutes, which made it difficult for Christians to condemn the entire class. Later moral reformers similarly uphold stories of penitent prostitutes and employ pathetic and ethical appeals to Christian duty to attain support for their efforts.

Ely's *Visits of Mercy* also depicted the tenuous plight of many women with moving stories of husbands deserting wives, young girls enticed to the city and ruined, tales of seduction, and the gruesome maladies suffered by women who had made their living as prostitutes. Stories such as these would later become common narratives in moral reform literature intended to both warn women and induce sympathy and support for the cause. Indeed, Ely frequently paired these stories with appeals for Christians to open a Magdalen asylum where prostitutes could be redeemed.[39] In one instance he writes, "Almost every day, I exclaim, 'Oh! For a Magdalen Hospital!'[40] Ely's inspiration for an asylum came from London and Philadelphia. In London reformers established a Magdalen hospital (which was not a hospital in the traditional sense) in 1758. By 1811 they claimed that they had admitted more than four thousand penitent prostitutes and that more than half of these women had been reformed and reconciled with family and friends or placed in respectable occupations. Inspired by London's success, the Magdalen Society of Philadelphia was formed in 1800 and eventually opened an asylum in 1808. It was the first organized effort to rescue prostitutes in the United States.[41]

Ely's pleas and sympathetic portrayals of prostitutes proved effective. Shortly after the publication of *Visits of Mercy*, the Magdalen Society of New York was established in 1812. The group's twenty-one-member board was led by physician Dr. Peter Wilson and other prominent New Yorkers active in benevolent endeavors. This group set out to establish an asylum that would afford penitent prostitutes a place of protection and support and provide them with the religious, moral, and practical training intended to bring about their complete reformation. Like the Magdalen hospital in London, the society envisioned that women leaving the asylum would either be reunited with family and friends or secure respectable employment.[42]

Details about the society's asylum and its management highlight challenges that early reclamation efforts faced. The society appointed a Standing Committee of men responsible for visiting the asylum and overseeing its operation. The board also appointed a Committee of Ladies who, along with a matron, was given responsibility for the general rehabilitation of the Magdalens, including their employment, diet, and dress.[43] The Committee of Ladies included wives of society board members as well as the powerful mother-daughter duo Isabella Graham and Joanna Graham Bethune.[44] Representatives from the Committee of Ladies and the men's Standing Committee were responsible for visiting the asylum twice a week to provide religious instruction, lead prayers, and sing hymns.[45]

By the *Second Annual Report*, members of the Standing Committee reduced their visits to once a week, and shifted most of their attention to fundraising and finances for the society. In essence, the men ceded oversight of day-to-day operations of the asylum to the Committee of Ladies.[46] This shift in responsibility is evident in the *Third Annual Report*: "The whole Board of Ladies meet monthly. They direct the internal arrangements of the Asylum; prescribe regulations from time to time for its management; correct whatever appears amiss; recommend to the Managers what *they deem necessary for the improvement of internal economy, or for the better accommodation of the Magdalens*; admonish, reprove, and instruct them; strengthen the hands, and confirm the authority of the Managers; and by examining into such matters as are exclusively the province of females, perform services essentially necessary to the well-being of the Institution."[47] In relegating control of the asylum and its charges to the Ladies Committee and in denoting such matters as "exclusively the province of females," the Magdalen Society of New York shows men's tendency to address moral reform from a distance. This points to another reason why moral reform eventually becomes gendered.

The Magdalen Society's asylum adhered to a strict regime aimed at instilling order and moral control. Magdalens were required to rise at six and go to bed at ten. They were required to work; the society considered idleness "a great inlet to vice."[48] The sewing and tailoring work the Magdalens performed was also intended to teach the women an honest livelihood.[49] Magdalens were also required to obey the matron and abide by a strict set of rules. While these rules were intended to protect the Magdalens from negative past influences and instill proper decorum and industrious habits, life in the asylum probably felt more like punishment than rescue to the women. Indeed, *inmate* was a term frequently used to refer to individuals residing in asylums and refuges, but these women probably felt more like inmates in its contemporary connotation. This may explain the asylum's difficulty in attracting repentant prostitutes.

Generally, an optimistic "if we build it, they will come" mentality surrounded the asylum. Whereas the society's annual reports expend much ink on bylaws, oversight, operating procedures, and rules for the asylum, there appears little thought as to how they might draw prostitutes to the asylum. Ely's appeals had intimated that there were multitudes of desperate women in need of assistance. In one entry Ely even estimated there were seven thousand prostitutes in the city and that an asylum could "save at least a few from what they deem the necessity of prostituting themselves for a piece of bread."[50] Yet the Magdalen Society of New York failed to acknowledge the complex motivations that led women to take up prostitution. The society simply viewed prostitution as a terrible sin and naïvely assumed women would seek salvation if given the opportunity. The society also gave little if any thought as to the difficult transition of moving from unrestricted street life to the asylum's rigid strictures.

During its first three years of operation, it proved far easier to attract donors than "penitent prostitutes."[51] Of the small number of prostitutes who entered the asylum, many ran away or were dismissed; few women were successfully reclaimed. Eventually, society members lost patience and interest. With Ely's appointment to pastor the Pine Street Presbyterian Church in Philadelphia in 1813 and the death of Isabella Graham in 1814, the society lost two of its strongest champions. In 1818 the society closed the asylum and ceased operations. Following its closure, different missions, ministries, and benevolent organizations assisted prostitutes. For instance, a House of Refuge, established by the Society for the Reformation of Juvenile Delinquents, took in teenage prostitutes, the majority of whom were orphaned or abandoned.[52] But none of these groups focused on prostitution, and it was not until 1830 that private citizens again took up the banner of moral reform.

While later reformers were likely aware of Ely's *Visits of Mercy*, they appear unaware of the Magdalen Society of New York and the asylum it operated. Ignorant of previous efforts to address societal problems, societies in the nineteenth century rarely learned from other groups' efforts, and frequently repeated previous mistakes.[53] And even though members of this former society were alive in the 1830s, none of them appear to have joined these later efforts. Nonetheless, this first attempt at moral reform foreshadows rhetorical tactics, challenges, and tendencies in later moral reform efforts.

FEMALE ASYLUM SOCIETY

Prostitution did not diminish in the city. If anything, it grew more widespread and more visible in the years following the Magdalen Society of New York's initial reclamation efforts. Between 1830 and 1834, five different groups emerged in New York City with the object of stemming the tide of prostitution. Prompted by the religious fervor of the Second Great Awakening and evangelical revivalists such as Charles Grandison Finney, who charged Christians with the responsibility of eradicating sin to save their communities and country, Christians in New York traveled to saloons, almshouses, slums, and prisons to evangelize and hand out Bibles and tracts. The dramatic social changes occurring in America were magnified in New York. Some worried that the shift from local agrarian communities to impersonal urban cities was shaking the foundation of American society.[54] Many evangelicals believed if you could save New York City, you could save the country.

One group of women established a Sunday school at Bellevue's female penitentiary. There they discovered that many of the penitentiary's occupants were prostitutes of all ages who had been arrested for vagrancy or drunken and disorderly conduct.[55] From their encounters with the inmates, the Christian women became convinced that some of the women could be rescued if they could provide them with a place of refuge after their release from the penitentiary. Consequently, the women established a Female Asylum Society in early 1830, and Elijah Pierson, a successful merchant, who had also worked as a prison visitor, rented a house to serve as an asylum. The Female Asylum Society struggled to attract sufficient financial support, so the effort remained small until John McDowall rallied support from some of the city's most prominent men.[56]

Like Ezra Ely twenty years before, McDowall was a young enthusiastic minister. A twenty-nine-year-old graduate of Amherst College and a ministerial student at Princeton University, he ventured to New York City to work as a missionary for the American Tract Society in the summer of 1830. While there, he held prayer meetings, went door-to-door handing out tracts and reading scriptures, and helped a group of women organize a Sunday school in Five Points. In his work, McDowall became acquainted with Arthur Tappan, John Wheelwright, and Abijah Smith, merchants and powerful men who supported the efforts in Five Points and occasionally accompanied McDowall on his visits to neighborhood residents.[57] Like Ely, McDowall was particularly struck by the plight of prostitutes and the difficulty they faced in altering their course. He shared his concerns with Tappan, who told him about Elijah Pierson's asylum house, which currently only had two penitent prostitutes in residence. McDowall encouraged ten additional prostitutes to enter the refuge. This success, combined with Tappan's support, resulted in the creation of the New York Magdalen Society in 1830, which replaced the struggling Female Asylum Society.

JOHN MCDOWALL
AND THE NEW YORK MAGDALEN SOCIETY

McDowall agreed to stay in New York and serve as the society's chaplain. Tappan served as president and Wheelwright and Smith served on the executive committee. Additionally, the society's first annual report listed twenty-five members, all male, and included wealthy merchants, physicians, attorneys, and bankers, many of whom were active in other benevolent organizations and crusades against intemperance, gambling, and breaking the Sabbath. No details about the society's reclamation program remain, but it likely pursued a course similar to the previous Magdalen Asylum in New York, which combined occupational training and religious teachings. Moreover, the asylum was likely run by women.[58]

Like earlier attempts, the number of successful reclamations was small. Only seventeen women "graduated" and either reunited with families and friends or entered service positions with families deemed pious. These successes were overshadowed by the twenty-eight women who left, were expelled, or sent away.[59] Additionally, the society's executive committee members, who came from different religious denominations, argued over the kind of religious instruction the asylum should provide.[60] But what ultimately led to its demise was the uproar that surrounded the publication of its first annual report, infamously known as the *Magdalen Report*.

The *Magdalen Report*, primarily written by McDowall, did not simply describe the society's mission, actions, and results, but presented a passionate case for moral reform. The *Magdalen Report* pointed a bright spotlight on New York City's vibrant sex trade, scandalously charging in all caps that there were TEN THOUSAND prostitutes in New York City.[61] Additionally, the report claimed that there was evidence that hundreds of domestics, seamstresses, and nurses in the most respectable families worked as harlots in "houses of assignation every night."[62] The report also alleged that the city's prostitutes had many wealthy patrons, and estimated the staggering sums men spent on prostitutes. McDowall believed he was making an urgent and persuasive appeal for moral reform in New York City, but he misjudged his audience. The report drew outrage rather than support; William Cullen Bryant bemoaned the fact that a report detailing such widespread whoredom was read in a meeting where the audience was primarily comprised of respectable ladies.[63] Former New York City mayor Philip Hone characterized the report as a "disgraceful document."[64] In response to the report's claims, public meetings were held in Tammany Hall and outraged city officials ordered their own survey of prostitution. Not surprisingly, the city's survey arrived at a much smaller number— less than fifteen hundred prostitutes—a sum that city newspapers derided as far too low.[65] Estimated numbers of prostitutes in the city were usually *too hot or too cold*; whereas moral reformers inflated numbers to try to raise concerns, city officials and police deflated numbers to lower concerns. Although the true number is elusive, today, considering the number of women who worked as part-time or occasional prostitutes to supplement their income or stave off destitution, the historian Timothy Gilfoyle estimates that 5–10 percent of all women between the ages of fifteen and thirty in nineteenth-century New York prostituted themselves, a calculation that lends credence to McDowall's initial claims.[66]

By publicly acknowledging New York's sex trade, McDowall had opened Pandora's box. The historian Marilyn Hill explains, "McDowall found himself in the middle of a controversy between reformers roused by a problem of seemingly near-plague proportions and respectable New Yorkers outraged by statistics they considered preposterous about a subject they viewed as obscene."[67] McDowall was not the first to make bold claims in hopes of attracting support,[68] but McDowall's assertion was made at a public gathering and appeared in an annual report to which many prominent men in the city had attached their names.

McDowall had hoped to "awaken compassion and zeal in the heart of every individual who fears God and loves his neighbor!"[69] Instead, he ignited outrage. His claims of widespread sexual immorality had crossed the line in a society that eschewed public discussion of sexual matters. Tappan and Dr. David Reese received threats after the *Magdalen Report*'s publication. Other society members withdrew their support, demonstrating that many influential men in the city were unwilling to endorse moral reform once it became controversial. Supporting an asylum to reform penitent prostitutes was one thing, but claiming a widespread prostitution problem existed or mounting an anti-prostitution campaign was something else altogether. Some of these prominent businessmen may have been complicit in the sex trade either through personal behavior or property holdings. McDowall resigned in September, and in November members voted to suspend all activities.[70]

With the *Magdalen Report*, McDowall played the role of whistle-blower—loudly condemning the city's vibrant sex trade that had long been silently accepted. The *Magdalen Report*'s publication also signaled a shift in moral reform tactics. The few prostitutes reclaimed in asylums had convinced McDowall and others that prevention through awareness and changing public attitudes about sexual immorality would prove a more effective course of action than rescue. Undeterred by the reaction to the *Magdalen Report*, in 1832 McDowall published *Magdalen Facts*—a collection of moral reform sermons, reports, letters, and prostitute case histories. Convinced that moral reform required the exposure of prostitution and other immoral behaviors, McDowall took on the social precept that deemed all discussion of sexual matters improper and taboo. Moreover, he outlined several measures that would become central tenets of prevention, including educating children about moral principles, preaching the seventh commandment from church pulpits, staying away from dances and theaters, refraining from pernicious reading, and avoiding bad company.[71] McDowall returned to his missionary work at Five Points, and rented a lecture hall to deliver a series of lectures. However, his efforts garnered little support. He was about to give up when he was approached by the Female Benevolent Society of the City of New York (FBS).[72]

THE FEMALE BENEVOLENT SOCIETY

With the founding of the FBS in December 1832, women began to take over the cause of moral reform. Women had always actively supported moral reform efforts—helping oversee Magdalen asylums, visiting prostitutes in prisons, establishing Sunday schools, handing out Bibles and tracts in Five Points and other centers of prostitution. With this new society, however, women took the lead. Yet having witnessed the public uproar leading to the Magdalen Society's collapse, they proceeded cautiously. Their stated aim was "the promotion of *moral purity* in the city of New-York, in a way both corrective and preventive."[73] To avoid denominational conflict, the FBS initially limited membership to Presbyterians, but later welcomed members from other denominations.[74]

The women decided to pursue both reclamation and prevention by opening an asylum to rescue prostitutes and by employing McDowall to oversee both the inmates' religious instruction and to educate the public about the need for moral reform. The women's decision to remain backstage and combat prostitution from a safe distance likely reflects their fear of public retribution. At first, they struggled to gain support for an asylum and achieved the same disappointing results as previous asylums—thirteen of the twenty-seven prostitutes admitted to their temporary asylum soon returned to prostitution. Moreover, McDowall seemed convinced that prevention was a better course of action than rescue, but the society was reluctant to wage a public campaign even though prevention was one of its stated objectives. In 1833 McDowall began publishing *McDowall's Journal*, which he used to continue to make a bold case for moral reform. He left his role as agent a few months later. McDowall's departure was contentious and led to a public feud that showed a growing rift between moral reformers who wanted to continue reclamation efforts and those who wanted to pursue broader prevention through public education and awareness.[75]

McDowall's departure actually ignited the FBS by forcing members to become more involved. Their active participation forged a stronger commitment, which helped the women attract support and secure funding for a permanent Magdalen asylum. Ultimately, the asylum fared better than previous reclamation efforts.[76] By its thirty-eighth anniversary, the women reported that their asylum had received two thousand women, six hundred of whom were placed in families as domestic servants, while four hundred were reunited with relatives.[77] In other words, the FBS successfully reclaimed or extricated from prostitution half of the women who entered the asylum. Averaged over thirty-eight years, this was roughly twenty-six women a year. Withdrawing from prostitution would have been difficult without the asylum's help. Without funds to relocate, there was nowhere for a former prostitute to go, and domestic service positions with respectable families required references so it would be tough for a former prostitute to acquire one of these positions without the asylum's assistance.

Nevertheless, if the number of prostitutes in New York City ranged somewhere between the higher estimates of fifteen hundred and ten thousand, then this small number of reclamations was doing little to stem the prostitution problem in the city. At the same time, it is important to note that women's efforts to reclaim prostitutes through Christian benevolence were readily accepted. The FBS continued to provide refuge for prostitutes for decades without encountering strong opposition. At different junctures, the society even received funding from the city. The FBS was cautious in its printed communications, which were primarily annual reports and occasional fundraising appeals. It upheld the view that sex was not a topic to be discussed publicly. While the FBS sought to reform prostitutes through rescue and reclamation, the only public attitude it tried to change was that view that prostitutes were irredeemable social outcasts.[78]

The FBS's efforts highlight an important distinction between women's approaches to moral reform and women's organizations in general. Anne Boylan delineates three categories of antebellum women's organizations: benevolent, reform, and feminist. Whereas the FBS operated more like a benevolent society, the AFMRS, which emerged from a split with the FBS, operated as a reform organization. Boylan notes that there seemed to be little overlap between these two functions. While women often joined multiple organizations, a woman "was either a benevolent lady or a reformer, seldom both."[79] Consequently, rescue and reclamation efforts became benevolent endeavors as the FBS focused on fundraising and directly assisting small groups of former prostitutes.[80] While these delineations help denote an organization's central mission, members' primary motivation, and views about women's proper roles, we should remember that women's organizations were fluid—adapting to the exigencies they encountered. For instance, in addition to promoting reform, the AFMRS performed several benevolent functions such as assisting families meet basic needs. The AFMRS also advocated more employment opportunities for women, generally categorized as a feminist objective.

JOHN MCDOWALL'S CRUSADE

McDowall left his position as agent for the FBS convinced that asylums were futile.[81] He resumed his prevention efforts, boldly condemning immoral behavior and ignoring the taboo against publicly discussing sexual matters. McDowall and later reformers considered silence an accessory to licentious behavior and exposure the most effective weapon. Proponents of prevention wanted to attract attention. They pursued moral reform in the same manner as temperance reformers. Instead of reforming drunkards, the temperance crusade sought to persuade the public about the evils of alcohol and attack purveyors including saloons and dram shops. Through *McDowall's Journal*, McDowall condemned brothels, assignation houses, theaters, and patrons of prostitutes.[82]

As his journal gained a following, McDowall remained a lightning rod for controversy.[83] His rift with the FBS continued, and he added fuel to the fire by publishing the quarrel in his journal. Likely instigated by his critics, in March 1834 a grand jury charged that *McDowall's Journal* was "offensive to taste, injurious to morals, and degrading to the character of [the] city."[84] While these findings carried no actionable consequences, they drew more attention to McDowall. In June, his critics brought charges before the Third Presbytery, the body that licensed McDowall to preach. While the Third Presbytery encouraged McDowall to continue pursuing moral reform, it advised him to cease publication of his controversial periodical. In response, McDowall gave his press and subscription list to a group of women who would later become the AFMRS. These women had recently split with the FBS over the McDowall controversy and their belief that prevention was a better course for moral reform.

McDowall continued his public feud, and his enemies brought more charges against him to the Presbytery, which finally decided to suspend him from preaching. He appealed the decision, but by this time the bitter public argument, along with McDowall's zealous pursuit of moral reform, had taken a heavy toll on his health. McDowall died on December 13, 1836, at the age of thirty-five. The AFMRS, which had hired McDowall to serve as a city missionary, honored him as a martyr to the cause of moral reform. Indeed, AFMRS auxiliaries sent money to his widow and purchased and circulated his memoir, aptly titled *Memoir and Select Remains of the late Rev. John R. M'Dowall, The Martyr of the Seventh Commandment, in the Nineteenth Century.*

THE SEVENTH COMMANDMENT SOCIETY

McDowall had also inspired a group of evangelical clergymen and laymen who distributed *McDowall's Journal* to families in church wards throughout the city. In October 1833 they established the American Society for Promoting the Observance of the Seventh Commandment, more commonly referred to as the Seventh Commandment Society. This group envisioned a national reform crusade that would combat the combined evils of sexual immorality, drinking, and slavery—all in an effort to purify the nation. The Seventh Commandment Society disseminated its proposed constitution to several hundred like-minded men across the country and sought to increase awareness and elevate moral reform to a level similar to that of temperance. As part of the group's envisioned moral purification campaign, it would urge parents to educate their children, clergymen to preach the seventh commandment from the pulpit, and members of respectable society to exclude all licentious individuals. However, the Seventh Commandment Society, whose leaders were also involved in abolition, soon relinquished the job of moral reform to the newly formed AFMRS, which had become an auxiliary to the Seventh Commandment Society.[85]

THE AFMRS AND THE GENDERING OF MORAL REFORM

Reluctant at first, women claimed moral reform as a women's movement. Upset by the ongoing dispute between the FBS and McDowall, several FBS officers, including Mrs. Charles W. Hawkins, Mrs. A. M. Roberts, Mrs. William Green Jr., and Mrs. D.C. Lansing resigned, and established the New York Female Moral Reform Society, later renamed the AFMRS. These women became officers for the AFMRS joining Lydia Finney, wife of revivalist Charles Finney, who was named first directress.[86] The women who established the AFMRS were also convinced that prevention was a more effective strategy to combat prostitution than reclamation.[87]

Attempts at prevention were more ambitious and controversial, focusing on places (brothels, saloons, theaters) and behaviors (drinking, dancing, reading romance novels) that moral reformers believed propagated licentiousness.[88] Pursuing their own prevention efforts required women to take center stage in a public and fiery moral reform campaign. "By challenging the benevolent ladies' assumptions about what women could and ought to attempt in the public sphere," Boylan declares, "reform-oriented women moved beyond benevolence and into active efforts to change basic social relationships."[89] In taking over the mantle for moral reform, AFMRS members helped forge broad social reform as a proper role for women.

While women numerically dominated most antebellum evangelical and benevolent endeavors, "moral reform was the first *reform* movement to become almost exclusively the cause of women."[90] The historian Daniel Wright argues, "unlike the other leading reform movements of the time—antislavery and temperance—moral reform quickly became a thoroughly feminized movement, not only in membership, but in leadership and agenda."[91] The history of early moral reform efforts in New York highlights the failure of several male-led initiatives; it also shows women's willingness to take charge of this cause. Drawing from both the factors contributing to New York's vibrant sex trade and the several failed efforts to combat it, which I have outlined, I want to suggest four reasons why moral reform was relegated to women's work, why women embraced it, and how AFMRS volunteers gendered the movement— transforming it from a male-led to a female-led reform effort. These include women drawing on their religious identities for ethos and armor, stressing the movement's commitment to women helping women, exerting pent-up frustration over gendered double standards, and using rhetorical tactics that were available and comfortable for women.

First, AFMRS women gendered moral reform by using their religious identities and perceived moral superiority as a source of authority and protection. The stigma attached to prostitutes was deeply entrenched in antebellum American society—so was the taboo against discussing sexual matters in polite company. Individuals were often implicated just by speaking about sexual immorality. While men were willing to donate money to establish asylums, and basically outsource the problem of prostitution to matrons and ladies' committees, most avoided any hands-on involvement and bristled at any type of broad societal reform. When John McDowall's *Magdalen Report* was met with public indignation, reputable merchants and other male business leaders made a hasty retreat. Indeed, opposition to moral reform brought together strange bedfellows. Not only did opponents include brothel madams, prostitutes, and their patrons who wanted to avoid exposure, but also wealthy landlords and business owners who profited from the city's sex trade and despised the intrusion on their livelihood. Conservative church leaders also believed that public discussions of licentious behavior encouraged it, and in some cases believed that female moral reformers had stepped beyond their proper sphere. Additionally, city officials were embarrassed by the city's lascivious industry and wary of riling their male constituents. Whatever the motivation, all opposition faced the same quandary—arguing in favor of prostitution was an untenable position. So, most opponents fervently claimed that publicly discussing sex was improper and even harmful. Others made fun of moral reformers, and some even absurdly condemned moral reformers as the group responsible for spreading licentiousness.

By pursuing an awareness campaign that exposed and publicly condemned prostitution and male licentious behavior, moral reformers often encountered personal scorn and harsh backlash. The women comprising the AFMRS, however, were more difficult to attack. Unlike men, they were not as vulnerable to claims that they were sexually interested in the women they were helping. Additionally, most were not worried about commercial enterprises or business reputations—or, in McDowall's case, a preaching license. And as far as maintaining respectability, which was vitally important in the nineteenth century, women were both motivated and protected by their belief that moral reform was their Christian duty. Women's elevation as models of piety in the nineteenth century and the religious fervor of the Second Great Awakening lent them ethos and emboldened women to defy certain social mores. Whereas women had previously been viewed as individuals who needed to be protected, the "evolving evangelical ideology of gender" made women's perceived moral superiority a strength and armament in the pursuit of moral reform. These religious identities enabled women "to rely on an authority beyond the world of men and provided a crucial support to those who stepped beyond accepted bounds," especially reformers. They acted under the conviction that God ordained their work. With this "spiritual armor," respectable middle-class women traveled to sections of the city previously off-limits and broached taboo sexual subjects, all in pursuit of moral reform.[92]

Second, AFMRS members gendered moral reform by emphasizing that they were helping other women. Women tended to take more personal interest than men in social outreach efforts, and they were especially drawn to causes that helped other women.[93] Moreover, women were the principal victims of licentiousness, so men did not relate to the issue in the same way women did. Women understood their sex's vulnerability in nineteenth-century society. Young women were admonished to remain innocent, even naïve, about sexual matters. Through education and awareness, AFMRS members believed they were protecting women. They warned them about behaviors that would put them at risk, alerted them to known libertines and seduction tactics, opened employment offices to help women find respectable positions, and lobbied lawmakers to pass anti-seduction and abduction laws. Railing against theaters, brothels, and gaming houses, female moral reformers also believed they were acting on behalf of mothers whose sons moved to the city for jobs and were easily lured into these dens of vice.

Third, AFMRS members also used their anger and frustration to gender moral reform. Women were outraged by a society that severely punished women for extramarital sex while ignoring men's indiscretions, by laws that targeted female prostitutes while disregarding their male customers, and by economic opportunities that made it nearly impossible for women to support themselves. AFMRS members' anger and frustration about these double standards is readily apparent in their periodical, *The Advocate of Moral Reform.* When the AFMRS began publishing these frustrations, they discovered a receptive and like-minded audience among women throughout the Northeast and Midwest, who were ready to break the silence on sexual double standards. Thus, this deep-seeded anger united women and roused them to take charge of moral reform.

Lastly, the rhetorical tactics the AFMRS used to pursue moral reform—publishing periodicals, circulating petitions, using their physical presence, forming auxiliaries, and establishing institutions—were also gendered, and offer a harbinger of rhetorical tactics female reformers would use throughout the nineteenth century. These were rhetorical means that were accessible to women; more importantly, women gravitated to these means because they were comfortable using them. While antebellum women had few avenues to pursue legal and economic reform, they used the rhetorical tactics that were available to them to shame men and to educate, organize, embolden, and protect women. In pursuing moral reform, women's ethos, motivation, and level of participation differed from that of men, and for several years female moral reformers endured the harsh backlash that accompanied their public prevention campaign. Instead of deterring them, opposition initially steeled their resolve by convincing them that the cause of moral reform was better suited for women.

The AFMRS persevered in their moral reform efforts far longer than any men's organizations. *McDowall's Journal* lasted just about a year, while the *Advocate of Moral Reform* was published for more than a century. Eventually, the AFMRS realigned its objectives and methods. Recognizing that limited economic opportunities was the root cause of many women's problems, the AFMRS opened a home for young, vulnerable women and orphaned and neglected children in 1847 and eventually changed its name to the American Female Guardian Society. With its home and its institutional rhetoric, which I discuss in chapter 5, the AFMRS placed women in employment situations and children in foster and adoptive homes. This home remained open for 128 years, shifting focus as needs changed. It eventually merged with several other organizations in 1974. Ultimately, the AFMRS's long history suggests that the women who pursued the controversial cause of moral reform not only embraced it as women's work, but were also more resilient and pragmatic than male moral reformers. Initially, however, women approached moral reform out of a sense of righteous anger, which I discuss in the next chapter.

Chapter 2

Radiating Righteous Anger in the Advocate of Moral Reform

And shall we, beloved sisters, sit down quietly in careless indifference, while thousands, and tens of thousands of dogs in human shape, have not only run naked with lust, but are biting and seizing from our own sex, victim after victim.

—Advocate of Moral Reform, 1835

An early issue of the *Advocate of Moral Reform* (*AMR*) compared immoral men in America to packs of mad dogs left unchecked to run the streets. The article exhorted readers to speak out and rid the nation of libertines, all the while admitting that antagonizing this mad pack would likely make them "bark louder, and bite harder."[1] Emotionally infused comparisons combined with references to Sodom and Gomorrah, "villains," "fiends," and "fornicators" filled the *Advocate*'s pages. Reading the periodical, one can feel the fury flying from its pages, which is surprising considering the time period and the genteel, white, middle-class, Christian women who led the AFMRS. These women were not extremists. Historian Nancy Hardesty notes, "these were ordinary middle-class wives and mothers fighting for their homes, their families, their less-fortunate sisters."[2] Yet, much like the impassioned Howard Beale in the movie *Network*, who raged, "I'm mad as hell and I'm not going to take it anymore," antebellum women's anger had reached a boiling point.

Out of this anger emerged the AFMRS's periodical through which female moral reformers sought to reach an audience of Christian women and men who shared their horror at the pervasiveness of sexual licentiousness. Periodicals were an accessible and acceptable medium for women; however, what distinguishes the *Advocate of Moral Reform* is the righteous anger that fueled its early issues and inspired women to push and even cross boundaries of acceptable behavior.

I define *righteous anger* as an emboldening anger bolstered by evangelical beliefs. In the *Advocate*'s early issues, this righteous anger is evident both in the periodical's tone and in the impulse that stirred women to openly discuss and strongly condemn immoral behavior. As a rhetorical tactic, righteous anger empowered and liberated female moral reformers to act out of Christian duty, and their Christian beliefs assured them that their anger was justified. In the remainder of this chapter, I first draw on scholarly examinations of anger to describe how expressing anger was both a daring and liberating act for nineteenth-century women. Second, I explain how periodicals became an important medium for nineteenth-century female reformers. And third, based on an in-depth analysis of the *Advocate of Moral Reform*'s early issues, I describe how the AFMRS used both its periodical and its righteous anger to create a public forum for women, publicly censure male philanders, claim moral authority and agency, condemn certain gendered double standards and exploit others, and encourage education and vigilance. Underpinning each of these tactics was the evangelical call to Christian activism and the use of Scripture to justify women's actions. Overall, this chapter claims that through its periodical, the AFMRS used righteous anger to motivate a national female moral reform movement.

EXPRESSING RIGHTEOUS ANGER

In the *Advocate of Moral Reform*, female moral reformers adopted a direct, confrontational tone, often targeted at men and male-led institutions, including churches and state legislatures. Their candid, unapologetic discussions of sexual licentiousness breached longstanding social taboos. This was especially daring considering the *Advocate*'s contentious lineage. When *McDowall's Journal*, characterized as "offensive," "injurious," and "degrading,"[3] came under fire because of its frank discussions of sexual licentiousness, John McDowall ceased publishing his highly controversial paper and gave his press and subscription list to the recently established AFMRS. The *Advocate*'s first issue, published in 1835, acknowledged this transfer, but rather than choosing a more cautious approach, the AFMRS continued to openly discuss immoral sexual conduct, a particularly unseemly act for respectable middle-class women. Moreover, they openly expressed their anger—another indecorous behavior for women at the time. Consequently, the AFMRS's early years can be viewed as a turning point and precursor of nineteenth-century women's rhetoric.

While using many of the methods women had effectively employed in benevolent organizations (forming local women's societies, visiting poor neighborhoods, distributing printed materials, and influencing family and friends), female moral reformers' rhetoric also signaled women's growing frustration with male dominance and societal double standards.[4] In their campaign against licentiousness, female moral reformers fused their evangelical beliefs with their frustration and outrage. Today, the word *evangelical* is a loaded term that is often used interchangeably with conservative Protestant or fundamentalist. Here, I am using it in the traditional sense to refer to the Christian call to save others and the belief that individual behavior is essential to salvation. According to David Bebbington, the four hallmarks of nineteenth-century evangelicalism included a "stress on the Scriptures as the source of faith, conversion as its beginning, redemption as its object, and activity as its consequence."[5] These four hallmarks are prevalent in the AFMRS's rhetoric. Indeed, early female reformers often believed their causes were inextricably linked to redeeming lost souls.

Like antislavery and temperance, moral reform was bolstered by the religious fervor of the Second Great Awakening. In churches and revivals in the 1820s and 1830s, especially Charles Finney's crusades throughout the Northeast, predominately female crowds heard an urgent call for Christians to save American society.[6] The revivalist connection with moral reform is especially evident through Lydia Root Andrews Finney, Charles Finney's wife, who helped found the AFMRS and became its first directress. Moreover, Charles Finney addressed an early gathering of the AFMRS in 1834, encouraging Christians to visit brothels and "fill them with Bibles and Tracts and make them places of religious conversation and of prayer, and convert their wretched inmates *on the spot*."[7]

Fueled in part by this call to Christian activism, the righteous anger that filled the *Advocate*'s early issues became an important rhetorical tactic for the AFMRS. Female moral reformers attacked immorality with a fury uncharacteristic of the charitable and benevolent endeavors women's organizations previously pursued. These women were outraged by male immorality exhibited most visibly by rampant prostitution in their city. In response, they did something women were warned not to do—they expressed their anger.

In "The Uses of Anger: Women Responding to Racism," a speech delivered in 1981, the writer and activist Audre Lorde described anger as an appropriate response to racism. "Every woman," she stated, "has a well-stocked arsenal of anger potentially useful against those oppressions, personal and institutional, which brought that anger into being."[8] Lorde believed the anger created by oppression, if tapped, could be generative, providing insight, energy, and a bond that could mutually empower women. Distinguishing between anger that generates hope and anger that generates fear, the activist Barbara Deming also believed that anger could be empowering if transmuted into a "determination to bring about change."[9] Anger proved a valuable resource for twentieth-century feminist activists. Indeed, Linda Grasso notes that through "essays, speeches, manifestos, and direct actions, [these twentieth-century] feminist revolutionaries liberated anger from pejorative connotations by *disassociating* it from fear, destruction, and masculinity, and reassociating it with courage, growth, and sisterhood."[10] One hundred and thirty-five years earlier, women considered their anger an appropriate response to prostitution, particularly the inequitable standards of conduct, gendered power relations, and limited economic opportunities for women that necessitated prostitution. Female moral reformers harnessed their anger and used it to reveal these social problems and to rally and unite women to pursue moral reform.

Historically, anger has been the prerogative of white men. According to Grasso in *The Artistry of Anger: Black and White Women's Literature, 1820–1860*, whereas white men have long used "righteous anger" to demand natural rights or raise concerns, anger expressed by women or other marginalized groups has often been dismissed, ridiculed, or used as evidence that these individuals or groups are irrational or incompetent.[11] For instance, when the Massachusetts's clergy condemned Sarah and Angelina Grimké's public speaking, the sisters were chided for both "assum[ing] the *place* and *tone* of man as a public reformer."[12] In other words, the clergy were not only upset with women speaking publicly but also openly expressing their outrage over slavery.[13]

This nineteenth-century gendered ideology of anger especially deemed anger unacceptable in the domestic sphere.[14] This sentiment is illustrated in Louisa May Alcott's *Little Women*. In an exchange where Marmee counsels her fiery daughter Jo about controlling her temper, Marmee admits, "I've been trying to cure it [her anger] for forty years, and have only succeeded in controlling it. I am angry nearly every day of my life, Jo; but I have learned not to show it; and still I hope to learn not to feel it, though it may take me another forty years to do so."[15] The root causes of Marmee's anger were likely her limited rights, voice, and opportunities as a woman, and societal norms that precluded her from outwardly expressing her anger probably exacerbated it.[16] Even if women could not "cure" their anger, the nineteenth-century domestic canon (women's magazines, conduct books, among others) ardently advised them to suppress it.

According to those who dispensed domestic advice, anger made women unfit wives and mothers. Women were supposed to be self-sacrificial and submissive—placing their families' needs above themselves. In fact, in her characterization of the "cult of true womanhood," Barbara Welter identified "submissiveness" as one of the cardinal virtues repeated in antebellum women's magazines and religious literature.[17] For example, women's tempers were a subject repeatedly addressed in the Ladies' Department of the *Christian Advocate*, a widely distributed periodical published by the Methodist Episcopal Church. In an 1827 column, "Reflection on the State of Marriage" by a Married Man, the author wrote, "The leading features in the character of a good woman, are mildness, complaisance, and equanimity of temper."[18] An 1831 *Christian Advocate* article also advised, "Sweetness of temper, affection to her husband, and attention to his interests, constitute the duties of a wife, and form the basis of matrimonial felicity."[19] Similarly, in the *Mother's Book* (1831), a domestic manual for American mothers, Lydia Maria Child advised, "It is important that children, even when babes should never be spectators of anger or any evil passion."[20] Here, notice how Child equates anger with evil. In a later chapter Child stated, "The simple fact that your child never saw you angry, that your voice is always gentle, and the expression of your face always kind, is worth a thousand times more than all the rules you can give him."[21] Grasso notes the irony of Child, whom she labels "one of angriest women writers in the nineteenth century," denouncing anger.[22] Indeed, the fact that Child herself dispensed such advice highlights the deeply held strictures against middle-class women expressing their anger.

Even today, expressing anger can be a dicey rhetorical move for women, but for antebellum women, social mores made this doubly so. The conventional binary that associates reason with men and emotion with women, negates the latter as a lower, even "feminine," form of persuasion. Thus, women who express anger are often portrayed as irrational, angry women. Jeffrey Walker's discussion of enthymemes of anger helps dispel this irrational view of anger. Drawing from Aristotle's treatment of anger in the *Rhetoric* and more recent philosophical considerations, Walker defines anger as "a complex intentional state, an invoked cognitive construct that rises enthymemically as the 'conclusion' from a number of beliefs that serve as 'premises' which may or may not appear to consciousness in overt propositional form."[23] Moreover, Walker cites Cicero's description of pathos as a 'perturbation' of the psyche" that is "provoked by some definite idea or set of ideas."[24] This is the case with female moral reformers' anger. Far more than an emotional reaction, their anger was a reasoned response based on their evangelical beliefs and the societal and economic double standards they experienced and observed. Consequently, to avoid being summarily disregarded as a group of angry women, female moral reformers pointedly directed their anger at libertines, immoral acts, and those they considered accessories to licentiousness, and they justified their anger with Scriptures and calls to Christian duty.

Nonetheless, voicing anger was liberating for female moral reformers. "Public expressions of anger," explains Grasso, "inform the larger culture that the individual or group are human beings of consequence who are seeking attention, respect, and equal rights and privileges."[25] Not only did female moral reformers' righteous anger highlight the problem that moral licentiousness posed, especially for women, but it also validated the anger many women felt, and affirmed their right to be angry. Frequently, women deny their anger because they do not feel their anger is justified; hence, seeing other women express their anger can help a woman feel justified in her own. Women are also more likely to discover their anger when the focus is shifted away from their feelings to a description of their situation in social or political terms.[26] Focusing on sexual double standards and the social and legal acceptance of libertines, the AFMRS showed women that their anger was warranted. Drawing on the Aristotelian concept of catharsis, Walker further illustrates the rhetorical nature of anger, claiming that the release or discharge of strong emotions through anger could be cathartic and even pleasurable when it "tends outward toward resolution in approvable, honorable, public action."[27] In other words, by enacting their Christian beliefs through public action, moral reform provided a cathartic release for the frustration and anger many women felt. For all these reasons, anger became an important rhetorical tactic for women.

PUBLISHING REFORM PERIODICALS:
OPENING A PUBLIC SPACE FOR FEMALE REFORMERS

The *Advocate of Moral Reform* was the primary venue through which women conveyed their righteous anger and waged a public moral reform campaign. During the nineteenth century, periodicals—multi-genre publications issued serially at regular intervals—became a means for reformers to gain public attention, promote a cause, and attract supporters. Reform periodicals were one of many specialized publications that emerged out of what Frank Luther Mott termed a "Golden Age of Periodicals." Encouraged by the invention of the cylinder press and an increasingly literate population, this proliferation of periodicals occurred between 1825 and 1850, when as many as four to five thousand magazines and newspapers were launched. While many magazines and secular and religious newspapers of the era condemned slavery and supported temperance, moral reform, and other reform efforts, unlike these popular publications, reform periodicals were wholly devoted to the causes they promoted.[28]

Appearing as early as 1819, antislavery periodicals were the first reform periodicals.[29] Most of these were religiously motivated; they stressed humanitarian objections and labeled slavery an evil and its perpetrators sinners. Much like other periodicals of the era, which had an average lifespan of two years,[30] reform periodicals were often short-lived. However, antislavery publications, including William Lloyd Garrison's *Liberator* (1831), the *National Anti-Slavery Standard* (1840), Gamaliel Bailey's *National Era* (1847), and *Frederick Douglass' Paper* (1851), continued for several years.[31] Like those vehemently opposed to slavery, temperance advocates launched numerous periodicals. The *National Philanthropist*, issued in 1826, was the first temperance paper, and only two antebellum temperance periodicals—the *Journal of the American Temperance Union* (1837) and the *Templar's Magazine* (1850)—enjoyed extensive runs.[32] Later in the nineteenth century, the Women's Christian Temperance Union's periodical, the *Union Signal*, first published in 1880, attracted more than ninety thousand subscribers. Evident from the *Union Signal's* broad distribution, periodicals had become an important rhetorical vehicle for nineteenth-century female reformers.

For women, periodicals were both an accessible and socially accepted media. Anyone who could write and gain access to a printer could start a periodical. And writing, particularly writing directed at other women, was generally considered a suitable female pursuit. More than six hundred American women edited nineteenth-century periodicals and thousands of women contributed content. These numbers confirm that periodicals became a widely accepted public space and forum for women. Additionally, periodicals often served as a site of rhetorical education for editorial staff, contributors, and readers. While many of these women's periodicals focused on family, domestic issues, religion, and literature, others took up specific reform causes.[33]

In her foundational study of women's reform periodicals, Bertha-Monica Stearns notes from 1830 to 1860 "a group of periodicals definitely addressed to women, and very largely edited by women, clamored loudly for some Right, or agitated vigorously against some Abuse."[34] Stearns examines a wide swath of women's antebellum reform periodicals, including the *New York Amulet* and *Ladies' Literary and Religious Chronicle* (1830), which sought to combat the evils of intemperance and infidelity; Lydia Maria Child's *National Anti-Slavery Standard* (1841); the *Olive Plant and Ladies Temperance Advocate* (1841); Jane Swisshelm's *Saturday Visiter* (1848), which railed against slavery and drunkards and advocated women's suffrage; Amelia Bloomer's *Lily* (1849), which promoted temperance and women's rights; and Paulina Wright Davis's

ADVOCATE of MORAL REFORM.

Vol. I. No. 3.]   **NEW YORK, MARCH, 1835.**   **[Whole No. 3.**

Published by the New York }
Female Moral Reform Society. }

For there is nothing covered that shall not be revealed ;
Neither hid, that shall not be made known.—Luke xii. 2.

{ A monthly periodical, price
{ $1 per annum, in advance.

THE ADVOCATE.

TERMS OF SUBSCRIPTION.

Price for one copy, $1 per annum to single subscribers. 75 per annum to any person who takes six copies. $6 66 to any individual taking not less than 25 copies enclosed in one wrapper, and sent to one person. $6 50 to any auxiliary Society taking not less than 20 papers, enclosed in one wrapper, and sent to one person.

N. B. Subscribers are distinctly to understand, that, if the friends of Moral Reform do not sustain this paper, and that if it fails for the want of support, they must consider whatever balance may be due them on their subscriptions, as a donation to the good cause we advocate. As our labors in this cause are wholly gratuitous, we hope that the benevolent person will object to this condition, on which we receive subscriptions.

The Advocate is to be supported not by donations, but by subscriptions, unless the subscription money should be inadequate to its existence. Therefore, we wish every person or society sending funds to us to be very particular in distinguishing between subscriptions and donations. Subscriptions will be acknowledged, not in the columns of the Advocate, but by a receipt sent in the paper to the subscriber. Donations will be publicly acknowledged in the Advocate. In case a person sends to us a certain sum, say $5, as a donation, with a request to send him or his friend a paper, we shall consider $1 as a subscription, and acknowledge $4 as a donation : in all cases subtracting from the amount sent, enough to pay for the papers ordered to be sent to the donor or his friends.

Country Subscribers.—Each country subscriber must tell us to what Post Office, and County, and State to send his paper. Sometimes we receive a letter requesting a paper to be sent to this writer; but the writer does not tell us where to send the paper. And when the Post-Master neglects to stamp or write on the letter the name of the town and state in which it was mailed, there is no way to determine whether the subscriber lives in New England, Canada, or the Valley of the Mississippi.

McDowall's Journal.—Those who have paid in advance for McDowall's Journal, for 1835, or for a shorter or a longer period then one year, will be supplied with the Advocate, to the place of that Journal, until their subscriptions have expired.

The Advocate is sent to all the old subscribers for McDowall's Journal, with the expectation that they will cordially accept of the substitute for that periodical, and afford all that timely and efficient pecuniary support which the state of our funds imperiously requires. This number not only exhausts every dollar, for the support of the Advocate, now in our Treasury, but imposes upon us a small debt. The mere statement of this fact is all that is necessary for our friends to know. They will immediately, by mail, please, each one, to remit to us the amount of their subscription for the present year, and that will enable us to accommodate ourselves, and to go forward with the Advocate.

Those who receive and retain this paper are considered subscribers. Those who receive it and do not wish to be considered as subscribers for it, are requested to return it to the Post-Master. The Post-Master is, by law, bound to return the paper to us, or to notify us by letter that you refuse it. If he neglects to notify us, he will be liable to pay us the amount of your subscription.

It is useless to send back this paper unless you write on it the name of the Post-office, county, and state where you live. We send donations to sustain our missionary operations, to pay rent for our hired house, and to defray a part of the expenses incurred by the females under our care.

N. B. The profits of this paper are to be devoted to the missionary work.

AN ILLUSTRATION OF DUTY.

It is said that a certain Jew went down from Jerusalem to Jericho, and fell among thieves, who stripped him of his garments, and wounded him half badly, and then departed, leaving him half dead. And it happened by chance that a certain priest came down that way, and when he saw the man who had been robbed, he very quietly passed by on the other side of the road. Soon after a Levite came along to the same place, and when he saw the man who had been half killed, he stopped and looked at him; and then, as the priest had done before him, passed calmly by on the other side of the way. But it was not long before a certain Samaritan, (between whose nation and the Jews there was a natural enmity) who was travelling along that road, came where the wounded man lay ; and as soon as he saw him he had compassion on him, and immediately went to him, and bound up his wounds, dressing them with suitable healing applications ; and then set him upon his own beast, and brought him to an inn, and took care of him. And not only this, but on the next day, when the Samaritan departed, he took out some money and paid the innkeeper for the expenses of the wounded Jew; and even gave him money in advance, telling him to take care of him, and promising, when he came that way again, to pay the innkeeper all the Jew's expenses until the Jew should be recovered.

Now this Samaritan treated his enemy, the wounded Jew, very *kindly* ;—and it was his *duty* to do so ;—he would not have acted on Christian principles if he had not treated him kindly. And we approve his conduct—and we are bound to approve it, simply because it was *right* ; and *not* because it was a work of supererogation. On the other hand, an indignation is excited against the Priest and Levite, because their treatment of one of their own citizens was exceedingly unkind and unchristian, and because it was morally *wrong*.

We are pleased with the good Samaritan, not so much because he gave relief in an ordinary case of charity, as because he took up a painful cross in aiding and assisting a man who was his natural enemy. But we are displeased with the Priest and Levite, because they *turned aside*, and *passed by their duty*, the one without even stopping to look at it, and both without discharging it. We admire the conduct of the Samaritan, because it is an example worthy of imitation. But we detest the conduct of the Priest and Levite, because it is an example which, if universally imitated, would banish all love, and holiness, and happiness from the earth, and fill it with hatred, sin, and misery.

Application.

Now, *dear sisters*, happy is she that condemneth not herself in that thing which she alloweth, or approveth. [For such is the meaning of Rom. xiv. 22.] Reader, if thou art a professor of religion, then we may address unto thee the language which Paul addressed to the Jews, Rom. ii. 17, etc., "Behold thou art called a Christian, and restest in the gospel, and makest thy boast in Jesus Christ, and knowest his will, and *approvest the things that are more excellent*, being instructed out of the gospel ; and art confident that thou thyself art a guide of the blind, a light to them which are in darkness, an instructer of the foolish, a teacher of babes, and that thou hast the form of knowledge and of the truth in the gospel. Thou therefore that teachest another, teachest thou not thyself? thou that preachest a man should not steal, dost thou steal?" Dost thou detest the conduct of the Priest and Levite, and yet wilt thou go away and imitate their example? Dost thou profess to be a follower of Jesus Christ, and to admire the conduct of the good Samaritan, and yet wilt thou refuse to follow the example of either?

"Beloved, we are persuaded better things of you, though we thus speak." (Heb. vi. 9) And if we now present before you an object that demands your attention, and your compassion, and your aid, we do confidently expect that you will not say unto us, or to the wounded Jew whom you hold in your hand, as Felix said unto Paul, "Go thy way for this time ; when I have a more convenient season I will call for thee." Acts xxiv 25.

But we rather expect that you will copy the example of Jesus in the case of the ruler of the synagogue's daughter. For when Jairus, the ruler, came and told Jesus that his little daughter lay at the point of death, and requested him to come and lay his hand upon her that she might live, Jesus not only listened and attended to his request, but immediately rose up and followed Jairus into his house, and took his little daughter by the hand, and raised her from the dead.

And now, beloved sisters, we come and present before you the sin of licentiousness, and the victims she hath either slain outright, or half killed, together with all the misery and wo, and desolation, which she hath brought upon the land. "For she hath cast down many wounded, yea, many strong men have been slain by her." Prov. iv 26. And we beseech you by the mercies of God, that ye will not, like the Priest, pass by the whole subject without so much as looking at it, nor yet like the Levite come and look at it, and then go away and do nothing.

True, licentiousness is an unpleasant, disagreeable, and even indelicate vice ; and we know of no vice or sin that is remarkably unpleasant, or agreeable, or delicate, in the

Una (1852) and the *Ladies' Advocate* (1855), two more early champions of women's rights. Stearns's study also highlights the *Advocate of Moral Reform*, which she identifies as one of earliest and most controversial women's reform periodicals. As a vehicle for the AFMRS's righteous anger, the *Advocate* became a powerful instrument for reform. The AFMRS used its periodical to create a public forum for women, censure male philanderers, claim moral authority, condemn certain gendered double standards and exploit others, and educate and encourage women's vigilance.

CREATING A PUBLIC FORUM FOR WOMEN

The AFMRS broke away from the Female Benevolent Society in large part because it believed prevention through public awareness and education provided a surer path to moral reform than efforts to reclaim and liberate prostitutes. Female moral reformers believed "vice should be exposed and the innocent protected from evil and warned of danger before it was too late."[35] Consequently, they deemed publicly discussing prostitution and sex unavoidable, believing they should pursue "a crusade against evil" through the press.[36] With the *Advocate of Moral Reform*, the AFMRS provided a venue in which women could express their anger and exchange ideas. The AFMRS encouraged its members to distribute the *Advocate*, an eight-page, semimonthly paper that typically included editorials, essays, sermons, cautionary tales, advice to parents on the proper moral education for their children, and warnings about practices or situations that might jeopardize a person's moral standing. Some of this material was reprinted from other sources (sermons, tracts, other periodicals, etc.), a common practice for periodicals of the era. At the same time, editorials, submissions written specifically for the *Advocate*, reports from auxiliary societies, and graphic reports from the society's city missionaries, who visited sordid neighborhoods and brothels, gave the periodical and the AFMRS its distinct character. The *Advocate* quickly became the AFMRS's voice and primary weapon against widespread immorality. With a circulation that climbed to 36,200 by 1840, it battled licentiousness beyond New York City and became one of the nation's most widely read reform periodicals.[37] When she was young, Lucy Stone's family subscribed to both Garrison's *Liberator* and the *Advocate of Moral Reform*—thus both reform periodicals nurtured one of the nineteenth century's most ardent antislavery and women's suffrage advocates.[38] Stone later supported moral reform as a member and secretary of the AFMRS auxiliary society at Oberlin College.

Initially, the *Advocate of Moral Reform* was edited by several AFMRS members with the assistance of ministers who supported the cause. However, in 1836 Sarah Towne Smith became its editor, and she continued in that role for nine years.[39] As editor, Smith not only wrote editorials and other sections, she also acted as the periodical's gatekeeper—soliciting and selecting content and copyediting. With the AFMRS board acting as publisher and Smith serving as editor, these women broke with traditional gendered roles and became public commentators.[40] In its masthead the paper proudly touted its female leadership stating, "The Advocate is, as it professes to be, "EXCLUSIVELY under the direction of the Female Moral Reform Society: it is edited entirely by a lady." With this emphasis, the *Advocate* was promoting itself as a public forum created *by* and *for* women. In its third annual report, the AFMRS explained that the paper is "needed to afford a channel of communication, in which the thoughts and feelings of females throughout the country may more freely mingle, than they could do in any other way. It will be obvious to all, that this can only be accomplished, to any extent, in a paper conducted exclusively by ladies, and devoted to their interests."[41] For nineteenth-century women's periodicals, acknowledging a female editor in chief was important to the publication's success. This was especially true when treading such controversial ground.[42]

The *Advocate of Moral Reform* provided a safe space for women to voice their concerns by extending the comfort women felt participating in all-female organizations to a textual, discursive space. This emphasis on an all-women organization also gave license to the AFMRS's female readers by claiming moral reform as appropriate work for women. While the editors printed articles written by men and encouraged men to subscribe to the *Advocate*, the AFMRS encouraged an exclusive female membership, believing that all-female groups were more productive and that moral reform was work better entrusted to women. Sharon Harris notes, "Periodicals were extremely important to women and girls of all ages as places for exchanges of ideas throughout the decades of the nineteenth century."[43] However, the reform-minded *Advocate* was unlike other mild-mannered ladies' magazines edited by women. Railing against male lechers and murderers of virtue, the *Advocate of Moral Reform* employed an outraged tone that resonated with its audience. In that sense, the *Advocate* operated as both a manifestation and an instrument of the AFMRS's righteous anger. The *Advocate* modeled anger as an appropriate response to sexual immorality and, in turn, readers flooded the paper with letters recounting stories of men who seduced and robbed women of their innocence. For instance, a submission in an 1837 issue of the *Advocate* told the story of Mr. A from R—, Vermont, who, during his profligate youth, ruined and abandoned a young woman. Years later after Mr. A had been saved by religion and a pious wife, his own daughter was seduced and ruined by a libertine. Thus, the article stressed retribution with the sins of the father being visited upon his daughter.[44] Another submission shared the story of a young man described as a "monster, by the name of S—," who graduated from a New England college and was employed as a teacher in a respectable academy in Massachusetts. According to the writer, the "infamous teacher," who was engaged to another woman, seduced the daughter of the family with whom he boarded. "By art and falsehood and promises of marriage, he triumphed over her virtue," and when exposure was inevitable, he fled.[45]

For many *Advocate* readers, these stories of women's vulnerability in antebellum society were generative; they prompted anger and provided a place to voice it. As Laurie Gries notes, "Publics are created and maintained by circulating discourses that unite strangers in a real or abstract sense."[46] The *Advocate of Moral Reform* made it possible for "geographically isolated women" to "communicate with like-minded women."[47] As such, the *Advocate* became a public forum that united and empowered ordinary antebellum women to speak out. "Lashing out through their periodical," Barbara Berg claims, female moral reformers "criticized, lectured, and instructed men in a manner unprecedented in American history."[48] This direct, confrontational style is especially evident in the *Advocate*'s first issue. Aware that its paper would stir controversy, the AFMRS defended the public forum it sought to create. On the first page of the *Advocate*'s inaugural issue, the AFMRS asserted "such a paper is absolutely necessary in order to call public attention to the vice of licentiousness, and aid in forming such a public sentiment as will banish this vice from the community."[49] Indicting religious papers and male editors, the AFMRS justified its paper's need, claiming, "Other papers *will not expose* this vice . . . if religious publications would do this, if they would cry aloud and spare not, and show the people their transgression, than we grant that no paper exclusively devoted to the sin in question would be demanded."[50] However, "*men will not do it.*" Indeed, the women who led the AFMRS had seen their ministers and even their husbands shy away from confronting sexual sin.[51] By publishing the *Advocate* female moral reformers superseded these men and the male-dominated periodical press that maintained silence on sexual licentiousness, a transgression that most negatively impacted women.

Declaring that licentiousness was running rampant and no one else was willing to expose it, female moral reformers claimed that exigent circumstances forced them to take such daring steps. In their anthology of women rhetoricians, Joy Ritchie and Kate Ronald note that exigency has often prompted women to make bold rhetorical moves and provided a justification for their actions.[52] Additionally, by portraying themselves as reluctant public actors, they employed another common topos used by female reformers and speakers throughout the nineteenth century.

As a forum for women, the *Advocate of Moral Reform* welcomed a woman's perspective. It empathized and took women's concerns seriously. Through publication, it transformed stories of seduction and betrayal, previously relegated as "rumors" and "gossip," into persuasive condemnation against male sexual license. Ultimately, the *Advocate* provided an outlet for women signaling that women's voices, concerns, and experiences mattered. In doing so, the *Advocate* released a floodgate of women's pent-up anger, which initially helped fuel the female moral reform movement.

PUBLICLY SHAMING MALE PHILANDERS

"For there is nothing covered that shall not be revealed; neither hid that shall not be made known." This passage from Luke 12:2, which appeared on the *Advocate*'s masthead from 1835 until 1837, could be characterized as the scriptural motto for the AFMRS's righteous anger. Believing there could be no remedy without exposure, female moral reformers took the audacious step of printing the names of confirmed philanderers in the *Advocate of Moral Reform*. For instance, an 1836 issue printed the name "John Stone, Jr. of Worthington" in bold letters then proceeded to accuse him of abandoning his legitimate wife and cohabitating with another woman.[53] Another issue condemned Benjamin Heely for abandoning his wife and three children to marry another woman, whom he also abandoned while she was pregnant with his child. The article then warned that Heely was on the prowl—recently spotted in Philadelphia "with a beautiful young lady, of highly respectable connections, who doubtless, was entirely ignorant of his character."[54] In addition to directing its righteous anger at these men and their brazen exploits, printing the names and crimes of libertines was a bold symbol of the AFMRS's commitment to end silence, particularly with regards to men's immoral actions. In one instance, the editor printed the name "S. M. Ensign" in bold letters above an article asserting: "This individual, it seems, is endeavoring to reestablish his claims to public confidence, and make it appear that he has been greatly injured by the article that appeared against his character in the *Advocate*. We thought at the time that we had ample confirmation of the truth of all that was alleged against him, and since the publication of that article, assurance has become doubly sure."[55] No shrinking violets, AFMRS women were unwilling to back down and again presented their charges and evidence against Mr. Ensign.

While women had no legal recourse, the *Advocate* allowed them to wield the power of public exposure. That power was also extended to the AFMRS's local auxiliary societies, which submitted the names of philanders in other cities and towns. In fact, the story of Benjamin Heely suggests that the AFMRS's network of auxiliaries and supporters worked in coordination to track the whereabouts of known libertines. Additionally, AFMRS missionaries and volunteers who visited brothels and stood vigil outside their doors often recorded patrons' names. Fear of public exposure became a deterrent to brothel customers, and the practice garnered the AFMRS even more acrimony. Anticipating this response, the *Advocate of Moral Reform*'s first issue announced and defended the practice: "Where it can be done with safety to ourselves and to the innocent, we may think it proper even to expose names, for the same reason that the names of thieves and robbers are published, that the public may know them. . . . We mean to let the licentious know, that if they are *not* ashamed of their debasing vices, we will not be ashamed to expose them."[56]

Notably, this article aligned libertines with thieves and robbers and delineated adultery, fornication, and rape as serious crimes. The AFMRS further emphasized its commitment to public exposure by printing a letter to the editor in which a reader questioned the AFMRS's practice of censure, suggesting that it also harmed the libertine's family and associates. In response, the *Advocate*'s editor pointedly questioned whether the names of every murderer should be carefully concealed because they too have families and friends. Juxtaposing libertines with murderers, the editor again elevated the seriousness of sexual licentiousness. With public censure, the AFMRS exerted power to which women were generally unaccustomed. Discrediting a man's reputation could have catastrophic effects. The historian Mary Ryan notes that in the 1840s the Mercantile Agency (the forerunner to Dunn and Bradstreet) "sentenced many a young man to business failure by denying credit on the basis of 'bad reputation' or 'running after women.'"[57] Using the eyes and ears of its local auxiliary societies and the national voice of its newspaper, the AFMRS attempted to hold men accountable for their moral behavior in the same way society held women accountable. Women were ruined in tandem with their reputations, so why not men?

Even when the *Advocate of Moral Reform* was not publishing names, it was constructing the immoral man as a vilified character (*ethopoeia*). With its righteous anger, the *Advocate* repeatedly characterized immoral men as "vile seducers," "practiced villains," "profligate pimps," "destroyers," and "murderers of female virtue." Rosenberg similarly notes, "Reckless," "bold," "mad," and "drenched in sin," were terms commonly used to portray men. Indeed, the AFMRS's rhetoric foreshadows temperance women's vivid depictions of violent and degenerate drunkards, which similarly helped rally sympathy and support for their cause.[58] The AFMRS used the *Advocate* to condemn immoral men in general and when possible to name libertines in particular. In doing so, it wielded one of the few means of power available to women—the shame of public exposure.

CLAIMING MORAL AUTHORITY AND AGENCY

By spotlighting acts of immorality, the *Advocate of Moral Reform* breached both religious and social mores that silenced all public discussions of sexual behavior. The AFMRS's righteous anger is especially evident in its defense of these actions and its claims of moral authority. Many Christians in antebellum America believed that sexual conduct was an inappropriate subject for public discourse. They contended that women should be kept sexually innocent, even naïve.[59] While adultery and prostitution had long been recognized as problems by Protestant faiths, male-led churches generally chose to remain silent on these subjects.[60] According to the *Advocate*, new ministers were even advised to avoid discussing these topics with their parishioners.[61] Many churches and Christians defended their silence, claiming that immorality was a "delicate subject" inappropriate for mixed audiences. They also insisted that publicly discussing sexual behavior could ignite passions and promote licentiousness.

While the AFMRS particularly took issue with men's efforts to silence the group, there were also women who opposed the AFMRS's forthright discussions. Many women, including editors of popular women's magazines, similarly condemned frank discussions of immoral sexual behavior. For instance, Sarah Hale, then editor of the *Ladies' Magazine* prior to taking the helm at *Godey's Lady's Book*, scorned the *New York Amulet and Ladies' Literary and Religious Chronicle* (1830), which in a milder manner also sought to combat the evils of intemperance and infidelity. Hale called the *New York Amulet* "one of the most noted infidel teachers," and scoffed, "there may be ladies among us inclined to infidelity and intemperance, and if so we advise them immediately to subscribe to the New York Amulet."[62] The ire Hale directed at the *New York Amulet* demonstrates that the *Advocate* and other women's reform periodicals were not only combatting social problems, but long standing social decorum that dictated what was appropriate for women to read, write, and hear.

Like the *New York Amulet*, the *Advocate of Moral Reform* was routinely attacked for contributing to licentiousness instead of combating it. Again, employing its righteous anger, the AFMRS tackled these concerns head on, asking critics to submit any evidence of individuals who had been corrupted by reading the *Advocate*.[63] The AFMRS also challenged the logic that sexual misconduct was an inappropriate subject for public discussion and that such discussions encouraged immorality. One *Advocate* article asserted, "To engage in this work of purification will not in the least endanger our own purity of heart or life. Its most probable effect will be, to make us aspire after the perfect freedom from the impurities of earth which alone can qualify us for the blessed society of heaven."[64] Rather than polluting its proponents, the *Advocate* argued that moral reform would purify them. The paper also called into question the convictions of ministers who would remain silent. One writer wryly chimed: "In my view, it argues a strong propensity to evil, *to say the least*, if a mind cannot come into contact with vice without embracing it. If the moral purity of him who ministers to me in holy things rests on such a frail foundation as this, viz: total ignorance of the evil, or silence with regard to it, let the temptation be presented; let him fall, and thus rid the ministry of one, who might, in his own parish, be taken in a snare, and not only destroy himself, but this flock also."[65] Both of these articles turn their detractors' own arguments back on them (*antistrephon*). The AFMRS espoused righteous anger. In harsh terms and tone, it questioned the faith and moral fortitude of those who would silence them and discourage action—one of the tenets of nineteenth-century evangelism. By defending itself and condemning those who would remain silent, female moral reformers were claiming their own moral authority and agency.

During the nineteenth century, women were often assigned the role of moral arbiters, and female moral reformers seized that authority. Amid the tide of the Second Great Awakening, acting as a moral agent was also a matter of Christian duty, so the AFMRS boldly cast moral reform as a means of enacting one's faith. "It is not time for cowardice or lukewarmness on the part of those who love the Lord," exhorted one *Advocate* article, "they owe it to the blessed Redeemer, to let it be distinctly seen, whose livery they wear and in whose service they are engaged."[66] Rather than averting their eyes and ears, the *Advocate* urged Christians to take up the work of moral reform. The *Advocate* took particular aim at the word *delicacy*, which was frequently used to silence discussions of sexual immorality. One article asserted, "*It is a delicate subject!*' True, and none have a deeper sense of this, than those who are now advocating the cause of Moral Reform; but they dare not offer this as a plea for neglecting to warn a licentious world of the enormity of this sin."[67] The *Advocate* even offered an alternate definition for delicacy—"To appear to know nothing about licentiousness, while you are daily associating with those you know to be habitually guilty of it."[68] Female moral reformers adroitly used Scripture to validate their moral authority and their methods. They claimed they were following God's example: "God does not advance his cause by miracles. It is by the operation of truth on men's minds, leading them to form correct opinions and act upon them."[69] They pointed out that the Bible, which is quite graphic in addressing sins of a sexual nature, including adultery, incest, sodomy, prostitution, fornication, and bestiality, is not deemed inappropriate.[70] In other words, God's word did not promote virtue through silence, so why should ministers or female moral reformers.

The AFMRS also stressed the inefficacy of silence. Again, using *antistrephon* to indict its opponents with their own arguments, the AFMRS asserted that rather than protecting innocent women, silence actually protects indecent men. The *Advocate* angrily asserted, "We now see, while we have been silently deploring the spread of iniquity among us, it has been steadily increasing."[71] Moreover, the AFMRS argued that the licentious and Satan were the primary beneficiaries of silence. One *Advocate* writer claimed, "Silence is just what the licentious wish: they don't expect the virtuous community will approve their vices: all they ask is . . . that their vices may be winked at and not exposed."[72] By situating the silent alongside the licentious and Satan, female moral reformers demonized those who demanded silence, suggesting they were in cahoots with the devil. Another *Advocate* article accentuated this point, posing the rhetorical question: "Must Satan be left to riot undisturbed in this, his chosen field, because Christians might soil their garments in exposing it?"[73] Classifying silence as a sin and the silent as sinful, the AFMRS exerted its own moral license.

By breaching the social mores of silence, the AFMRS also revealed silence as a male prerogative. The AFMRS's unapologetic trespass on the subject of sexual conduct opened it to harsh and unremitting attacks. Female moral reformers, instead of the libertines they condemned, frequently became targets of rebuke. Because of the society's bold tactics, women were threatened to avoid participation in moral reform lest their own moral standing be called into question.[74] "When clergymen and laymen joined the vituperative attacks on the society, castigating members for unladylike behavior," Anne Firor Scott writes, "the women were unmoved, reminding their critics that since men were in the habit of holding women responsible for improving the moral tone of society they could hardly complain when they assumed that responsibility."[75] The AFMRS and its auxiliary societies also pointed to this opposition as evidence of the movement's success; female moral reformers clearly struck a nerve with sinners and those who knowingly and unknowingly protected them. Accusations against the AFMRS bolstered the women's belief that they could not trust men to pursue moral reform and that it was men who stood in the way of moral purity.

The AFMRS assumed a role it believed the church had abdicated. By urging Christians, particularly women, to confront and combat licentiousness in their communities, moral reform offered the churchwomen, who overwhelmingly comprised church membership, another avenue for exerting moral authority. Thus, they wrested power away from the church and its clergy. One of the more interesting aspects of the AFMRS's righteous anger was how often it was directed at ministers and churches. *Advocate* articles chided churches for not reproving the libertines among their ranks.[76] In a direct address to one minister, an article charged, "May not that ruined young man, who went down to a profligate's grave from your congregation, and who will say when called to answer for his deeds, that he never heard one word on the subject of the 7th commandment from his pastor; may not he charge you with being, at least, accessory to his destruction?"[77] The AFMRS condemned these spiritual intermediaries for their censure of God's commandments. Moreover, female moral reformers claimed moral authority over men and institutions that they believed were derelict in their Christian duty. In doing so, they disrupted the social mores that called for silence on all sexual matters and the institutions that had maintained that silence. The AFMRS used the *Advocate* to dispel the reasons used to justify this silence, to highlight its inefficacy, and to call into question those who attempted to silence them. Female moral reformers supported each of these actions with calls to Christian duty and with Scripture, thus assuming the authority to interpret the Bible for themselves. Moreover, these actions demonstrate the confidence and collective consciousness that emerged from the combination of anger and evangelical activism.

CONDEMNING CERTAIN DOUBLE STANDARDS, EXPLOITING OTHERS

As part of its righteous anger, the AFMRS vehemently condemned the gendered double standard for sexual conduct. According to the long-standing social narrative, women who engaged in sex outside of wedlock were believed to be utterly defiled; they were often rejected by their families and friends and forfeited any hope for respectable marriage or employment. Conversely, men were rarely publicly exposed or ruined; for them, sexual conquests were often a tacit badge of honor. These drastically different standards that wrought such severe consequences for women help explain why women were especially drawn to moral reform.

The AFMRS's efforts to eliminate this double moral standard that primarily penalized profligate women mirrors the argument for a single moral standard that Sarah and Angelina Grimké, Lucretia Mott, and Antoinette Brown Blackwell later used to defend their right to speak publicly.[78] Both groups of women were attacking the logic that an action (sexual behavior or public speaking) could be morally acceptable for men and not women. In essence, female moral reformers were making an early argument for equality. Stipulating that whatever disgraced a woman should also disgrace a man, moral reformers argued for a uniform standard of sexual conduct. That said, the AFMRS was not advocating more sexual freedom for women or even acknowledging women's sexual desires; rather, it was condemning men's sexual freedom and the society that turned a blind eye to their wanton behavior. While affirming "a traditional view of respectable womanhood," J. Shoshanna Ehrlich notes that female moral reformers attempted to "rein in male lust" and "the presumed right of male access to the youthful female body."[79] In other words, they were asserting "the right to control the mores of men."[80] Espousing righteous anger, one *Advocate* writer reminded readers that "no effort need be made to fasten disgrace upon the licentious woman; she is disgraced already, and effectually shut out from all communication with the virtuous of the other sex: but the licentious man, as guilty and polluted as the woman, is still permitted to move in respectable society."[81] These different societal standards especially outraged female moral reformers and became the movement's central rallying cry.

While underscoring society's unequal treatment of men and women, the AFMRS also emphasized women's own complicity in this double standard. A report submitted to the *Advocate* by the AFMRS's Rochester auxiliary chided, "And may not the exceeding prevalence of this sin in the other sex, be greatly owing to the courteous and respectful treatment they receive from virtuous females? Scarcely could they wish for greater license to sin than has thus been given them, while the guilty of our own sex have been branded with infamy, and banished from society."[82] The *Advocate* demanded that female readers exercise their righteous anger by banishing disreputable men from respectable society. The AFMRS even asked its members to commit to this action in their membership pledge. The pledge, which became a rhetorical act, included the following passage: " in cases of licentiousness, fully believing the male is *equally*, and in most cases *more guilty* than the female, we will withdraw from all unnecessary intercourse with the vile of both sexes, except with a view to reclaim them."[83] Like the temperance movement, the AFMRS instituted a pledge that asked members to affirm their support of the movement's main tenets. This oath was intended to unite and embolden the society's members; it emphasized the movement's commitment to religious activism and the ways women could individually enact moral reform. The pledge, like the AFMRS's other array of tactics, sought to end the double standard for immorality and make life miserable for those men who continued immoral acts by publicly shaming them. Although limited, the AFMRS continually called on women to employ the means of power available to them.

While railing against double standards applied to sexual conduct, the AFMRS shrewdly used other social narratives and gendered double standards to their advantage. In addition to seizing on the perception that women were more moral, the *Advocate of Moral Reform* exploited the view that women were pure, trusting, open-hearted, and without sexual desires in order to reverse the perception of prostitutes as vile seducers of men. Instead, female moral reformers depicted prostitutes as victims of men, inequitable social systems, and economics. The *Advocate* printed countless cautionary tales of girls seduced, defiled, and abandoned by libertines from which a narrative of the woman ruined and relegated to prostitution emerged.

An 1835 issue of the *Advocate* shared the story of a young female orphaned, who was placed under the care of a, Mr. *** in Newberg and his young family. "Though possessed of wealth and influence, and respected as a citizen, and considered, by a casual observer, to be a moral man," the story explained that when the girl was fourteen, Mr. *** "consummated her ruin," and for years continued to force himself on her until he eventually turned her out of his household for fear that his horrid crime would be discovered. The girl, homeless and friendless, came to New York, where she "had been living in sin for two years," when the writer encountered her. Acknowledging that readers might doubt the young woman's story, the writer attested, "She was under deep conviction, and in the anguish of her soul when she related to me the sad story that I have been writing; and I believe every word of it.—Some may say, such creatures will lie. I know they will. But I shall never forget the manner in which she told it. It was while the Spirit of the living God was present."[84] The writer offered to find the young woman a place in an asylum, but the woman admitted, "I can't bear to be with those who despise me—I can't bear to look virtuous persons in the face—I feel I am fit for no society but this in which I live." The next time the writer inquired after the young woman, the writer learned that she had committed suicide.

The story depicts the tragic life of a child orphaned, a young girl repeatedly raped, and a defiled woman discarded and relegated to a life of prostitution. Clearly the intent was to generate sympathy by revealing this prostitute as a victim. In fact, today it may be difficult to fathom why so much rhetorical effort was necessary to portray this woman as a victim. However, nineteenth-century society maintained a rigid view of fallen women. In addition to prostitutes, fallen women in antebellum society might include a rape victim, a participant in a pre- or extramarital affair, a widow engaging in sexual relations, or even a woman condemned for being too flirtatious. "Regardless," María Carla Sánchez notes, "once women in the nineteenth century had fallen, they stayed fallen; it rarely mattered how they got that way."[85] There simply were no gradations where female promiscuity was concerned.

Nonetheless, the AFMRS tried to elicit sympathy for fallen women. *In Reforming the World: Social Activism and the Problem of Fiction in Nineteenth-Century America*, Sánchez suggests that antebellum moral reform writing, while attempting to document actual events, appropriated many elements from fiction and popular novels of the era such as *Pamela*, *Charlotte Temple*, and *The Coquette* to generate sympathy. Ironically, moral reformers continually railed against novels, accusing them of glamorizing sin.[86] However, like the novelists Samuel Richardson, Susanna Rowson, and Hannah Webster Foster,[87] female moral reformers wanted readers to identify with the young women in their articles and alert them dangerous situations that existed for women. Similarly, *Advocate* narratives were intended to show that under certain circumstances, this fallen woman could have been anyone—a daughter, sister, or friend. The fallen women depicted in the *Advocate* came to symbolize women's vulnerabilities. By doing so, the AFMRS attempted to redirect women's righteous anger away from the fallen women to the perpetrators and situations that caused their fall. The heartrending story of the orphaned girl strongly condemned the man who repeatedly raped her and then turned her out onto the streets with little prospect other than prostitution. Moreover, the narrative showed how easily women could fall victim to villainous men. The AFMRS's focus was on prevention—preventing men and women from committing immoral acts. Even as the AFMRS sympathized with prostitutes and would gladly assist them in finding an asylum that might assist in their reclamation, the *Advocate*'s objective was prevention.

Another story published in the *Advocate* shared the sad tale of a foolish young wife, Jane, who was seduced by her brother-in-law, Mr. V. Highlighting common moral reform themes, the narrative provided the circumstances that led to the woman's fall. For instance, Jane had been raised by "a misjudging mother, who lavished on her every external decoration and accomplishment while [her] mind was left quite unfurnished, or cheated only with the semblance of food, in the form of novels and romances."[88] Readers also learned that her blaggard brother-in-law had a reputation as an infamous gambler and libertine. Thus, foolish Jane became his easy prey. Once the affair was discovered, Jane was forced to leave her home and abandon her children. To support herself, she was relegated to a life of infamy in a distant city. From there, the article notes her rapid decline, "in less than three years from the time that her guilt became public, she was carried to the grave."[89] Nudging readers to sympathize with this foolish young woman, the writer implored, "The story of Jane W. is but one of thousands. I have felt it deeply, because a companion of my childhood was the victim, but each of the loved and lost had a circle of friends to whom she might have been an ornament and blessing."[90]

Even if readers could not identify with the adulterous wife, they could identify with the tragic loss of a friend or a mother torn from her children. Moreover, they could identify with society's double standard for women and men. While Jane was condemned to a life of infamy and a tragic death, her seducer, Mr. V, was forgiven by his wife. Claiming that Jane had seduced him, the scoundrel was welcomed back into his home and respectable society. No doubt, the double standard in this story was intended to incite readers' wrath. On the other hand, Mr. V's wife may have had little choice. Women without a husband in the nineteenth century were often relegated to poverty. Thus, she may have considered living with a libertine the lesser of two evils.

In both stories, the prostitute dies. Clearly, there were few narrative options. While some prostitutes did die untimely deaths, and quitting prostitution was difficult, some prostitutes were welcomed back by family members, some began new lives—moving to different sections of the city or new cities altogether, and some former prostitutes even married. But these endings did not serve the AFMRS's rhetorical purposes. The *Advocate*'s sentimental narratives were intended to transform prostitutes from vixens to victims. By doing so, the AFMRS shifted anger away from the sinful woman to the male perpetrator who cast her down that path. One *Advocate* article even argued that the libertine was more contemptible than the murderer because he not only has defiled a woman but in most cases, has "consign[ed] her to a life of infamy here, and almost certain perdition hereafter."[91] With its depictions of prostitutes as victims of male seduction, entrapment, rape, and abandonment, the AFMRS hoped to shift contempt to immoral men. This not only redirected anger to men and women's vulnerability but also affirmed the need to prevent other women from suffering the same fate.

The AFMRS's efforts to redefine prostitutes as victims overlooked other circumstances that drew women into prostitution. Most women turned to prostitution out of economic necessity, not because they were defiled. As I noted in chapter 1, even amid dramatic economic changes in cities during the first half of the nineteenth century, women's opportunities remained limited, making prostitutes and brothel madams the best paid women in nineteenth-century cities. Occasionally stories in the *Advocate* depicted this sad reality of women relegated to prostitution out of necessity as well as shame. For instance, one of the AFMRS's city missionaries reported "an affecting interview" with a mother whose two daughters "had recently been driven by poverty, and want of employment" to prostitution in order to "procure their daily bread."[92]

Although they were both stories of oppression—economic and sexual—the narrative of the prostitute trying to earn a living was not nearly as compelling as the woman victimized and relegated to prostitution by the lustful libertine. Consequently, the AFMRS primarily chose the most persuasive frame as it rallied support for moral reform.

ENCOURAGING EDUCATION AND VIGILANCE

Just as the narrative of Jane W. insinuated that her mother's indulgence contributed to Jane's fall, to save women from the grips of male seduction, the AFMRS stressed the importance of education and upbringing. Again, emphasizing those rhetorical means available to women, the AFMRS believed that women could reform the culture through their children.[93] Even these pleas are tinged with righteous anger as the *Advocate of Moral Reform* urged mothers to instruct and prepare their children. Numerous articles appeared under the title "A Mother's Influence." In an address before the Brooklyn AFMRS, which was printed in the *Advocate*, Reverend C. S. Macreading stressed the need for mother's vigilance—posing a series of rhetorical questions: "Is it ever too early to eradicate the seeds of sin? Do we practice on this principle in other things? Does the mariner overlook the leak because it is small? Does the gardener wait till the weeds have reached their full growth ere he digs them up? Shall the fire be neglected till it emblazons the whole house, before it be extinguished? Nay let the first stir of the serpent alarm you. Let nothing prevent you from doing your duty."[94] The AFMRS repeatedly stressed that a mother's duty included the moral instruction of her children. Another article admonished, "Ought not mothers feel, that ignorance of danger is no security against it—and should they not endeavor, notwithstanding the apparent difficulty of the task, to make their children understand, on every point."[95] In addition to stressing exigency, these pleas also affirmed women's roles as moral authorities and mothers' roles as reformers. For female moral reformers, motherhood became a justification for their participation in moral reform and an appeal to other women to similarly protect their children. Women repeatedly claimed that they were merely acting in their special roles as mothers and guardians to promote the spiritual and moral welfare of society for their children.

In the same way that the *Advocate* had condemned silence and concerns about delicacy with regards to public discussions of sexual conduct, the AFMRS's righteous anger attacked mothers' reluctance to discuss sexual conduct with their children. It especially condemned the notion that girls should be kept naïve. One anecdote which described a woman's escape from a villain's grasp asserted, "Miss — attributes her escape from this snare, simply to moral reform principles and the faithful instruction of a pious mother."[96] By calling for boys to be instructed in the same manner as girls, the paper also attacked the double standard customarily employed in children's upbringing, which implied that "purity in man is not as desirable as purity in woman."[97] An article titled "An Unjust Distinction" argued that by granting them greater latitude in action and expression, boys were taught "what would be indelicate and improper in a sister, was only an exhibition of boyish spirit in them, of which they might be justly proud, or at least for which they had not cause to blush."[98] In essence, the AFMRS was attempting to nip in the bud the gendered double standard for moral behavior.

The moral instruction of both boys and girls especially became a concern for mothers in a commercial era that drew many of their children to cities in search of employment. The *Advocate* itself assumed an instructive role for young women and men. It shared numerous cautionary tales as well as prescriptive advice to avoid "seductive" activities such as going to the theater, reading romance novels and other salacious fiction, and attending parties, particularly those that encouraged close dancing. The *Advocate* also revealed common tactics employed by male seducers and the missteps of their female victims. Articles repeatedly warned women to be wary of men who wanted to separate them from their parents or promised to marry or take care of them. The paper shared numerous cautionary tales of women who ran away with men, but were abandoned soon after the liaison was consummated. Articles also warned about the dangers of traveling alone. One writer counseled, "A women should be on her guard when traveling in our stage coaches, packet boats, cars and other public conveyances . . . I assure you that men journey to and fro through the country, who have no other object in view than the pursuit of unprotected females."[99]

The *Advocate of Moral Reform* also advised readers of the dangers women faced when coming to cities in search of employment. The *Advocate* printed countless anecdotes of young girls taken in by brothels posing as boarding-houses. One article told the story of an innocent girl decoyed to a brothel, lamenting "here her virtue found its grave."[100] The *Advocate*'s effect in prompting women to action is evident in a report from the Buffalo, New York, auxiliary moral reform society, which shared the story of a girl lured to a brothel by a gentleman who offered her a job. Members of the Buffalo auxiliary, who successfully rescued the girl, warned, "the net is spread in our streets and the snare laid in our public houses to catch the unwary and decoy the innocent."[101] Stressing the need for vigilance, they added, "O when will the Christian be as much engaged to warn and instruct the ignorant, as vigilant to save the inexperienced, as these harpies are to destroy them?"[102]

In addition to dispensing advice and cautions to young men and women, these warnings provoked outrage and vigilance among readers. The effect is evident in stories of individuals who intervened to protect young girls on the verge of danger. One article told the story of a woman traveling on a steamer, who noticed a young girl staying in a stateroom with an older gentleman. Taking an opportunity to talk with the young girl, the woman discovered that the man was an acquaintance of the girl's father, and he had persuaded the girl to accompany him on the journey so she could see the country. The woman instructed the girl on the danger of her situation. Then, with the assistance of other ladies and the boat's captain, the woman secured the young girl in another room beyond the gentleman's reach. When the man angrily confronted the woman about her interference, she asserted that she was simply a mother taking care of another's child. Furthermore, she stated that "She was also a friend of Moral Reform, and found, as she supposed that the child was ignorant of right principles, and ignorant of his villainous intentions."[103] These types of stories showed women that they *should* act, and that they *could* rescue girls through their efforts.

In cities and villages, women also formed AFMRS auxiliary societies. Many of these auxiliaries turned their vigilance into action by opening employment offices and offering to serve as clearinghouses for girls looking for respectable employment.[104] Other societies began submitting to the *Advocate* recommendations of respectable boardinghouses in cities, and safe public houses and inns where women should stay while traveling. Chapter 4 discusses the important role auxiliary societies played in the moral reform movement. Here, their efforts show how the anger and frustration the AFMRS expressed in the *Advocate* reflected sentiments shared by women across the country.

Antebellum women's rhetorical means were limited. Nonetheless, they used their roles as mothers, and they stressed the moral superiority society had granted them Female moral reformers also drew on their religious beliefs and their vast scriptural knowledge, women's shared experiences, their sympathy and identification with fallen women, and their anger. These became generative resources for the AFMRS as it published its periodical. By expressing their righteous anger, women asserted their independence. And by publishing the *Advocate of Moral Reform*, the AFMRS showed that women's experiences mattered, and that those individuals and social practices that harmed women should to be called out and condemned. The next chapter discusses another resource readily available to women that became a potent rhetorical tactic in the moral reform movement—women's presence.

Chapter 3

Being Present

I was led to speak plainly and faithfully to a man who had a family, but was known to be keeping a mistress at the same time. My age made me feel that as he was thrown in my way, there was no impropriety in attempting to set his sin before him. But it provoked his anger and he repeatedly threatened my life.

—*Walks of Usefulness, Or Reminiscences of Mrs. Margaret Prior*

While traveling in New York City in her role as a city missionary for the AFMRS, Margaret Prior confronted an adulterer about his transgression, and the man threatened her life. Although Prior was not easily frightened, afterward she admitted that she had avoided the vicinity of the man's house until the day when she received a note asking her to come to his residence immediately. Although she feared "a plot had been laid to ensnare [her]," she reports, "after commending the case to God, I went as requested."[1] There she found the same man on his deathbed pleading with her to pray for him, admitting that he was not prepared or fit to die. Recorded in one of Margaret Prior's missionary reports, and later her memoir, this story exhibits Prior's commitment to moral reform. Publicly confronting and reproving a man was an audacious act for an antebellum woman, yet her willingness to condemn the adulterer had persuaded this man of both his immoral behavior and her steadfast faith; thus, he sought her help as he faced his own mortality. Through her work as an AFMRS missionary, Prior repeatedly put herself in unlikely places, and her presence and fearlessness helped persuade those she encountered and those who read her missionary reports.

For individuals who feel excluded from political, economic, and other means of power, inhabiting unlikely places has often become an effective rhetorical tactic, enabling them to draw attention to broader societal problems. Southern lunch counters, factory floors, Wall Street, the streets of Washington, DC, and town squares throughout the Middle East have all served as sites where individuals' presence became powerful sources of persuasion. Historically, this has especially been the case for women. From early temperance crusaders who prayed and sang hymns inside taverns to Jane Addams's residency in Hull House to the Silent Sentinels who stood outside the White House advocating women's suffrage, women have used their presence to highlight social problems, particularly those negatively impacting other women. While antebellum women were absent from most public forums such as courtrooms, legislative chambers, and church pulpits, upper- and middle-class white women used their presence in slums, almshouses, and jails to persuade individuals to change immoral behaviors. Without professional titles, credentials, and sometimes little formal education, women used their presence to build ethos. Women persuaded audiences directly through their conversations and actions along with the opinions and observations they published and disseminated to broader audiences.

In this chapter, using what I refer to as an "ethos of presence," I highlight Margaret Prior, the AFMRS's first female missionary, to illustrate how presence became an important rhetorical tactic used by early female moral reformers. My conception of an ethos of presence shows how the authority women garnered with their immediate physical audiences also helped them attain authority with distant readers. Ultimately, I show the interplay between physical presence and the presence created through textual depictions. For Prior's immediate physical audience in the neighborhoods that she frequented, she relied on a *situated ethos* that drew from her reputation and actions. Excerpts from her missionary reports provide glimpses of Prior's situated ethos in these neighborhoods by showing her holistic approach to assistance and her fearlessness. These actions drew the attention of her immediate audience and sometimes even emboldened them. For *Advocate of Moral Reform* readers, Prior created an *invented ethos*, in which she intentionally constructed her character within the discourse.[2] In constructing this ethos, Prior not only recounted her actions, she made other rhetorical choices, such as showing that her assistance was requested, presenting her work as part of an unfolding narrative, and providing explicit descriptions. In addition to showing the dire needs in the neighborhoods and the importance of the AFMRS's work, these rhetorical choices also present Prior as a reliable narrator who knows (and is known) in the communities she serves.

In the following pages, I introduce Prior and describe the rhetorical training that prepared her to become the AFMRS's first female missionary. Then, I explain how and why presence became a rhetorical tactic for antebellum women, and through a synthesis of discussions on ethos I show the relationship between ethos and presence. Drawing on missionary reports published in the *Advocate of Moral Reform* and Prior's memoir, *Walks of Usefulness, Or Reminiscences of Mrs. Margaret Prior,* this chapter then examines the tactics that comprise Prior's ethos of presence. Ultimately, this chapter presents Prior as an illustrative example to show how female reformers used their presence to persuade.

TAKING WALKS OF USEFULNESS

By walking through some of New York City's poorest areas, Prior and other female moral reformers entered places rarely visited by respectable middle-class women. In *The Practice of Everyday Life*, Michel de Certeau conceives of walking around a city as a "pedestrian speech act" in which individuals highlight or avoid certain spaces through the act of walking. He suggests that the paths individuals choose make statements; in other words, their steps compose, argue, and persuade.[3] Similarly, in his study of contemporary activist groups, Kevin Deluca claims that bodily presence can be used as a form of public argumentation.[4] Through Prior's and other women's presence, which occurred during what tract and benevolent societies commonly referred to as "walks of usefulness," female moral reformers argued that these neighborhoods and the people living there were worthy of attention and assistance. During these walks of usefulness, Prior and other AFMRS women highlighted the victims of inequitable social and economic systems in some of the city's neediest sections. Even though its primary mission was combatting immoral sexual behaviors, the AFMRS construed its mission broadly, as did its first female missionary. Not only did Prior walk door-to-door in some of the city's poorest and most sordid neighborhoods distributing tracts and issues of AFMRS's semimonthly periodical, the *Advocate of Moral Reform*, she evangelized, provided counsel, visited the sick, attained assistance for the needy, organized prayer meetings and Sunday schools, helped locate suitable jobs and lodgings for women, confronted libertines, reproved gamblers, and ardently encouraged temperance. Prior documented these efforts in her missionary reports, which were printed in the *Advocate*. Consequently, her words and actions extended far beyond the people she visited.

AFMRS members "traveled to 'low' brothels of Corlears Hook and Five Points, the most powerfully tabooed spots for women in the entire city, to stand outside and read Scripture, to pray and to urge repentance on all who entered and exited."[5] Their presence in such unlikely places attracted the attention of the residents in these poor neighborhoods and individuals who later read their reports. The power of their presence is a rhetorical tactic women learned through early religious and benevolent efforts. As far back as the Revolutionary War, women's groups used door-to-door solicitations to raise funds. Even though these groups disbanded after the war, women, more than men, continued to rely on their presence on door stoops and dram shops to advocate and persuade. Motivated by both societal concerns and religious revivals, women's Bible and tract societies, missionary societies, Sunday school societies, benevolent organizations, and other female associations, which emerged during the first three decades of the nineteenth century, provided women's initial path into public life. "Visiting," which drew women out of their homes and into the homes of others, became a vital tactic for women's voluntary societies. Women distributed printed materials, raised funds, evangelized, and assisted the poor. Indeed, many early female benevolent organizations stressed the importance of systematic visiting, and "visitor" was often an official position alongside director, corresponding secretary, and manager. Other organizations assigned their managers responsibility for visiting and assessing needs, and societies that distributed material and monetary assistance typically divided their cities into districts with a manager assigned to each area.[6]

Even when visiting was employed in pursuit of organizational goals, it was a familiar and comfortable practice for women. Women had customarily carried out social visits, and home visits to needy neighbors were an individual act of charity long before benevolent and reform groups systematized the practice. Additionally, visiting relied on conversation. As Jane Donawerth has convincingly shown, conversation served as a model for much of women's public discourse. Conversation was an accepted and comfortable rhetorical practice for women—usually informal and taking place in household settings, among individuals or small groups.[7]

In churches and benevolent organizations where men retained control, visiting, canvassing, selling Bibles, distributing tracts, proselytizing, and fundraising were entrusted to female volunteers. Male leaders may have believed that women had more time available for such tasks. Women were also willing to do this work and proved their effectiveness. Some male organizations relied heavily on women for fundraising while others entirely delegated their fundraising to female auxiliary organizations. At the same time, women also used this power to hold male leaders accountable. "As the primary laborers, and often essential fund-raisers," the historian Marilyn Westerkamp notes, "women could and did require that the associations' goals and strategies conform to their own expectations." In addition to withholding their funds, women could threaten to withhold their presence and labor.[8]

Women's efforts as visitors, fundraisers, and alms distributors allowed them to expand their reach and influence to different neighborhoods and social classes and even to city governments as they appealed for public assistance. "Although some females succumbed to pressure and sought male protection when they walked in their cities' poorer areas," Barbara Berg asserts, "the overwhelming majority of women visited in wretched neighborhoods alone. Disregarding the inherent risks, they entered districts conspicuous for disease, alcoholism, and crime."[9] Frequently, they encountered opposition, jeering, insults, and even threats as Margaret Prior's report at the beginning of this chapter attests. Nevertheless, they persevered sustained by their religious beliefs and the needs they witnessed.

In visiting people in need, women in benevolent organizations believed they were establishing congenial relationships. Women's groups often recorded the deaths of longtime clients in the same manner as longtime group members. During their visits, women heard heartrending stories relayed by thousands of poor women in cities across the country. They observed social and economic problems, and saw women's suffering and the effects of female subjugation firsthand. Not only did these experiences rouse an early feminist consciousness in some women, they also prompted new efforts and institutions, including schools, orphanages, and shelters to assist orphans and widows. Women also expanded their visits from homes to almshouses, asylums, hospitals, and jails. There, some found new callings, including the group of women who in 1830 initially established the Female Asylum Society in New York to help prostitutes, and Dorothea Dix, who in the 1840s became an advocate for the mentally ill when she found insane persons imprisoned alongside thieves and prostitutes throughout several states.[10]

Countless numbers of women joined benevolent and reform organizations to address pressing social needs and to enact their religious convictions during the first three decades of the nineteenth century. In doing so, they bravely stepped beyond the domestic sphere and expanded their rhetorical influence and boundaries. Sadly, today, most of these women remain nameless, and their influence is often overlooked. Even when records from women's reform and benevolent groups exist, they primarily detail membership, money raised, or the number of tracts distributed, which offer only scant traces of women's contributions and their modes of persuasion. By studying Margaret Prior's memoir and missionary reports, we can gain a broader conception of female reformers, their public advocacy, and their rhetorical tactics, especially the way women used their physical presence.

GARNERING AN ETHOS OF PRESENCE

I contend that presence allowed Prior and other antebellum women to garner ethos, sometimes among audiences that might be reluctant to grant women authority. Nedra Reynolds's discussion of location and discursive authority claims, "Locating *ethos* in written texts requires attention to the mediation and negotiation that goes on in the spaces between writers and their locations." This requires us to examine the "rhetorical strategies writers use to locate themselves, their texts, and the particular discursive communities they are mediating between."[11] In the case of Prior's missionary reports, location was a critical component of her persuasion.

Through her walks of usefulness, I argue that Prior exerted an "ethos of presence," which undergirded the appeals she made to her different audiences. Prior's willingness to traverse the city's seediest sections, call on any person, and address any need demonstrated her faith and commitment to serve and "save" others. Thus, her regular presence became an ethical resource that helped her proselytize, pursue moral reform, and promote temperance in the neighborhoods she visited. Moreover, the authority Prior garnered through her presence in these neighborhoods and her interactions with residents helped her demonstrate the value of her work through the AFMRS and reveal the dire economic conditions that existed to individuals who read her missionary reports in the *Advocate of Moral Reform*.

Since ancient times, rhetoric has been a bodily art.[12] Along with pathos and logos, ethos is one of three modes of persuasion that Aristotle delineates in his *Rhetoric*, and the one that he deems most important. Drawing from Aristotle's discussion of ethos, Michael Halloran suggests, "In its simplest form, ethos is what we might call the argument for authority, the argument that says in effect, Believe me because I am the sort of person whose word you can believe."[13] Hence, ethos involves a negotiation between a speaker/writer and audience. Examinations of ethos either explicitly or implicitly acknowledge the significance of presence. For instance, Halloran notes the importance of bringing a good reputation to a rhetorical situation. Historically, reputations have been established in areas where individuals' actions are associated with their names. Indeed, a person may leave a place in order to escape a bad reputation. By stressing the communal nature of ethos, Karen LeFevre similarly acknowledges the value of a person's presence in a community. "For Aristotle," she explains, "ethos refers not to the idiosyncrasies of an individual, and not to a personal and private construct such as is often meant by 'personality'; rather, ethos arises from the relationship between the individual and the community."[14] In Prior's case, her actions, her reputation, and the relationships she established in the communities she served all contributed to her ethos.

Risa Applegarth's study of ethos in American novelist and essayist Mary Austin's nature writing shows how place can also become an ethical resource for rhetors by exemplifying their participation, values, and commitment. In this sense, ethos draws "persuasive power from the shared symbolic resonance of such places."[15] With her definition of rhetorical space, Roxanne Mountford similarly argues that rhetorical spaces are not only "the geography of a communicative event," they may carry cultural and material dimensions as well as "a physical representation of relationships and ideas."[16] Both Applegarth and Mountford acknowledge how a rhetor's presence in a particular place contributes to the way the rhetor is perceived by their audience. Through her ongoing presence in the city's neglected areas and through the descriptions of those areas, these places became an important source of ethos for Prior because they symbolized her commitment to those in need, her Christian beliefs, and her pursuit of moral reform.

Of course, conceiving of some of antebellum New York City's poorest neighborhoods as ethical resources may seem peculiar because these were not locations where power resided—they were neglected and disadvantaged. However, Reynolds shows that rhetors can exert discursive authority from "positions not traditionally considered authoritative."[17] Prisons, insane asylums, brothels, factory floors, porterhouses, and the ramshackle dwellings inhabited by the city's poorest residents—these were the marginalized locations Prior visited and described in her reports, and in my conception of an ethos of presence, these locations became sources of her authority. Prior inscribed who she was—a good Christian committed to combatting sin and suffering, by showing where she was—poor neighborhoods, prisons, brothels, etc. Ultimately, all the elements described in these discussions of ethos—actions, reputation, communal relationships, and the symbolic nature of place—contribute to understanding how Prior and other antebellum female moral reformers successfully exerted ethos from their presence in New York City's marginalized locations.

HIRING THE AFMRS'S FIRST FEMALE MISSIONARY

Prior, who was a sixty-four-year-old widow at the time she was hired by the AFMRS, seems an odd choice to become the organization's first female missionary. A letter from a friend included in *Walks of Usefulness* explains that the AFMRS had trouble finding women who were suitable and willing to serve

Mrs. Margaret Prior

FIGURE 3. Margaret Prior became the AFMRS's first female city missionary in 1837 and continued in that role until her death in 1842. Courtesy of the American Antiquarian Society.

as city missionaries, and Prior eventually decided it was her duty to undertake the work.[18] Prior was a devout evangelical Christian and an ardent supporter of moral reform who served on the AFMRS's first board of managers in 1834.

Prior had been active in several benevolent organizations in the city. She served on the New York Orphan Asylum Society's board of managers.[19] She also helped establish an asylum for half-orphans (children of single parents unable to care for them) and served as an official visitor at the House of Refuge for delinquent children. Indeed, her desire to assist children stemmed from her own tragic losses. Prior, who had lost seven children, was said to have vowed after the death of her last child that she would become a "mother to the motherless."[20] Prior's benevolent work not only provided emotional catharsis—it also equipped her with rhetorical training. Recent scholarship, including Jess Enoch's *Refiguring Rhetorical Education: Women Teaching African American, Native American, and Chicano/a Students, 1856–1911*, Shirley Wilson Logan's *Liberating Language: Sites of Rhetorical Education in Nineteenth-Century Black America*, and David Gold and Catherine Hobbs's collection, *Rhetoric, History, and Women's Oratorical Education: American Women Learn to Speak* expand previous conceptions of women's rhetorical education and encourage researchers to ask: What counts as rhetorical education? And where does rhetorical education take place? Enoch acknowledges that scholarly examinations beyond traditional sites "offer a new vision of rhetorical education that interrogates the not-so-simple relationship between learning rhetoric and entering public life."[21] According to Gold and Hobbs, rhetorical education is not just "formal instruction in writing or speaking or derived from classical rhetoric, but any form of education designed to promote rhetorical competence, be it writing, speaking, reading listening, or . . . movement of the body."[22] These descriptions broaden rhetorical education beyond institutions and texts to the embodied educational experiences of many women in antebellum America.

This type of experience is evident in Prior's memoir, which notes that she was "early enlisted in the temperance cause and labored untiringly to persuade men, women, and children, to sign the pledge," a document in which individuals pledged to abstain from alcohol.[23] Prior also participated in early antislavery efforts. She served as a delegate to the 1837 and 1838 Anti-Slavery Convention of American Women. The 71 delegates and 103 corresponding members attending the 1837 convention comprised a who's who of antebellum female reformers, including Lucretia Mott, Sarah and Angelina Grimké, Lydia Maria Child, and the AFMRS's own Sarah Ingraham.[24] At the 1838 women's antislavery convention in Philadelphia, Prior was named a vice president for the proceedings. She offered the opening prayer on the second day, and was involved in one of the most contentious debates over a resolution that asked women to abstain from attending services at churches that allowed slavehold-ers to preach or receive communion.[25] The controversy and danger surround-ing these antislavery conventions are underscored by the fact that Pennsylva-nia Hall was burned by an angry mob the night before the women's antislavery convention's conclusion. In fact, the managers of Temperance Hall, where the meeting was being held, refused to open the doors the following morning, fearing the safety of their building, so the women concluded their convention in a nearby schoolroom instead.

While Prior's participation at the antislavery conventions afforded ad-ditional experience speaking publicly and debating, her membership in the Methodist Church along with her work as a religious-tract distributor pro-vided her formative rhetorical training. As a Methodist, Prior acquired what Vicki Tolar Burton defines as spiritual literacy—literate practices directed at spiritual growth such as memorizing Scripture and other religious texts, read-ing Scripture and delivering prayers in public, and offering public testimony, exhorting, and hymn singing.[26] Indeed, Prior's memoir notes her intense Bible study through which she acquired a wide corpus of memorized Scripture and her participation in class meetings, prayer meetings, and other religious gath-erings through which she gained experience delivering "heartfelt and power-ful exhortations" and "effectual" prayers.[27]

Every person who joined a Methodist society became a member of a small group called a *class* where members were "invited, encouraged, and expected to pray aloud and to narrate publicly their struggles, problems, and hopes."[28] These forums especially helped women find their voices by inviting and requir-ing "that each individual speak for herself."[29] Within this nurturing narrative structure, women were emboldened to also speak publicly offering testimony, counsel and, if necessary, to reprimand and instruct others.[30] The historian Cynthia Lyerly explains, "It is difficult to overestimate the way Methodist be-liefs infused women with purpose and power."[31] Ultimately, the Methodist Church served an integral site for Prior's rhetorical education; there, she ac-quired several spiritual literacy practices and evolved into a deliberate and confident speaker who recognized the power of her words.

Prior's experience visiting door-to-door as a tract visitor provided the sec-ond major site of her rhetorical training.[32] As a tract visitor, Prior honed her spiritual literacy practices and garnered additional skills, including canvass-ing neighborhoods, assessing a wide variety of audiences, and applying differ-ent rhetorical appeals. Here, Prior learned the power of a continual presence in neighborhoods because tract visitors usually disseminated tracts through-out assigned districts. Religious tracts were a popular form of evangelism be-cause they were cheaper and easier to distribute than Bibles and easier for readers to understand. In his book *Faith in Reading: Religious Publishing and the Birth of Mass Media in America*, historian David Nord writes that tracts were "simple, free, something light to catch the attention of the busy sinner in an unguarded moment."[33] Typically four to eight pages, tracts relied on narrative and dialogue to deliver the gospel. Antebellum evangelicals believed that reading had the power to save souls, so they aggressively distributed Bibles, religious books, and tracts. In fact, by 1852 American evangelical societies claimed to have distributed forty million Bibles and hundreds of millions of pages of tracts.[34]

Tract visitors were recognized as important religious emissaries, second only to ministers.[35] The stated qualifications for tract visitors included "acquaintance with Scriptures—and skill in communicating to the apprehensions, and impressing on the hearts of others, the Gospel method of salvation."[36] In other words, it was not enough to know the Bible—effective visitors needed scriptural *facilitas* that would enable them to converse, answer questions, draw supporting evidence and examples, and counter opposition. Additionally, they were instructed to bring children to Sunday schools, persuade residents to attend public worship, encourage individuals to read the Bible, and bring sinners to Christ.[37] Whereas the Methodist Church had equipped Prior with spiritual literacy practices, her experience canvassing as a tract visitor taught her how to best apply those skills and how to use her presence in her assigned tract districts to earn residents' trust. Both these sites equipped Prior with valuable rhetorical training, which she brought to her role as an AFMRS missionary.

Initially, the AFMRS dispatched male missionaries such as John McDowall to make visits and distribute the *Advocate of Moral Reform* throughout the city. Female members often accompanied these men, and in 1837, by hiring Prior as its first female missionary, the AFMRS signaled its belief that women could serve as missionaries on their own. The move to hire female missionaries, which was a paid position, was also motivated by a desire to expand women's employment options. From its visits and interactions with prostitutes and poor women, the AFMRS's leadership came to recognize limited economic opportunities as a root cause of prostitution and women's destitution. In addition to female missionaries, the AFMRS hired a female editor for the *Advocate*, female agents to organize auxiliary societies, and female typesetters and bookkeepers, all of which were occupations customarily filled by men. Women-run movements believed that women were qualified for such roles; antebellum antislavery and temperance societies paid female speakers and agents, and as women's organizations opened asylums for poor women and orphans, they paid matrons and teachers.[38]

As a paid city missionary, Prior was required to write and submit reports detailing her actions, from which extracts could be published in the *Advocate*. Prior admitted that she had written little in many years, and at her advanced age felt unable to write reports suitable for publication. So, society leaders suggested that she ask someone to write for her, and Sarah Ingraham, who would later compile Prior's memoir, became Prior's "amanuensis," enacting what Buchanan terms a "productive collaboration," which enabled Prior to produce persuasive texts. Ingraham was the AFMRS's corresponding secretary and *Advocate* editor for many years. [39] In Prior's memoir Ingraham describes the collaborative dictation and composing process they used:

> Her reports, as given verbally, were briefly narrated, together with her remarks, and then read to her for correction and alteration, so that the statements and sentiments expressed might be entirely her own. She generally came to us with such a variety of incident, that after hearing her through, it was somewhat difficult to begin and end right. She perceived this, and often while we were writing would sit in silent prayer, with her eyes closed, asking the Lord to make the communication she had given *fully understood*, and what was said about it, the means of doing *good*.[40]

As a devout church member and former tract visitor, Prior understood the value of affective narratives and illustrative examples. Moreover, the AFMRS convinced her that publishing extracts from her reports in the *Advocate* could "do good"; however, Prior asked that her name be withheld from these reports, and certainly she never imagined that her reports would eventually become part of a memoir.

Prior continued her work as a city missionary until her death in 1842. After her death, selections from her reports were compiled and published in *Walks of Usefulness, Or Reminiscences of Mrs. Margaret Prior* (1843), which was printed in numerous editions. Prior's memoir, which was frequently cited in the *Advocate*, extended her influence even further making her a strong female role model for AFMRS members and other women.[41] The decision to publish *Walks of Usefulness* indicates both the popularity of Prior's missionary reports and their perceived rhetorical power. Indeed, the importance of missionary visits is repeatedly acknowledged by the AFMRS's auxiliary societies. For instance, in a letter printed in the *Advocate*, the North Attleborough, Massachusetts, auxiliary claims: "Next to the Advocate, we believe your Missionaries are doing the greatest possible amount of good. We have read those tales of woe which you have depicted before us, and our hearts have been touched on behalf of those fallen ones . . . it is our own sex, who are thus degraded and fallen, and shall we make no effort to secure the innocent from danger, and save, if possible, those which have fallen?"[42] In this instance, the

North Attleborough auxiliary not only acknowledges the effect of these missionary reports, but by posing a rhetorical question demonstrates its own turn to advocacy. Reports from auxiliaries also frequently cite missionary reports as motivation for material and monetary donations, which are often designated for distribution by missionaries and visiting committees.[43] The AFMRS's 1840 annual report also attests to the effectiveness of this labor.

> To those employed [as city missionaries] it has been arduous and self-denying, but not without its reward. During the past year, between four and five thousand families have been visited, many temperance pledges obtained, over 80 children gathered into the Sabbath school, and one hundred and fifty respectable seamstresses and domestics provided with places, where a religious influence is exerted over them. The pressing wants of the needy have been relieved to some extent; papers, testaments, bibles, and a large quantity of tracts given to those visited, and some of the seed sown has already sprung up ... there have been reported sixty-three hopeful conversions. Of this number twenty-four have occurred during the last year.[44]

Reports such as this one denote not only the influence Prior and others had on the individuals they visited, but also signal their influence on the AFMRS. Clearly, the AFMRS's officers believed that visits by Prior and other city missionaries carried out an essential part of the organization's mission. Ingraham's opening letter in *Walks of Usefulness* also notes that the memoir came about because of several requests, which likely came from AFMRS members and *Advocate* readers.

Prior's 324-page memoir is primarily made up of extracts from missionary reports she compiled from 1837 until her death in 1842. With the publication of *Walks of Usefulness*, Prior was immortalized and the AFMRS continued to reference her and hold her up as a model during meetings and in *Advocate* stories. In fact, an 1853 *Advocate* issue reported that AFMRS volunteers assisting a needy widow and her child discovered that Prior had initially encouraged the widow's conversion. According to the widow, Prior "had often conversed and prayed with her urging her to give her heart to God." In response, AFMRS members acknowledged, "we could not but feel privileged in being permitted to water the seed sown by her, so long since."[45] An article in an 1854 *Advocate* issue describing a visit to the city prison notes an old bookcase Prior placed in the women's prison fifteen years earlier to establish a small library of religious books. The writer muses: "Who can tell but that her kind eye even now sometimes looks down from her home above and lingers about these familiar walks and cells, where she once plead so lovingly with youthful wanderers from the path of right, saying, '*I speak to you as a mother.* I love your soul's welfare: oh! do be persuaded to read and obey the precious words of your Saviour, and then, when you once get out, you will never come here again.'"[46]

Both examples underscore the power of Prior's model still evident a dozen years after her death.

Though Prior felt called to the role of missionary and clearly left an indelible impression on those she helped and those who observed her efforts, the job of city missionary was not easy. In a letter included in *Walks of Usefulness*, an AFMRS member explains, "As a missionary, proclaiming the gospel from house to house, she was wonderfully successful; yet she did not please all— even good people sometimes treated her coolly. Her feelings were often tried by indifference or open opposition, so that she was moved to tears; and her only solace was found in committing the matter to the Lord." Indeed, Prior often cheered herself with the mantra "'No cross, no crown.'"[47] Her devotion to the work is illustrated in a story retold by a friend in *Walks of Usefulness*. According to the story, Prior stopped at the house of a fortune teller to drop off some tracts, yet she was distressed by the lengthy line of ladies waiting to have their fortunes read. Prior began encouraging the women to turn away from black magic and look to their own souls to discover their destinies. Her passionate exhortations, which brought some of the women to tears, convinced almost all of them to leave. However, when the fortune teller emerged from his chamber to see his customers walking out the door, he grew irate and chased after Prior. She managed a quick escape out a back door that led to an alley. Yet Prior halted her getaway when she encountered a group of men gambling in the alley. Again, she seized the opportunity to share the gospel and pass out copies of the *Advocate*. Even as some of the men berated her with insults, she continued, aware that others in the group were listening. Driven by her religious convictions, Prior was not easily deterred. She traveled wherever she was dispatched and wherever she saw people in need.[48]

Using Prior as a representative example of how presence became a rhetorical tactic for female moral reformers, the remainder of this chapter delineates Prior's ethos of presence by showing the many ways her presence contributed to her actions, reputation, and relationships, and demonstrated her compassion and Christian beliefs. I discuss Prior's holistic approach to assistance, her fearlessness and the emboldening influence she had on other women, the acknowledgment that her assistance was sought, the way she situated her reports as part of an unfolding narrative, and her explicit descriptions. Altogether, these narrative choices emphasize the persuasive power of presence.

PURSUING A HOLISTIC APPROACH TO ASSISTANCE

In one report, Prior states, "I have made it my business to follow to their homes numbers of poor, ragged children, found begging in the streets."[49] What she discovered and described were scenes of abject poverty, disease, and drunkenness, from which children were relegated to begging to support themselves and their families. During her walks of usefulness, Prior assisted families living in the most degraded conditions. She helped destitute mothers and widows obtain food for their children and heat for their homes. She helped individuals secure lodgings, find suitable employment, orchestrate adoptions, and even arrange funerals. Evident in countless reports, when Prior saw a need, she made it her business. Consequently, Prior's missionary reports provide proof of her presence, the compassion and care she exhibited in the neighborhoods she regularly visited, and the reputation, or situated ethos, she garnered among residents. If she ran out of resources, she gave from her own pocket, solicited contributions and, in some cases, even took women and children home with her to feed and shelter them.[50]

Prior's assistance came without conditions. Although she was motivated by her Christian beliefs, Christianity was not a prerequisite for her care. For example, she provided food for a poor widow with four children, reporting, "For a week they had lived only on a few potatoes, received from the ward committee. One little child of two years and a half had been sick for some weeks, and was pining away from actual want. Their distress was alleviated for the time, and they were earnestly exhorted to seek the bread of life."[51] In this instance, Prior first attended to the family's temporal needs, and then she addressed their spiritual needs. This approach resembled the methods female foreign missionaries later used. During the modern mission era, as women were dispatched to posts abroad, their approaches to the communities they served tended to be personal and holistic—focused on both immediate needs and evangelism.[52] This holistic approach was clearly linked to the women's presence. They were not debating solutions in government chambers or theorizing approaches in the administrative offices of a church or national charity. Like Prior, they were looking directly at individuals in need, and their efforts helped engender residents' trust. Long after Prior's death, the AFMRS continued this holistic approach as it encountered individuals in need, which contributed to its reputation as a reliable source for assistance.[53]

Even though it was not a prerequisite for her aid, Prior undoubtedly believed that religion was a powerful form of assistance. Like other AFMRS members, Prior's faith motivated her moral reform efforts. In addition to evangelizing, her reports show her praying, reading Scripture, and singing hymns. She reports a visit to one family where the daughter took care of her mother, whose rheumatism had rendered her an invalid. The older woman was angry and depressed. When Prior suggested that she might find solace in reading the Bible, the woman admitted that her poor sight and arthritic hands made it impossible for her to read or hold a Bible. Persistent, Prior bought the woman a pair of spectacles and found a carpenter who, at no charge, constructed a stand that would enable the woman to hold her Bible. According to the woman's daughter, reading the Bible put her mother at ease and completely changed her demeanor.[54] Prior's efforts in this case highlight her sincere desire to help. Overall, the array of compassionate acts outlined in her missionary reports offer evidence of Prior's ethos of presence and the relationships she cultivated in the communities she served. As Halloran notes, "To have ethos is to manifest the virtues most valued by the culture to and for which one speaks."[55] In Prior's case, her presence symbolized her sincere commitment to helping others. For residents, both the religiously inclined as well as those individuals who might have felt ignored by churches and people claiming to be Christians, they saw Prior in their neighborhood *practicing what she preached*. Thus, her presence and her holistic approach contributed to her situated ethos.

EXHIBITING EMBOLDENING FEARLESSNESS

At times, this commitment put her in harm's way, but Prior's missionary reports portray her as fearless. Under the mantles of moral reform and religious revivalism, Prior ventured into areas usually considered off-limits to respectable women. She confronted adulterers, bar owners, brothel madams, and anyone else who impeded her assistance, evangelism, and reform message. In one report, she admits going to an area "considered so degraded, that the tract agent could find no visiter [*sic*] willing to take it."[56] Countering the view that antebellum women's reform and benevolent endeavors were gentle, peaceful, and generally unseen—what Lori Ginzberg terms the "rhetoric of female benevolence"—Prior's reports show an ardent reformer willing to travel anyplace and confront any sinner.[57] In one instance, Prior attempted to take some issues of the *Advocate of Moral Reform* into a brothel, but when some of the prostitutes spotted the words *moral reform*, they locked the doors—claiming Prior as their prisoner.

According to Prior:

> For a moment my heart was tremulous. I said nothing till the risings of fear were quelled, and then replied pleasantly, "Well, if I'm your prisoner I shall *pray* here, and would sing praises to God if I were not so hoarse. Yes, bless the Lord! his presence can make me happy here or anywhere, and you can have no power to harm me unless he gives it. This is a dreadful place, to be sure, but it is not so bad as hell; for there, there is no hope. The smoke of their torment ascendeth up for ever and ever! What compassion in the blessed Jesus that he spares us, when our sins are every day so great!" I talked to them in this way till they were glad to open

the door as a signal for my release. Indeed, they seemed quite ashamed, and tried
to apologize for their rudeness by saying that they had nothing at all against me, it
was only the paper that displeased them.[58]

By turning her fear into a powerful demonstration of faith, Prior's presence
unnerved and persuaded her captors. Transforming these women's mal-
ice into shame, Prior exerted an influence that was anything but gentle and
peaceful. Additionally, this incident shows how "the paper," the *Advocate*, was
perceived as a threat by prostitutes.

Just as Prior's escape from this brothel required rhetorical savvy, so did
gaining entry to other brothels. For instance, when other attempts failed, Pri-
or was admitted "by sending word that an old lady had 'jewels for them,' referring to the society's tract." On other occasions, she would disguise herself as a
washerwoman or enter by a back-alley door.[59] Here it is important to acknowledge that Prior often used her age to her advantage. According to a friend's
recollection in *Walks of Usefulness*, Prior once counseled a young woman who
wanted to follow her example: "It would not become *you* to do *my* work. I am
an aged person, my appearance is plain, my countenance grave [and I may
add, a person commanding and dignified]; I can go through the markets and
public places and no one dare insult me; whereas your youthful appearance
might provoke insult. Serve God, my dear in that sphere of life in which you
are called to move."[60] At the same time that Prior cautioned the young woman
that she would likely be insulted whilst walking the streets alone, Prior did
not dissuade her from action or using her presence in an appropriate sphere.

Prior often used her presence to embolden women who otherwise might
be afraid to act on their own. For instance, after she visited a drunkard's suffering family, Prior went to the local grocer to urge him to stop selling rum.
When she found the merchant's wife waiting on customers, Prior reports, "I
begged her to go and visit this wretched abode, and witness the fruit of her labors."[61] After visiting the family and taking them some groceries, the woman
told Prior she would never sell rum again. In this case, Prior used the woman's
own presence to persuade—demonstrating the power of observing these situations firsthand.

On another occasion, a woman told Prior that if she would accompany her,
the woman would have the courage to confront her husband, who had been
seeing a prostitute at a nearby brothel. The story of this encounter turns into
an amusing tale. When Prior and the wife went to the brothel, the wife angrily
accosted the woman she believed her husband had been seeing. The accused
woman adamantly denied that she was a prostitute and denied knowing the
wife's husband. Seeing the two women quarrel, Prior decided the issue would

not be resolved in that manner, so she suggested that they all pray. However, as they knelt, the wife spied her husband hiding under the bed. Initially, he refused to come out until "that moral reform woman had left the room," which further indicates Prior's reputation and situated ethos in the neighborhood. When he finally emerged, the wife and husband conversed, and the husband promised to reform his ways.[62] In both examples, Prior used her presence to prompt the woman she was accompanying to act. The AFMRS encouraged women to form auxiliaries, because women were often emboldened by the presence of other women. Moreover, because women comprised the majority of the *Advocate*'s readers, the AFMRS hoped Prior's reports would similarly inspire them.

RESPONDING TO REQUESTS FOR ASSISTANCE

The fact that Prior was known in the neighborhoods she visited is often evident in her reports' opening lines. She frequently acknowledges individuals asking for assistance, suggesting people or places she should visit, or reporting the impact of a previous visit. Prior likely included these requests as a way of showing the value of the AFMRS's work. At the same time, these acknowledgments demonstrate her relationships, influence, and reputation in the neighborhoods in which she traveled. In that sense, these details contribute to her invented ethos, which extended her credibility beyond her physical presence to *Advocate* readers and, later, her memoir's audience. For example, in one report Prior notes how a woman who overheard her talking to a family that lived in the apartment downstairs asked Prior if she would come speak to her husband, who was confined to his bed with a badly sprained leg. Prior reports, "I went up, not knowing what the Lord had for me to do," but she soon discovered that the man was intemperate, and his present injury had resulted from a drunken bout. Prior began counseling him and then asked if he had ever taken the temperance pledge. According to her report, "He answered no, for he did not think he could keep it if he did, but if I thought it was of the Lord he didn't know but there was some hope." She encouraged him to commit to the pledge, and as he signed it he "uttered a whispered prayer, 'Lord, help me keep it.'" Prior notes, "My heart was full for I had never before seen an habitual drunkard pray as he put his hand to the pledge, and I was more than ever convinced that the hand of the Lord was in all this."[63] By including this incident in her missionary report, Prior affirmed the power of Christianity and the good work done on behalf of the AFMRS. This exchange also demonstrates her ability to engender trust with the husband, whom she admonished, and with the wife, who overheard Prior speaking to her neighbors and then sought her assistance. Especially in the nineteenth century, a drunken husband and father could have a disastrous impact on a family, which underscores the wife's motivation in seeking Prior's help. As with most missionary reports, Prior was not simply observing, but actively assisting and, in this instance, reforming. Moreover, using what Applegarth terms the "strategy of attestation," Prior's missionary reports repeatedly locate her within the communities she serves.[64]

In another instance, an *Advocate* subscriber asked Prior to visit a sick young woman who was a boarder in her home. Prior, who realized the woman's recovery was unlikely, spoke to her earnestly about preparing to die. Noting the distressing situation, Prior describes the scene: "She wept as I spoke of a dying hour, and confessed that she was unprepared." Prior adds, "She seemed grateful for my call, and desired me to come again."[65] Similarly, another report tells the story of a woman suffering the final stages of consumption who sent for Prior. This young mother asked Prior if she would promise to find good homes for her three children after her death. Prior consented to the charge, and helped comfort the woman.[66] Chapter 5 discusses the Home for the Friendless, which the AFMRS opened in 1848 to help place orphaned and neglected children in adoptive and foster homes, and this incident foretells why female moral reformers were drawn to this need. In their efforts, they frequently encountered orphaned and homeless children.

Ultimately, each of these cases show, when facing difficult situations—addressing an intemperate husband, telling a woman she was about to die, or agreeing to oversee the welfare of a dying mother's children—people sought Prior's help. By acknowledging these requests for assistance and locating herself amid these trying circumstances, Prior demonstrated her ethos and the respect she had garnered. Readers far removed from these situations saw that residents in the neighborhoods Prior visited knew her; they trusted Prior, and individuals who were reluctant to listen to others often listened to her.

PRESENTING AN UNFOLDING NARRATIVE

Prior also used her reports to show the fruits of her labor, which were not always immediately apparent. By referencing individuals and stories that had previously appeared in the *Advocate of Moral Reform*—often citing the particular issue of the paper—Prior documented the impact of earlier visits.[67] In that sense, presenting her reports as an unfolding narrative was another rhetorical choice Prior used to invent her ethos for readers. For example, she reports visiting a house where "I supposed I was among strangers," when a woman reminded Prior of a visit she had made to a nearby house seven months earlier. During that previous visit, Prior had found a group of fashionable young ladies working around a quilting frame. While Prior conversed with the mistress of the house, the young ladies made fun of her. Before leaving, Prior "pointedly warned them of their coming wrath, and pressed upon them the duty of repentance." Reminding Prior of that earlier scene, the young woman told Prior, "the remarks then made, were sent by the Spirit directly to her heart," and remained with her until her conversion. Prior ends this report by making a direct address to the readers: "What encouragement does this fact present to the faithful exertions of tract visiters [sic], who may by a word in season save a soul from death, and hide a multitude of sins."[68]

By highlighting her continued presence in the neighborhoods she visited, Prior modeled the power of persistence—encouraging Christians and reformers to continue their efforts even if the impact was not readily apparent. This is especially evident in another report in which Prior relays a conversation she had while visiting a sick gentleman.

> When I inquired kindly whether he expected to recover, he replied, it was quite immaterial to him whether he should get well or not. "But my friend are you prepared to die?" "None of your business," said he roughly. "O yes," I continued, "the Lord makes it my business to care for the souls of my fellow-beings, and it is my duty to say to you that if you do not repent, and love the Lord Jesus Christ you will be lost for ever." He replied, "I do not believe in Christ." "Then," said I, "it is useless to talk to you, for you are now a lost man!"[69]

Prior turned to leave, but says, "on opening the door, the conviction was so strong that the Lord would have me pray with him," so she knelt and prayed out loud next to the man's bedside and then left. She felt inclined to return in a few days and discovered the man completely changed, to which he credited Prior's prayer for sending conviction to his soul.[70] Prior's faith and persistence not only paid off in this instance, they also distinguished her from other evangelicals. During the antebellum period, it was not uncommon for religious and secular reform groups to visit poor neighborhoods in order to evangelize, hand out tracts, or evaluate potential recipients for relief funds.[71] Prior performed all of these actions as well, but her continued presence and commitment, which is acknowledged and documented in her missionary reports, set Prior apart and helped her engender trust.

Although Prior never aspired to be a minister, her reports show that the people she visited often granted her ministerial authority. The introduction to *Walks of Usefulness* even lauds that few ministers had brought as many to salvation as Prior.[72] This authority was also linked to Prior's presence. In her study of three contemporary female preachers, Mountford describes how one of the women stepped outside of the pulpit, traditionally a masculine space, and moved closer to the congregation to preach. Mountford claims that her movement "served a mimetic function—it simulated that movement of the divine to the people and therefore evoked an emotional response."[73] Prior's walks of usefulness performed a similar mimetic function—extending Christianity to individuals who were often excluded, or those unwelcome in churches. For instance, a woman whom Prior had helped convert to Christianity thanked Prior for her visits and kind instruction, stating that no one had conversed with her about her soul or told her about Christ and heaven.[74] In another case, a friend asked Prior to go with her to visit an elderly blind woman who wanted to repent her sins. According to the blind woman, "the preaching she had heard had not reached her soul, and she now desired to see some Christian female who knew by experience the value of a Savior, that she might open her heart to her, and obtain instruction."[75] Prior proved to be the right woman for the job; her testimony and presence persuaded the blind woman, who finally felt the Lord's compassion and forgiveness. Ultimately, Prior conveyed an authenticity that resonated with the people she encountered. This is also evident in another moving account shared in a letter included in *Walks of Usefulness*. The letter describes how Prior attended to the letter writer's dying child: "I have myself experienced while watching over the dying bed of a beloved child, how deeply she [Prior] could sympathize with the afflicted; and I can not better describe the effect these visits had upon that dear child, than by quoting her [my daughter's] own words. One day after Mrs. Prior had left the room, she [my daughter] exclaimed, 'Oh mother, if it is so sweet to meet Christians here, what will it be in heaven?'"[76] This moving example offers a glimpse of Prior's care and impact. Even though she was not an ordained minister, Prior's presence and actions became powerful symbols of Christianity, and her audiences frequently granted her ministerial authority, exhibiting further how presence became an ethical resource and an important part of the persona she constructed for readers.

PROVIDING EXPLICIT DESCRIPTIONS

Another facet of Prior's invented ethos came through the explicitness of her reports. Prior's work as an AFMRS missionary occurred amid a severe economic depression that stretched from 1837 to 1842, and her firsthand accounts provided her readers with grim images of suffering that most may not have seen otherwise. For example, one of her reports vividly describes this dire scene: "At the farther extremity of a dark alley, and up two pair of outside stairs, so broken as hardly to afford safe passage, we found a poor woman afflicted with rheumatism. She was lying upon the floor, with a log of wood for

her pillow. She had been obliged to part with her bed, and most of her clothing, to procure bread; and all she had left, which was a few old garments, she
had spread under her on the floor, and over her hard pillow."[77] Firsthand accounts such as these bolstered Prior's ethos of presence by locating her there.
At the same time, her detailed descriptions made these grim scenes *present*
in her readers' minds. Similar to the way Chaim Perelman explains the power of rhetoric to create a presence in the consciousness of audiences,[78] Prior's
presence not only makes her reports credible, it also makes tangible the conditions and problems she describes. Through her presence, she attempts to draw
attention to the residents in these neighborhoods and the grim conditions in
which they live.

In another report, Prior describes visiting a poor family living in a dank
basement. "On entering the apartment, and beholding its emaciated and sor-
rowing inmates," she confesses, "my heart grew sick. In one corner sat a feeble mother, with tattered garments, bending over her sick infant, who was
apparently near its happy release from want and wo [*sic*]. On the other hand
was another little one, nearly blind. Three other half-clad and half-starved
children made up the group."[79] Noting that the family's drunkard father was
in prison, Prior describes her efforts to raise the funds necessary to relieve the
family's suffering. This scene, like many other sad circumstances illustrated
in Prior's reports, made a strong pathetic appeal. Though women are often
associated with "emotion-laden appeals," Patricia Bizzell suggests that ethos
can provide another avenue for understanding the persuasive impact of these
appeals.[80] Through her presence, Prior not only attached faces and suffering to
the city's economic and social problems, she lent credibility to these accounts.
These were not simply emotional appeals, but ethical appeals as well. Prior's
walks and observations substantiated these scenes, but more importantly, in
the same way that de Certeau suggests that walking speaks, Prior's walks of
usefulness argued that ignoring these types of living conditions was uncon-
scionable. In essence, she added moral authority as well.[81]

It is no coincidence that many of Prior's reports detail women's dire circumstances. The nineteenth-century patriarchal economy made women de-
pendent on male wage earners. Few employment opportunities existed for
women outside of domestic service, sewing, washing, and light factory work,
and these paid little; thus female-headed households were almost always
poor.[82] Prior's reports provide stories of women "ruined" and abandoned by
men, imprisoned husbands, intemperate husbands who spent all their income
on alcohol, and women unable to support themselves through any respectable means. Hence, her reports underscore why women were drawn to moral reform and temperance and how these efforts are directly linked to early

calls for women's rights. In one report, Prior describes the situation of two orphaned sisters who lived in one small rented room that they could not even afford to heat. "We found them engaged in sewing on fine shirts, which they were making at sixty-two cents apiece, and by their utmost endeavors they could only pay for their food and rent."[83] In a direct address to readers, she asserts, "It is painful to see the deserving of our own sex, when dependant [sic] upon their own efforts, oppressed and doomed to unrequited toil . . . there needs to be radical reform on this score."[84] Evident here, Prior also used her reports to highlight and denounce the limited economic avenues available to women.

Indeed, by showing how economic and social systems conspired against women, Prior's missionary reports contributed to the feminist consciousness that emerged out of the AFMRS. The conditions among the city's poor, particularly women and their children, that Prior and other AFMRS members observed and reported influenced the AFMRS's reform agenda. Eventually, the group moved away from moral reform to focus on the plight of poor women and children. Women's involvement and presence in reform efforts, especially those that moved them beyond their households and neighborhoods, shaped their views about social and economic issues. Seeing social problems firsthand or even through the eyes of reliable narrators like Prior, made women more confident in speaking out, thus demonstrating the effect of presence on women's perceptions of themselves.

USING PRESENCE FOR PUBLIC ADVOCACY

With reform and revivalist endeavors, antebellum women broadened their spheres of influence and enacted their religious convictions. According to Susan Hill Lindley, they also carried "some of their own 'female' values of personal concern, neighborly charity, and nurturing into the public sphere, which they believed needed more of those values."[85] These values are evident in Prior's missionary reports, as is her frustration with the economic and social structures that relegated so many individuals, particularly women and children, to such desperate situations. With her steps, Prior composed her missionary reports. She provided AFMRS members and *Advocate* readers with a glimpse of different sections of the city and humanized an array of urban problems. At the same time, she showed how individual efforts could make a difference.

Altogether, Prior's missionary reports highlight how presence operated as a rhetorical tactic for early female moral reformers, enabling them to establish ethos in the communities they served and to transfer that ethos through print. As Applegarth notes, "*Ethos* is a situated practice, never fully and freely chosen nor yet thoroughly determined, but shaped through the interaction between individual rhetors and the social and material environments within which they speak."[86] Prior's audiences used her presence to judge her connection to the community, her level of commitment, her religious convictions, and even her treatment of nonbelievers. Her readers took their cues from the people she served, or at least her depictions of their interactions. Like many antebellum women who lacked social standing, positions, titles, or any formal rhetorical education, Prior earned trust through repeated actions in local neighborhoods and then conveyed that trust to a broader textual community. In doing so, she foreshadowed ways that female religious and social reformers could exert a powerful ethos from their location as women and from other marginalized locations, such as urban neighborhoods, North American Indian missions, and foreign missions halfway around the world.

Prior's path also demonstrates how presence operates as public advocacy. Prior's regular presence in an unlikely place captured attention, and she used this attention to persuade the people she encountered and to make visible to *Advocate* readers the inequitable economic systems that existed and their consequences. Like the protestor's placard that projects alarming facts or images, Prior's missionary reports tried to make the appalling situations she observed real and untenable. In their discussion of alternative discourses, Michael De-Palma, Jeffery Ringer, and Jim Webber point to the power of nondeliberative rhetoric, claiming that it "sets out to make itself visible, heard, felt, smelt, tasted. It does not seek a reasoned posture nor does it aim to maintain a respectful tone in persuasion. It *acts*."[87] Prior and other female moral reformers boldly walked to New York City's poorest neighborhoods; they entered barrooms, brothels, and sickrooms. They visited prostitutes, confronted libertines, and entered the dirtiest and most dire dwellings to read Scripture, kneel in prayer, and offer comfort to individuals on their deathbeds. In other words, *they acted*, and they acted in a fashion uncustomary for most antebellum women.

Female moral reformers used their feet, their faith, their sweat, and their tears to motivate and, in many instances, they changed the individuals they encountered. Moreover, by infusing themselves and their subjects' desperate situations into the *Advocate of Moral Reform*, they exhorted readers to demand change as well. All the while, their audiences judged their intentions by the steps they took. For many women, their first step was joining together with other women. The next chapter discusses women's efforts to establish and act collectively through auxiliary societies, which became another important rhetorical tactic for female moral reformers.

Chapter 4

Igniting Auxiliary Power

Do any such here, doubtingly ask, what a few females can do to alter the state of morals among us, I answer—the influence we might exert if all our powers were brought to exercise, cannot be told.

—Westfield, Massachusetts, AFMRS auxiliary, 1839

In 1833 a group of evangelical clergymen and laymen in New York established the American Society for Promoting the Observance of the Seventh Commandment ("Thou shalt not commit adultery"). More commonly referred to as the Seventh Commandment Society, the group, which got its start supporting prostitutes' rehabilitation, began to envision a national reform crusade that would combat the combined evils of sexual immorality, drinking, and slavery—all in an effort to purify the nation. The group disseminated its proposed constitution to several hundred like-minded men across the country. Yet an interesting thing happened on the road to moral purification—the Seventh Commandment Society encountered some women. No, not sirens or vamps, but kindred reformers, who established the New York Female Moral Reform Society in 1834. These women aligned their new female organization with the Seventh Commandment Society by becoming its auxiliary. However, with its popular and controversial periodical, the *Advocate of Moral Reform*, this sister auxiliary quickly usurped the Seventh Commandment Society, asserting itself as the primary voice in moral reform. Within a few years, female moral reformers had attracted more than five hundred of their own women's auxiliary organizations, and thus changed their society's name to the American Female Moral Reform Society to reflect its national character. By this time, the Seventh Commandment Society had disbanded.[1]

With moral reform, women moved out from behind men's coattails. Instead of simply remaining an auxiliary organization to a male-led movement, they took center stage in moral reform and established the first women's national reform organization. At the same time, the AFMRS recognized the important roles women's auxiliaries could play in supporting and expanding moral reform. Numerous scholars, including Anne Firor Scott, Lori Ginzberg, and Anne Boylan, have shown the important role early nineteenth-century women's organizations played in giving women voice, empowering them to public action, providing them with business and organizational skills, and endowing them with a sense of identity beyond their domestic roles.[2] In this chapter, I focus more closely on the role of auxiliary organizations.

An auxiliary organization is usually defined as a group that performs an "ancillary" and or "adjunct" function such as providing "voluntary assistance to a church, hospital, charity, etc."[3] The term came into common usage in the early nineteenth century when benevolent and reform organizations began to flourish in the United States. For instance, the American Bible Society (1816), the American Sunday School Union (1824), and the American Tract Society (1825), were massive national institutions that relied on local auxiliaries to found Sunday schools, and to purchase and widely distribute their centrally published materials.[4] Frequently, women and men established separate auxiliary societies, which I will discuss later, but over time, *auxiliary* has become a gendered term because auxiliary societies are often assumed to be female. In fact, the word *auxiliary* has often been paired with the possessive *ladies'* or *women's*.

Becoming an auxiliary society to an active national organization was usually quite different from establishing a freestanding benevolent or reform organization in the sense that women were joining a cause with a preexisting structure. In the case of the AFMRS, I argue that mobilizing auxiliaries became a rhetorical tactic that women used to help sustain and expand the moral reform movement. The mutually beneficial relationships the AFMRS established with its auxiliaries provided a way for women to take a public stand in favor of moral reform, created an affirming network, expanded and financed the moral reform movement, and provided sites for women's rhetorical education, which enabled auxiliary societies to broaden their moral reform efforts. Rather than performing an "auxiliary" function, local societies viewed themselves as active partners with their parent society in New York.[5] Drawing on reports from AFMRS auxiliaries published in the *Advocate*, I discuss each of these rhetorical functions. I begin by explaining how and why women's auxiliaries became integral to antebellum reform efforts and how the AFMRS initially organized auxiliaries. Altogether, this chapter shows how mobilizing auxiliary societies created a vital network that encouraged women's rhetorical activities and propelled the AFMRS's national moral reform campaign.

CREATING SEPARATE WOMEN'S AUXILIARIES

By joining an auxiliary, women widened their webs of interaction and often their rhetorical endeavors. J. R. McNeill and William H. McNeill define webs of interaction as "a set of connections that link people to one another," and through these connections they "communicate information and use that information to shape their future behavior."[6] Membership in a local organization expanded women's interactions in their communities, and if the society was part of a national organization, it expanded their interactions within and across states. Women's organizations had long relied on communications between family and friends to share organizational ideas and documents. These helped prompt the proliferation of women's voluntary organizations across the country with similar organizational forms, constitutions, and operating structures.[7]

While women were establishing their own independent charitable and benevolent societies as early as the 1790s, women also established organizations as auxiliary societies to men's organizations. In many instances, women formed auxiliaries to lend support to societies established by their husbands, male relatives, or ministers. Additionally, men's groups recruited women's auxiliaries, especially for fundraising, visiting, and distributing printed materials.[8] Because of women's societal standing as moral arbiters, women's auxiliaries also lent moral ethos to a cause; hence, women's advocacy as well as their labor was valued and sought.[9] Nancy Woloch notes that during the first half of the nineteenth century, women's societies were frequently "absorbed as 'auxiliaries' into large, male-dominated, national, non-sectarian federations—such as the American Bible Society, Tract Society, Home Missionary Society, or Sunday-School Union."[10] Additionally, Nancy Hardesty claims that this antebellum "Benevolence Empire" was sustained by the voluntary and fundraising efforts of women.[11]

A pamphlet published in 1824 offers an example of this type of auxiliary support. In a footnote to a fundraising appeal made by Reverend Elias Cornelius on behalf of the Salem Massachusetts Society for Moral and Religious Instruction, Cornelius recognized the women's auxiliary that visited the poor, provided a large part of the Sunday school instructors, ran a female adult school, and contributed to the society's funds. From this description, the women's auxiliary appears to be making a substantial contribution to the society, but the women's auxiliary only receives a footnote reference. Indeed, male organizations relied heavily on women's efforts, yet women's auxiliaries have often been relegated to footnotes in history because they are deemed support or adjuncts. However, the AFMRS's own history illustrates that women's auxiliaries assumed a wide array of functions. Some performed vital supporting roles, some became important forums where women read about and discussed issues, and other groups used the association to pursue their own initiatives.[12]

In forming female auxiliary organizations, women often sought more active roles and independence. Sometimes women established auxiliaries because they were not allowed to join men's organizations or simply because they felt more comfortable in women-only organizations. In mixed-gender organizations, women were precluded from most leadership positions, and women were reluctant to speak freely, offer ideas, or exert control for fear of indiscretion. In its third annual report, the AFMRS acknowledged this problem stressing the importance of women-only auxiliaries. "If ladies act *only* in concert with the other sex," asserted the AFMRS Board, "half their usefulness and efficiency will necessarily be lost . . . They ought to speak and pray and labor with each other, and there are many reasons why this can only be done where none but ladies are present."[13] Reports from AFMRS auxiliaries affirmed this sentiment. For instance, a report from the Wadham's Mill, New York, auxiliary demurred, "Our society consisted of both sexes the past year, and of course was conducted by gentlemen. But after mature deliberation, we felt that the ladies could do more good in a separate capacity, and accordingly took the management of the Society into our own hands."[14] The Carthage, New York, auxiliary did the same, explaining, "we felt that females could do more good in a separate society."[15] Frustrated by their secondary status in male-led societies, women formed their own. In women-only auxiliaries, women assumed leadership and the same responsibilities as men except for delivering addresses at public gatherings.[16]

While there are some instances of women working alongside men, in the three largest antebellum reform efforts—temperance, antislavery, and moral reform—women repeatedly gravitated to separate female organizations. In temperance, women supported men's efforts in female auxiliary societies until the latter half of the nineteenth century, when the Woman's Crusade took place and the Woman's Christian Temperance Union was established in 1873. In the 1840s, when men formed Washingtonian societies and the Sons of Temperance, women formed Martha Washington and Daughters of Temperance auxiliary societies. Nonetheless, women were still frustrated by men restricting their activity. In fact, the temperance movement launched Susan B. Anthony's public career and pursuit of women rights when the men at a Sons of Temperance convention admonished women that they were there to learn, not to be heard.[17]

With antislavery organizations, "Women did not wait for men to ask them to organize," according to the historian Beth Salerno.[18] In her book *Sister Societies: Women's Antislavery Organizations in Antebellum America*, Salerno notes that before the American Anti-Slavery Society (AAS) was established in 1833, at least six female antislavery societies had already organized, including a black women's society in Salem, Massachusetts. Additionally, several female literary and free-produce societies existed. [19] Initially, men did not invite women to join the AAS even though four women attended the organizational meetings in Philadelphia. Lucretia Mott, who was one of the four women, suggested changes to the organization's declaration of sentiments and purposes, but neither she nor any other woman was invited to vote on the document, sign it, or become a member of the society despite the bylaws, which stipulated that all "persons" might participate. Thirty years later, Mott remarked, "I don't think it occurred to any one of us at that time that there would be propriety in [women] signing the [declaration of principles]." In other words, while men customarily excluded women, most women did not expect to be included and continued to gravitate to all-female organizations. Indeed, Mott helped found the Female Anti-Slavery Society in Philadelphia in 1833, and Maria Weston Chapman and her three sisters established the Boston Female Anti-Slavery Society as an auxiliary to the male-led New England Anti-Slavery Society the same year. Early on, a few combined male and female antislavery societies did exist, but only one had a female officer, and a clear delineation of men's and women's responsibilities existed. In Massachusetts, women in at least five mixed-gender societies decided to form women-only societies. "Many women felt that if they wanted to get something done, they had to do it themselves," explains Salerno. Eventually Lydia Maria Child and other women would advocate women's equal membership in male antislavery societies "fueling a major division in the anti-slavery movement."[20]

The AAS, which sought to eliminate slavery through "moral suasion," encouraged women to form female antislavery societies, recognizing women's moral standing as an asset. By 1837 at least 139 female antislavery societies were established. Many of these were formed as auxiliary societies to the AAS or local male societies, yet they established vital networks with other female antislavery societies through correspondence and joint efforts such as antislavery fairs. Even some transatlantic networks were established with British women, who had helped lobby for the British Slavery Abolition Act in 1833 and began encouraging and counseling their American sisters. Women's societies, including the Female Anti-Slavery societies in Concord, New Hampshire; Salem, Massachusetts; Philadelphia; Boston; and Ashtabula County, Ohio, mentored new societies by providing advice, document templates, and suggested reading materials. In fact, new women's societies often chose to attach themselves to female antislavery societies as auxiliaries instead of becoming auxiliaries to men's societies. Temperance and antislavery efforts show how mobilizing auxiliary societies became an important rhetorical tactic for female reformers in the nineteenth century. This is especially apparent with the AFMRS, the first national women's reform organization.[21]

MOBILIZING AFMRS AUXILIARIES

The Oberlin Female Moral Reform Society (FMRS) provides an illustrative example of how both local auxiliary societies and the AFMRS benefitted from this relationship. Two moral reform societies formed at Oberlin soon after the AFMRS organized: the Oberlin FMRS and the Young Men's Moral Reform Society of the Oberlin Collegiate. The men's society was one of the few male societies that became an auxiliary to the national AFMRS; however, the Oberlin men's society was not active and quickly ceded the job of moral reform to the women's society. By 1840 the Oberlin FMRS's membership comprised 380 women, and by 1854 it exceeded 850 women.[22]

The Oberlin FMRS's membership was diverse—including the wives of Oberlin professors and presidents, married women from the town, and female students at the college. Alice Welch Cowles, wife of Professor Henry Cowles, was principal of the Female Department, and the Oberlin society's president. Up until her death in 1843, she presided over most meetings. Marianne Parker Dascomb was also part of the original group that formed the society, and served as principal of the Female Department from 1835 to 1836 and again from 1853 to 1870. Lydia Root Andrews Finney, wife of the popular evangelist Charles Finney, and one of the founding members and the first directress of the AFMRS in 1834, became active in the Oberlin society after the Finneys moved to Oberlin. Eliza C. Stewart, wife of Oberlin cofounder Philo Penfield Stewart, was also an active member. Students active in the Oberlin FMRS included the first three women to receive college degrees: Caroline Rudd, Mary Hosford, and Elizabeth Prall. The Oberlin FMRS also became training ground for well-known nineteenth-century reformers Lucy Stone, who served as the society's secretary and treasurer in 1845, and Antoinette Brown Blackwell, who served on the society's executive committee in 1848 while attending Oberlin College.[23]

FIGURE 4. Oberlin female graduates, 1855. Marianne Parker Dascomb, front row, center, was one of the founding members of the Oberlin Female Moral Reform Society, which remained active for twenty-five years. Photo courtesy of the Oberlin College Archives.

The Oberlin FMRS, like other societies in college communities,[24] had the opportunity to influence a large body of students. In its constitution members pledged "to cultivate and promote purity of feeling, of action, and dress, both in ourselves, our associates, and all who come within the sphere of influence." As principal of Oberlin's Female Department, Alice Cowles believed an active moral reform society could encourage virtuous behavior among Oberlin's co-eds. To that end, she delivered lectures to the society on modest attire and sensible views of marriage. In its constitution, the Oberlin FMRS also vowed to reclaim "those who have wandered from the path of virtue," and indeed, three reclaimed women were brought from New York City and enrolled as students at Oberlin College.[25]

The Oberlin FMRS also helped expand and underwrite moral reform by disseminating tracts and copies of the *Advocate of Moral Reform*. By 1854 the Oberlin FMRS subscribed to more than one hundred copies of the *Advocate*. The group also supported the AFMRS with both financial and material donations. In fact, when a crisis occurred in the national organization over the mishandling of funds, the Oberlin FMRS sent a letter of encouragement and an additional financial contribution to the AFMRS.[26] The Oberlin FMRS was also a site where women could use and develop their rhetorical skills. Members regularly delivered lectures and composed original essays to read at society meetings. The Oberlin society hosted outside speakers, kept detailed meeting minutes, and submitted reports and letters, which were often published in the *Advocate*. Representatives from the Oberlin society also attended AFMRS conventions. In 1842 and 1843 the Oberlin FMRS helped spur a petition drive across the state, encouraging the Ohio legislature to legally punish seducers. Because of Ohio female moral reformers' petitioning efforts, a bill to suppress crimes against chastity was introduced; although it never made it out of legislative committee.[27] Ultimately, the Oberlin FMRS answered the AFMRS's initial call to form an auxiliary society, and through this society local women supported the AFMRS and pursued their own moral reform efforts.

Reports from auxiliaries published in the *Advocate* similarly denote the benefits of mobilizing auxiliary societies. From the start, the AFMRS envisioned moral reform as a national movement. Shortly after its formation in 1834, the AFMRS drafted a circular stating its objectives and printed two thousand copies to distribute. Many of these were sent to newspapers and bundled and mailed to principal cities. Addressed to "the ladies of the United States," the circular made an urgent plea for women "to wield a power that can be wielded by no one else." Acknowledging efforts to silence discussion with claims of indelicacy and ministers' unwillingness to broach the topic, the circular called on women to "disseminate light" on the topic through conversation and printed materials and to condemn libertines by excluding them from all society. The circular concluded, "Thus we have attempted to lay before you our views and plans. If they meet the approbation of our sisters, we cordially and earnestly entreat those of every denomination to unite with us in energetic and determined action without delay."[28] The AFMRS was inviting women to join them and become activists. Female moral reformers also used the *Advocate* to recruit women to the cause.[29]

In the *Advocate of Moral Reform*'s first issue, the AFMRS again called on women across the country to act collectively to fight licentiousness: "We hope to exert a preventive influence by endeavoring to persuade virtuous females throughout the country to organize themselves into auxiliary societies to discountenance this sin, and bring the weight of public odium to bear upon the licentious."[30] Thirty-four auxiliaries, stretching from Maine to Ohio, answered these initial calls. Even as the movement grew, auxiliaries were heavily concentrated in New York, New England, and Ohio's northeastern counties.[31] Like antislavery and radical temperance organizations, female moral reform societies were absent in the South. Southern women's organizations were usually confined to charitable endeavors and rarely questioned the economic, legal, and social systems that sustained white privilege, especially the authority of wealthy, white men.[32]

Moral reform societies were especially popular in northern industrial cities. At the same time, rural communities throughout the country worried about the fate of daughters and sons they sent to these large, impersonal, industrializing cities. These concerns were exacerbated in 1836 by the media attention that accompanied the brutal murder of Helen Jewett, an elite prostitute. The media sensation surrounding Jewett's murder and the trial of the young man accused of committing the gruesome crime directed a bright light on the city's thriving sex trade.[33] Seizing on this *kairotic* moment, the AFMRS published a twelve-page pamphlet titled "An Appeal to the Wives, Mothers, and Daughters of Our Land." Addressed to "Beloved Sisters," the pamphlet presented the AFMRS's objectives and appealed to women to "endeavor, as far as your influence extends, to form auxiliary societies."[34] A year later, at its quarterly board meeting, the AFMRS continued encouraging the formation of auxiliaries appealing to "our Christian sisters in all parts of the land, to form themselves without delay into such societies, that we may thus more effectually cooperate in raising a barrier against the tide of licentiousness, which threatens to overwhelm our beloved country."[35]

In addition to using its periodical and pamphlets, AFMRS officers and female agents traveled throughout New York and New England meeting with existing societies and helping establish new ones. For instance, during the summer of 1837 Sarah Ingraham, the AFMRS's corresponding secretary, and Miss M. I. Treadwell, one of the AFMRS's missionaries, visited thirty-six local societies and helped establish new auxiliaries—logging almost one thousand miles in the process.[36]

As the number of auxiliary societies grew, the semimonthly *Advocate of Moral Reform* began printing correspondence and annual reports submitted from its auxiliaries, thus encouraging this exchange. An important part of the *Advocate*'s rhetorical function was creating a network that connected the AFMRS to its auxiliaries and connected the auxiliaries to each other. Auxiliary reports appeared on the sixth and seventh pages under the column heading Annual Reports of Auxiliaries. With each report, the society's name appeared at the top in a bold subheading under the words *For the Advocate of Moral Reform* in small type, signifying that this correspondence was written specifically for the *Advocate* and intended to be shared.

Reports from local auxiliaries followed a common pattern and contained similar content. New auxiliaries usually include excerpts from their constitutions and names of officers. Established auxiliaries often recount a brief history, including how and when the auxiliary was formed, initial membership numbers, current membership numbers, descriptions of opposition faced as well as the auxiliary's success in swaying public opinion. Reports also note speakers who had addressed the auxiliary and actions taken to locally promote moral reform, such as distributing the *Advocate*, visiting door-to-door circulating petitions, and raising funds. Auxiliaries often report specific examples of licentiousness in their communities and the exigence for moral reform. Many also direct praise, encouraging words, and prayers to the parent society in New York, and affirm their own Christian motivation for pursuing moral reform. Some groups also apologize that their auxiliary has not done as much as it could do or should do to promote moral reform. The reports conclude with the name of the society's corresponding secretary, which not only lent credibility to the report but also represented a bold stand in some communities.

The report genre that emerged in the *Advocate* highlights four distinct rhetorical functions auxiliaries performed, which underscore why mobilizing auxiliary societies became a vital rhetorical tactic for the AFMRS. First, auxiliaries became a means of advocacy, enabling women to take a stand particularly with regards to a controversial social issue like moral reform. Second, auxiliaries became an affirming network that bolstered female moral reformers amid the strong opposition they faced. Third, auxiliaries financially underwrote and geographically expanded the moral reform movement. Fourth, auxiliaries became important sites for women's rhetorical education and activity. In the remainder of this chapter, I examine each of these four rhetorical functions, drawing on numerous examples from the auxiliary reports published in the *Advocate of Moral Reform*. These reports provide the primary archival evidence of AFMRS auxiliary societies' actions. Because copies of the *Advocate* are not readily available, I cite numerous examples to demonstrate AFMRS auxiliaries' reach and rhetorical roles. Throughout this discussion, I refer to auxiliaries and local societies interchangeably. This was a common practice by the AFMRS; it also signifies the dual nature of auxiliary societies. Auxiliaries gave women guidance and license to act as well as the freedom to choose their own actions based on local situations.

TAKING A STAND

By mobilizing auxiliaries, the AFMRS offered women beyond New York City a way to voice and enact their support for moral reform. For antebellum women, whose public voices were often silenced or restricted, becoming auxiliary societies to national organizations provided an important means of public advocacy. Salerno shares the example of the Ladies' Anti-Slavery Society of Norwich, Connecticut, which in 1829 declared itself an auxiliary to the American Colonization Society. Before the national AAS was established in 1833, Salerno suggests that the American Colonization Society provided "an early space for women to agitate against slavery even if they did not support the goal of colonization."[37] For many antebellum women, aligning themselves with national reform movements by forming and joining auxiliary societies became a way to advocate. By establishing a local auxiliary to the AFMRS in 1838, the women in Pittsfield, Massachusetts, recognized their membership as a rhetorical act, stating, "The organization of this society was a public avowal of our disapprobation of vice, in all its various forms."[38] Similarly, women in South Attleborough, Massachusetts, viewed their membership in a local auxiliary as a public testimony, asserting, "While we regret that so few have been found inclined to enroll their names in the cause of virtue, we rejoice that even these few have been willing to testify to the world their abhorrence of licentiousness, and their adherence to the principles of chastity."[39]

Previously, women had formed auxiliaries to support local benevolent causes and national, male-led evangelical enterprises, including Bible and tract societies, missionary societies, and Sunday school societies, and their efforts raising funds and distributing printed materials were recognized as integral to these efforts' success. However, antebellum women seldom encountered opposition or rebuke for their support of benevolent or Christian causes.[40] Yet, in the case of controversial movements like moral reform and antislavery, the stakes were raised. Because of widespread opposition, ridicule, and threats of retribution, joining an AFMRS auxiliary society was not a step a woman took lightly. Indeed, the female moral reform society in Torringford, Connecticut, reports that few had come forward to labor in this "unpopular" cause.[41] Women in Flint River, Michigan, also faced tremendous opposition, including a group of young men who formed an Anti-Moral Reform Society and declared they would not associate with young ladies who belong to the local moral reform society.[42] Similarly, the auxiliary in Brockport, New York, explains, "We soon found that our cause and its firm supporters were not unfrequently the subject of jest and ridicule. Nor did we escape the notice of the press." Under the strain of public criticism, the Brockport society reports that some members withdrew.[43] At the same time, the society in Nelson, Ohio, admits that it deferred announcing the formation of its auxiliary society "for want of courage to meet the opposition."[44] The society in Forestville, New York, also reports, "The powerful opposition we have met, has in some cases disheartened the timid," nonetheless it notes a courageous few had "determined to face the frowns and insults of a wicked world."[45] As these reports attest, the decision to form or join an AFMRS auxiliary did not go unnoticed in communities. For many women, membership became a courageous rhetorical act, something easily overlooked if women's membership is not placed in the context of these auxiliary reports. Because the AFMRS sought to warn and educate women about licentious behavior, particularly cunning employed by male libertines, moral reform was not a discreet movement. Thus, women had to weigh the prospect of public ridicule against their desire to condemn and curtail what they perceived as rampant licentiousness.

To join an auxiliary, women usually signed their names to a constitution modeled after the AFMRS's constitution.

> *Whereas*, The sin of licentiousness has made fearful havoc in the world, "corrupting all flesh," drowning souls in perdition, and exposing us to the vengeance of a holy God, whose law in this respect has been trampled on almost universally, not only by actual transgression but by the tacit consent of the virtuous, and by the almost perfect silence of those who He has commanded to "cry aloud and spare not";
>
> *And whereas*, It is the duty of the virtuous, to use every consistent moral means, to save our country from utter destruction: We do therefore form ourselves into a society for this object.[46]

With their signatures, women pledged their support through their collective efforts and personal example. The constitution also equated moral reform to a Christian duty. Women relied on their religious convictions to ballast themselves against opposition—viewing opposition as a test of their faith and fortitude. Mirroring the AFMRS's organizational constitution and the *Advocate of Moral Reform*'s contents, reports from auxiliary societies were replete with scriptural references, evangelical language, and supplications to God. Women used these religious appeals to remind each other that while men and genteel society might try to dissuade or even shame those who took a public stand against licentiousness, their calling came from an infinite, higher power.

Using call-and-response, the Buckland, Massachusetts, auxiliary asks, "Shall we be ashamed to be found in the ranks of moral reform?" They emphatically answered, "No! Certainly not! We will not be ashamed of the cause of virtue! We will not cease our efforts to correct an erroneous public sentiment, so long as the libertine is privileged to commit his foul deeds with impunity." The Buckland auxiliary report concludes, underscoring society's gendered moral standards, "O, I would bless God that the dawn of that day has already appeared when the licentious gentleman shall take the place of his guilty victim in society."[47] The Malone, New York, society also drew strength from the belief that they were pursuing a God-ordained mission. They exalt that against loud, organized opposition, "we have found that *truth is mighty.* Our sisters wielded this instrument with a reliance on an Almighty arm, and persevered in their course."[48] Ultimately, as female moral reformers took a stand in favor of moral reform, they claimed that with God on their side, opposition was nothing to fear.

Viewing moral reform as Christian duty, auxiliaries were especially exasperated when they encountered opposition from other Christians. Auxiliaries used reports to call out local ministers and Christians who renounced their efforts. Bemoaning the fact that local clergy were unwilling to join them and "the Lord" in their fight for decency, the Greenport, New York, society claims, "our motto shall ever be 'onward' till we gain complete victory."[49] The Albany, New York, auxiliary also reports that they faced opposition from most of the city's ministers.[50] Similarly, announcing the formation of its moral reform society, the auxiliary in Geneva, New York, writes:

> We meet with opposition where we least expected. Those to whom we have been accustomed to look for aid and encouragement in our plans of benevolence and mercy, not only withhold their influence, but set their faces against us. It is truly painful to engage in any thing without the approbation of those we love and revere; and though this renders our self-denying efforts doubly trying, yet while the Bible sanctions, Heaven forbid that through the fear of man we should relinquish our purpose.[51]

As these excerpts indicate, without the approval and assistance of the men and clergy, who usually supported their benevolent and evangelical efforts, advocating moral reform often forced women to operate independently. Thus, women's willingness to take a stand was both daunting and liberating. In many communities, they were on their own except for the bonds, literal and imagined, that they formed with other female moral reformers in their local communities and region, and across the country.[52]

CREATING AN AFFIRMING NETWORK

As the AFMRS mobilized auxiliaries, it created a mutually affirming network. One of the rhetorical functions of a network is to remind individuals that they are part of something larger than themselves. This was especially important for antebellum women who dared to pursue broad societal reform. From reading the *Advocate*, local societies were well aware of the struggle their leaders in New York faced. Hence, the steady stream of letters and reports from local societies assured AFMRS leaders that *they were not alone.* The society in Honesdale, Pennsylvania, writes:

Dear Sisters—Engaged as you are in an arduous self-denying and unpopular cause, it may perhaps cheer you, in your onward course, to know that there are those in Northern Pennsylvania who deeply sympathize with you, and from whose hearts prayer unceasingly ascends to the throne of the God of purity in your behalf, that your hands be stayed up and that your spirits sink not under the vast responsibilities you have assumed.[53]

Like the women in Honesdale, female moral reformers referred to each other as sisters, a familial reference they used to unite themselves. Moreover, the designation clearly signified moral reform as a women's movement. Calling themselves sisters, fellow laborers, and partners, the Napoli, New York, auxiliary writes, "Beloved Sisters—As laborers in the same part of the vineyard of our Lord we greet you; as partners of your joys, we rejoice with you, and as partners of your sorrows we sympathize with you."[54] Likewise, the South Deerfield, Massachusetts, auxiliary assured the AFMRS with its "wish to be considered as *co-workers* in this effort."[55] Underscoring their unity, the auxiliary members in Holden, Massachusetts, passed a resolution, stating, "That in view of the appalling and destructive sin of licentiousness, we will tender our sympathy to those dear sisters who stand as pioneers in this self-denying work of reform, and that by prayer and exertions, we will do all in our power to sustain them."[56]

Auxiliaries acknowledged and affirmed their parent society through their correspondence. While most assurances were directed at the women in New York City, these public affirmations, printed in the *Advocate of Moral Reform*, also strengthened the auxiliaries that discussed, composed, and approved them as well as the other auxiliaries and supporters that read them. In addition to corresponding with their parent society, auxiliaries often corresponded with each other. The *Advocate* published the names of corresponding secretaries for each society, which helped facilitate exchanges between societies. Local society members also attended meetings of other societies. For instance, Westmoreland, New York, and Clinton, New York, held a combined meeting.[57] The Rindge, New Hampshire, auxiliary also noted the "interesting and extensive correspondence" it carried on with other societies as well as "by way of delegations."[58] In fact, at one point it reported that women from fourteen different towns had attended its meetings.[59] Similarly, the Peruville, New York, auxiliary reported that a schoolteacher from nearby Etna attended a meeting and then returned to her village to organize a local society.[60] This type of interaction and correspondence further reinforced the bonds of sisterhood.

Again, highlighting the movement's strong religious grounding, auxiliaries supported each other through religious disciplines such as prayer and fasting. Women in Mount Morris, Michigan, note that their "dear sisters in New York City" have become special subjects of their prayers during their monthly meetings.[61] The Utica, New York, auxiliary set aside a day of fasting and prayer to demonstrate its support for the AFMRS's semiannual meeting that was to be held in Utica and called on other local societies to do the same.[62] And prior to the 1840 AFMRS annual convention, the Litchfield, Ohio, auxiliary wrote, "We design to hold a prayer-meeting on the 13th of May, in behalf of your Annual Meeting, that the Lord would strengthen your hand and encourage your hearts to go forward with a single eye to his glory, in this great work of purifying the world, and that you may have wisdom and grace to execute all your plans in that way which will best promote the interests of the Redeemer's kingdom."[63] Even as the distance between New York and Ohio precluded Litchfield auxiliary members from attending the convention, they used their own gathering and prayer to unite with the assembly in New York.

Another way auxiliaries bolstered the movement was by documenting their societies' growth. Reports printed in the *Advocate* announce the formation of new societies and increases in the membership of existing societies. For instance, the North Attleborough, Massachusetts, auxiliary, which began with twenty-seven members, reports that its membership quickly grew to seventy. An auxiliary in West Chazy, New York, reports that it began with ten members and now has eighty. The Peru, Massachusetts, auxiliary reports that its society grew from fourteen members to forty-five to eighty-eight.[64] Societies formed throughout New York and New England, but they also extended westward into Pennsylvania, Ohio, Michigan, Illinois, and Wisconsin. As families moved west, women carried copies of the *Advocate* and their commitment to reform with them. Case in point, one announcement of a new society explained how a woman who had recently moved to Michigan contacted another woman in western New York asking for copies of the *Advocate*. With the two copies she received, the woman in Michigan attracted interest, and ultimately formed an auxiliary.[65] The rapid expansion of auxiliaries especially occurred between 1836 and 1839. In 1836 108 local societies formed, taking the total number of auxiliaries to 226. Three years later, the total rose to 519 auxiliaries. Between 1837 and 1841 563 different auxiliaries are mentioned in the *Advocate*.[66] Beyond affirming the AFMRS, this network of auxiliaries enabled the movement to expand its reach—making moral reform a national campaign.

These auxiliaries also confirmed that prostitution, seduction, and all manners of licentious behavior existed well beyond the boundaries of New York City. This was especially the case in emerging industrial centers, which mirrored New York City's problems on a smaller scale. A report from the female moral reform society in New York Mills, New York, explains, "The state of society in this place is peculiar to manufacturing villages. Multitudes of youth are here collected, who need light and instruction on this subject, and our population is constantly changing."[67] The auxiliary in another manufacturing city, Utica, New York, used its annual meeting to present facts on the state of morals in its city with the object of motivating "greater diligence," and the Springfield, Massachusetts, society formed a visiting committee, which verifies "licentiousness, both in high places and low places."[68] Beyond urban areas, rural auxiliaries also corroborated the need for moral reform. A letter from the Winchendon, New Hampshire, auxiliary states, "We are far from believing that the sin of licentiousness is *confined* to cities and large towns—a careful observation for years has led us to a different conclusion."[69]

Reports show how the call for moral reform struck a unifying chord of frustration with women from small communities. The Forestville, New York, auxiliary reports that "Many painful circumstances have occurred in our own little village and vicinity, as evidences that the destroyer is even here, that licentiousness is not confined to the large cities alone, but is even at our very doors blighting and withering every thing in its path. None are safe, while the libertine goeth about as a roaring lion, seeking who he may devour."[70] Likewise, the West Chazy, New York, society laments, "There are near this place a number of families supported by virtuous wives, who have been deserted by their perfidious, false-hearted husbands . . . leaving their weeping families to find their way through a cold-hearted world alone."[71] Notably, these latter reports were not complaining about prostitution and the sex trade—problems especially endemic in cities. Instead, they complain about men's moral conduct (seduction, desertion), and the disastrous effects these behaviors had on women and families as well as the lack of consequence for their actions. These frustrations with male behavior attracted women to the movement and united them in a common cause.

These frustrations also explain why moral reform auxiliaries drew a more inclusive membership than most women's organizations. While moral reform was predominantly made up of middle-class, white women, the movement also drew women in urban and rural communities; single and married women; Congregationalists, Baptists, Methodists, and Presbyterians; upper-class women and working-class women including schoolteachers, boardinghouse keepers, and textile and factory workers. Shortly after the formation of the AFMRS, a group of African American women at Zion's Church in New York City formed an auxiliary. Two years later, this auxiliary had 138 members, and at one point its members considered hiring their own city missionary. The Albany, New York, auxiliary's managers represented eleven different churches, the Gardner, Massachusetts, auxiliary's membership included an equal number of married and unmarried ladies, and the Geneva, New York, auxiliary, which was initially started by a group of young ladies, recruited several "Mothers of Israel" who were also willing to "proffer their influence and support." Conversely, the Nelson, Ohio, auxiliary amended its constitution, so it could include young ladies as members. And like the Oberlin auxiliary, the Dartmouth auxiliary brought together professors' wives and female students. Membership in a local moral reform society expanded women's webs of interaction, and these webs became support that reinforced and strengthened the movement.[72]

EXPANDING AND UNDERWRITING MORAL REFORM

Mobilizing auxiliaries helped underwrite and expand the moral reform movement. The AFMRS, which considered the *Advocate of Moral Reform* its primary vehicle for moral reform, encouraged its auxiliaries to extend the publication's reach. Even the least active auxiliaries sold subscriptions to the *Advocate* and purchased copies for their members to read and distribute gratis. This provided crucial financial support and helped underwrite the cost of the *Advocate*, which was the AFMRS's chief operating expense in its early years. Occasionally the AFMRS even enlisted its auxiliaries' assistance in collecting payment from delinquent subscribers. Auxiliaries also supported the AFMRS by paying annual dues, taking up collections, and by purchasing lifetime memberships. Lifetime memberships, which cost $10, provided a way for auxiliaries to both raise funds and honor local members. These lifetime memberships also became a public endorsement—the name of the individual being recognized, as well as the society that purchased the membership, were published in the *Advocate*. In fact, the popularity of lifetime memberships during one period necessitated a special section on the *Advocate*'s back page. Societies found other ways to raise money for the AFMRS. Some women turned their needles to reform. The Rockford, Illinois, auxiliary formed a sewing society to help raise funds with its members' handiwork, and the Cato, New York, auxiliary held a fair where it raised $32 for the AFMRS by selling handmade articles.[73]

Selling subscriptions to and distributing the *Advocate of Moral Reform* made auxiliary members active spokespersons for moral reform in their communities. Reports in the *Advocate* proudly state the number of periodicals local societies purchased for distribution. The Boylston, Massachusetts, auxiliary considered circulation of the *Advocate* its priority, because they believed that ignorance on the subject of moral reform was "the greatest barrier in the way of their success." Their members purchased twenty-five subscriptions, which they read and then "scattered as widely as possible."[74] Similarly, the Zion's Church auxiliary, an African American society in New York City, asserted "we will give the Advocate a wider circulation, until we succeed in waking up a general interest in the cause."[75] Beyond selling, purchasing, and distributing the *Advocate*, local societies continually testified to the paper's import. An annual report from the Philadelphia auxiliary reported that the *Advocate* saved one girl by alerting her mother to the dangerous situations that girls searching for employment in the city encountered. The Philadelphia auxiliary wrote, "This mother blesses the Advocate, and so, we doubt not, will thousands and tens of thousands in time and in eternity."[76]

Another way auxiliaries sought to expand moral reform was by persuading local ministers to preach on the seventh commandment. The Utica, New York, auxiliary sent a letter to pastors in the city asking them to preach on moral reform, and the West Chazy, New York, auxiliary listed among its accomplishments getting seven ministers to preach on the subject of adultery. Similarly, the Attica, New York, auxiliary touted that a prominent minister delivered a sermon on the seventh commandment to a large congregation. Local societies used the *Advocate* to recognize these ministers and hopefully encourage others to do likewise. The Troy, New York, auxiliary even sponsored a writing contest that offered $50 for the best written tract on the "the Duty of Ministers and Physicians in relation to the cause of moral reform and their responsibilities for promoting it." Of course, it is ironic that women would use tracts to convert ministers to active moral reform proponents.[77]

Auxiliaries also expanded the moral reform movement through a variety of local initiatives. As AFMRS auxiliaries, women received both guidance and license to act. By sharing its own actions and demonstrating effective means for pursuing reform, the AFMRS acted as a rhetorical mentor and model for local societies. Inspired by the reports from city missionaries like Margaret Prior, many local auxiliaries appointed visiting committees responsible for visiting door-to-door throughout neighborhoods in their community. These visitors distributed copies of the *Advocate*. They also recruited women to join their society and asked both women and men to donate and sign the moral reform pledge. Like visitors in New York, some local visiting committees traveled to neighborhoods and observed for themselves situations and conditions most had never seen. A group of women in Farmington, Connecticut, visited a "well-known *thoroughfare of ill-fame*" in their city and used their presence to try to awaken consciences.[78] Likewise, a Northfield, Massachusetts, auxiliary discovered houses of ill repute in its midst. They contacted city officials to little avail, and thus explain, "we nerved ourselves to visit them, that if possible the inmates might be reformed and broken up." The women spoke to prostitutes and reported that one of the houses was eventually vacated.[79] It is unclear whether the auxiliary was responsible for closing the brothel; nonetheless, the example demonstrates how women *nerved* themselves to take actions they would not have contemplated apart from participation in a local auxiliary and without the suggestion and encouragement from a parent organization.

Auxiliaries in Philadelphia and Albany, New York, also followed the example of the AFMRS by opening their own offices of direction, employment offices, to help women find respectable employment. Women new to an area often turned to offices of direction to find positions as domestic servants, but the *Advocate* repeatedly warned that these offices were frequently used to lure unsuspecting women to brothels.

The Dunbarton, New Hampshire, auxiliary borrowed another tactic from the AFMRS; when one of its own members became pregnant by the man who employed her as a housekeeper, the society published the libertine's name in capital letters writing, "Men whose characters are stained, as is JOHN NE-SMITH'S, we think, find it difficult to 'maintain an erect position,' in any of the cities or villages of our land."[80] This bold, even snide, public defamation again shows women taking actions far beyond the conventions of the day. Similar to AFMRS members in New York City, who were known to stand watch outside of brothels, women in the Utica auxiliary began monitoring the behavior of men living in local boardinghouses.[81]

Encouraged by the actions of the AFMRS and other auxiliaries, many local societies initiated their own reform endeavors. Some societies explored possible avenues for moral education beyond reading the *Advocate*. For instance, the New Hudson, New York, auxiliary appointed two members to visit each school district in the area, the Utica, New York, auxiliary created an evening school to provide moral reform education to domestic servants, and several societies established juvenile societies as a way to educate youth about proper moral conduct.[82] The Boston auxiliary even began publishing its own monthly paper, *The Friend of Virtue*, in 1838. The AFMRS congratulated the society,[83] but later when some New England societies inquired about becoming auxiliaries of the Boston Female Moral Reform Society, it voiced concern about splintering the movement. In a carefully crafted response, the AFMRS explains:

> In giving an answer, we are aware that we risk the imputation of selfishness, but as we are conscious of no motive but a desire for the greatest good of the whole cause, so we dare not from personal consideration refuse to express our opinion. . . . We say, then to our auxiliaries, that if the cause of Moral Reform were a sectional matter, we should not object to its being bounded by geographical limits, and divided by states and counties; but we have never considered it. We do not look upon it as a New York effort, or a New England effort, but as a Christian attempt to remove a moral evil; and in our appeals to the community we have not attempted to arouse

New England feeling, or southern, or western feeling, but *Christian* feeling in view
of a deep and deadly sin . . . we cannot dispense with the assistance of our friends
and patrons in New England . . . wherever its [moral reform's] advocates are found,
they are recognized as sisters in a common bond of union, far stronger than that
which binds together the inhabitants of a state or section of country.[84]

In addressing Boston and other New England societies, the AFMRS was trying to hold together a national movement. Eventually, what would become
the New England Female Moral Reform Society in Boston attracted approximately sixty auxiliaries, including five which transferred their membership
from the AFMRS.[85] This regional association foreshadows later women's organizations such as the Women's Christian Temperance Union and the various
women's suffrage associations that created hierarchies of regional and state associations.[86] Even as the number of auxiliaries grew, the AFMRS maintained
direct correspondence with its auxiliaries. While trying to avoid regional
fragmentation, in addressing its active Boston auxiliary, the AFMRS was also
negotiating a careful balance. The AFMRS encouraged auxiliaries to pursue
independent actions that would help expand the movement all the while remaining part of this national organization.

BECOMING SITES FOR WOMEN'S RHETORICAL EDUCATION

Mobilizing auxiliaries also created numerous sites for women's rhetorical education and activities. Selling and distributing the *Advocate*, canvassing neighborhoods door-to-door, persuading ministers to preach on the seventh commandment, and even writing the reports themselves can all be characterized
as rhetorical actions that women learned and applied as members of AFMRS
auxiliaries. Auxiliaries also prepared women to advocate for moral reform
through the act of composing constitutions, by educating them on moral reform, by encouraging them to discuss issues contributing to moral reform,
by asserting their views about moral reform in writing, and by circulating
petitions as a means of exerting political pressure.

   In forming an auxiliary, women wrote constitutions, elected officers, conducted meetings, and submitted regular reports to the AFMRS. In its annual report and pamphlets, the AFMRS widely distributed its constitution as a
model. While societies typically adopted the AFMRS's constitution, they also
amended it. Hence, the amendment became a rhetorical tool that auxiliaries
used to assert individual identities. The AFMRS encouraged this individuality
through its publishing practice, which was to only publish the additions auxiliaries made to the AFMRS's constitution. Through this publication practice,

the AFMRS was urging its auxiliaries to "own" the cause. The newly formed Heath, Massachusetts, auxiliary shared its preamble, which stressed the calling its members felt. The society explains, "Feeling the cause of moral reform to be the cause of God, and that we are loudly called upon by our sisters already in the field to put our hands to the work, and stay if possible the progress of licentiousness, which is sweeping over our land, threatening us with the fate of Sodom and doom of Gomorrah."[87] Similarly, the newly formed society in Springfield, New York, shared a pledge its members composed.[88] Societies also used amendments to highlight particular areas of concern or focus. In an article in its constitution, the Monson, Maine, auxiliary pledges to "refrain from attending" balls and parties that included dancing because they believed these "haunts of gaiety and mirth often prove an introduction to licentiousness."[89] Similarly, the South Deerfield, Massachusetts, auxiliary uses its constitution to stress parents' responsibility "to instill virtuous principles into the minds of our children."[90] And the Groton, New York, auxiliary pledges not to keep "unseasonable hours" during visits, rides, or parties and to "wholly disapprobate the receiving of visits from gentlemen after the usual hour of retiring to rest."[91] (The implication being that late hours led to immoral behavior.) Ultimately, these amendments show that writing and approving constitutions were not perfunctory exercises for auxiliaries. Members not only learned how constitutions were constructed and amended, they put thought and time into discussing and composing their addendums—knowing that the words they wrote and approved would be published and read.

Most auxiliaries held monthly or quarterly meetings. These regular meetings provided a means for educating, organizing, and motivating members. The Willoughby, Ohio, auxiliary explains that the effect of its first meeting was "to harmonize our views on the subject, and more deeply impress our minds with a sense of its vast importance to our domestic, social, moral, religious, and political interests."[92] As is the case with most reform movements, education and motivation were intertwined, so it was important for women in Willoughby and the rest of the country to see how moral reform touched their domestic and social spheres, aligned with their moral and religious convictions, and underlined some of their political frustrations. Societies created numerous opportunities for members to learn more about issues related to moral reform. In addition to sharing copies of the *Advocate*, several societies purchased copies of popular tracts and John McDowall's memoir.[93] The Rockford, Illinois, auxiliary passed around publications in hopes that women joining the society could become "efficient members."[94] Repeatedly, auxiliaries stressed the importance of learning more about moral reform in order to converse intelligently on the subject and persuade others to support the cause. In addition to reading, local auxiliaries invited speakers to address their groups.

Local societies often looked to clergy to deliver lectures on topics pertaining to moral reform. However, as I noted earlier, ministers were sometimes reluctant to address the topic. Several societies encouraged their own members to lead discussions or write and present essays on moral reform. In 1837 a group of women gathered in Addison, Vermont, to hear remarks from a member of the neighboring AFMRS society in Bridport, Vermont. Afterward, the women in Addison decided to form their own auxiliary society.[95] The following year the new Addison auxiliary reported a meeting during which its group heard "some very interesting remarks" from one of its own society members.[96] Female speakers became the norm in these two Vermont societies. Similarly, the Sheffield, Ohio, auxiliary reported that society members "take up the different subjects connected with moral reform" and present their views in written articles to the society. The Sheffield auxiliary explains that the examination of these subjects is intended "to prepare ourselves for laboring more successfully and efficiently in the cause." Evident in this example and others, auxiliary meetings provided a safe, liberating space for women to speak and deliberate. Indeed, the Sheffield auxiliary acknowledges how this approach had increased attendance and "freedom of remark" among its members.[97] Several local societies discovered that female speakers drew larger crowds. Whereas male clerics delivered talks to silent female audiences, female speakers stimulated participation and conversation. Women's attraction to these more active forums may signal women's changing expectations. In the same way that women chose to form their own organizations instead of remaining quiet supporters in male-run societies, women may have begun to turn deaf ears to male orators who spoke *at* female audiences, but did not share their same experience or invite or listen to their comments.

Writing and sharing essays was a frequent practice in women's literary societies and in some antebellum female seminaries,[98] but moral reform auxiliaries linked this literate practice to reform. In her study of black women's literary societies, Shirley Wilson Logan recognizes this connection between rhetorical skill and activism. She writes, "The women understood that finely tuned rhetorical skills could serve the abolitionist cause, and many used the societies as training groups for, if not sites of, antislavery work at the same time."[99] Women in many auxiliaries similarly understood that equipping members with education on moral reform, confidence, and rhetorical wherewithal was essential to further the cause. Societies in Griffins Mills, New York; Gardner, Massachusetts; and Rindge, New Hampshire, regularly asked members to write on subjects pertaining to moral reform and present these compositions to the society.[100] Thus, asking members to write deepened their commitment to moral reform. The Rindge auxiliary reports, "Twenty of our members have, from time to time, written on this subject, and the reading of these articles has added much to the interest of our meetings."[101] The Gardner auxiliary assigned questions to its members—"What are the evils, moral and physical, arising from the sin of licentiousness?" and "What is usually the first step by which females stray from the path of virtue?"—to be discussed at the next meeting.[102]

Recognizing the value of this type of active participation, the AFMRS promoted it in the *Advocate of Moral Reform*. In an editorial note introducing an article, the *Advocate*'s editor explained that it was written by a member of an auxiliary society, and commended the "practice of handing in written communications on the various subjects connected with moral reform" as a way to increase interest in the society's meeting while also increasing "the personal improvement of those who write."[103] In that sense, the AFMRS understood the strong connection between women's rhetorical education and reform. Other societies read articles from the *Advocate* and examined different aspects of moral reform at their meetings.[104] The Monroe, Ohio, auxiliary asked its members to bring a passage of Scripture to read and discuss—a practice that provided members with scriptural evidence they could use to support moral reform.[105]

By encouraging women to write, speak, and converse about moral reform, auxiliaries showed women that they could be effective writers and speakers. This is especially evident in a report published in an 1837 issue of the *Advocate*. According to the report, when some women in West Boylston, Massachusetts, were frustrated in their efforts to find a lecturer to address moral reform, "Miss S. . . . being on a visit in a neighboring town, proposed to the ladies of this place if they would appoint a meeting, that she would attend and give us some information on the subject." The report notes, "Miss S. met and addressed us, to the very great satisfaction of all present, and to the conviction of some, who had before been uninterested, that a woman can be eloquent when pleading for the debased and suffering of her own sex." Following the address, the group voted in favor of forming a society.[106] Excluding the woman's full name may indicate the controversy surrounding female speakers, particularly a single woman, at the time. Nonetheless, Miss S., who was likely a member of another local auxiliary, exhibited eloquence and effective persuasion. Thus, she demonstrated how moral reform auxiliaries gave women both the opportunity to exercise and attain rhetorical skill.

Conventions provided another opportunity for auxiliary members to hone their rhetorical skills by deliberating on issues, voting, and offering resolutions. At these conventions, auxiliary members also heard from female leaders in the movement, and learned about moral reform efforts across the country. While the AFMRS had always invited members to attend its board meetings, in 1838 it organized a convention in conjunction with its annual meeting, noting that many sister societies had requested a general meeting. Part of the motivation may have come from the Anti-Slavery Convention of Women held in New York in 1837 and the one scheduled to be held in Philadelphia in 1838. At least half a dozen female delegates, who attended the AFMRS's first convention, were delegates to the first women's antislavery convention the previous year.[107] However, women's antislavery societies, which did not have a national parent society like the AFMRS, were much more fragmented.[108] The AFMRS's invitation to auxiliaries conveyed hope that the meeting would foster stronger unity and enable the group to discuss important subjects including female education, the education of children, maternal duties, conjugal and filial obligation, and "the relative position of females as members of society."[109]

Approximately twelve hundred persons attended this first convention, including three hundred men, whom the AFMRS had not expected. Wright claims that this male presence was an attempt to reassert male oversight.[110] Notably, the AFMRS resisted this effort and retained control, indicating their confidence as the rightful leaders of the movement. To accommodate the men, while preserving an all-woman meeting led by the AFMRS's officers, the AFMRS invited the men to open the first day's session with prayers and remarks then to withdraw, which they did. Delegates from local auxiliaries and other women in attendance primarily came from New York and nearby states.[111] The Clinton, New York, auxiliary remarked that sending delegates to the convention both strengthened and encouraged its group.[112] And even auxiliaries that could not send delegates recognized the value of conventions. The Walton, New York, auxiliary asserts that "if conducted in a right spirit, it will be the means of giving a new impulse to the cause over the whole land."[113] Women's obligations as the primary family caretaker and the cost and difficulty of travel, especially for women who were discouraged from traveling alone, made it especially hard for them to attend conventions.[114] The AFMRS recognized this challenge, as well as the value of bringing women from different auxiliaries together, and began to hold semiannual meetings outside of New York City. The following year, the AFMRS held a semiannual meeting more than two hundred miles north in Utica, New York.[115]

Auxiliaries unable to send delegates to conventions learned about the proceedings and the resolutions that were passed from excerpts published in the *Advocate*. Many of the resolutions from the first convention seem intended to bolster women's resolve, including resolutions expressing that women could assert and maintain the rights of their sex without neglecting their duties, women must banish licentious men in the same way that licentious women are banished, and reading and conversing about moral reform is in no way corrupting. Resolutions also gave auxiliaries marching orders. One resolution encouraged members to place a copy of the *Advocate* or *Friend of Virtue* in the hands of every family, while another resolved that petitions should be prepared and circulated to encourage state legislatures to make seduction and adultery punishable crimes.[116]

Petitioning became another form of rhetorical instruction for auxiliaries. By mobilizing local auxiliaries to circulate petitions and lobby legislators, the AFMRS was teaching members how to exert political power. In her study of women's antislavery petitions, Susan Zaeske argues that in early nineteenth-century America, "petitioning had emerged as a potent instrument through which minority political causes and people denied the full rights of republican citizenship could exert considerable pressure on their representatives by appealing to the power of public opinion."[117] Although petitioning, which relied on door-to-door visits and conversation, fell within the boundaries of acceptable social behavior for women, by instructing women how to circulate petitions the AFMRS was encouraging women to enter political debate through one of the only avenues available to them. Circulating petitions also provided another means for women to educate, create awareness, and promote moral reform. Noting this opportunity, the Oppenheim, New York, auxiliary avows, "we highly commend this practice for the opportunity it affords of disseminating knowledge on the subject, even if nothing is accomplished by obtaining names."[118] Auxiliary members became visible and vocal advocates, and by persuading other women to sign their names, female moral reformers were also encouraging women in their communities to state independent opinions, assert "their existence as political individuals," and make themselves present in a deliberative space from which they were excluded.[119]

Women had previously claimed their rights as subjects of the new republic through petitions that voiced their concerns about widow's pensions, the need for orphanages, Indian removal, and slavery.[120] Indeed, women's antislavery petition campaigns in Great Britain and the United States are widely known, but female moral reformers also mobilized large petition drives. They even used women's successful antislavery petitioning in Britain to encourage members.[121] In its petitioning efforts, the AFMRS set its sights on state legislatures and used the *Advocate* to encourage and equip its auxiliaries. An 1839 issue of the *Advocate* published a copy of a petition to be circulated and submitted to the New York state legislature.

To the Hon. _____ The Legislature of the State of _____

Whereas, certain vices exist in this community, viz. Seduction and Adultery, which are most degrading to moral and accountable beings, and destructive of the best interests of individuals, families, and society at large; and whereas, hours of infamy are tolerated to an alarming extent, and are the known cause of ruin to multitudes of the rising generation; and whereas, no efficient measures have been taken by your honorable body for the suppression of these evils, in consequence of which their continued prevalence is filling alms-houses and penitentiaries, and prisons, with the victims of want and crime, rending the hearts of fathers and mothers, and causing unutterable anguish to be felt through all the relations of life; and whereas, the enforcement of salutary laws would tend greatly to diminish this amount of human woe, and suppress extensively those sins which are "a reproach to any people"; And whereas, the Legislature of this State has the constitutional power to enact such laws as the nature of the cause imperiously demands:

We therefore, the undersigned residents of this State, and the County of _____ respectfully and earnestly pray your honorable body, at this Session of the Legislature, to pass an act, whereby the perpetrators of the crimes referred to viz. Seduction and Adultery, including also the keepers and tenants of houses of ill-fame, shall be punished with imprisonment, for such term of time as shall be sufficient to make the penalty "a terror to evil doers."[122]

Evident from the wording, these petitions became a means for both public advocacy and political persuasion. The instructions accompanying this petition note that they are printed on half sheets of foolscap paper, and the blanks should be filled in before soliciting signatures. The instructions conclude, "We invite our auxiliaries to make immediate arrangements for having them extensively circulated in every town and county in the State."[123]

Auxiliaries regularly reported tallies from their petitioning efforts in the *Advocate*. The Walton, New York, auxiliary acknowledged that their drive had exceeded their expectations. The AFMRS's 1840 annual report recognizes both the Ohio auxiliaries and New York auxiliaries for their efforts circulating thousands of petitions.[124] Petitioning was an ongoing effort as each legislative session marked the beginning of a new drive. In 1840 the AFMRS urges, "Let the attempt be made to obtain 50,000 names the present year, and let it be distinctly understood that the cry will annually come from an increasing number, till our voices are hushed in death, or our prayer is answered."[125] Persistence became another tactic for women; female moral reformers showed lawmakers they were not going away. The AFMRS persuaded its auxiliaries that petitions gave them political voice and provided those lawmakers who supported their cause with valuable firepower. "If these petitions should be laid on the table by our lawmakers, they will have a voice to speak even there to the inmost heart of the whitewashed libertine."[126]

During the decade-long campaign in New York, female moral reformers acquired expertise in organizing statewide petition drives and lobbying legislators. Eventually, their public-awareness campaign and petition drives paid off when legislatures in several northern states took up anti-seduction, adultery, and abduction legislation. In 1843 the Pennsylvania legislature, and in 1844 the Michigan legislature, passed anti-seduction laws. In New York, two bills outlawing seduction and abduction passed by large majorities in the New York House and Senate in 1848 following ten years of petitioning by AFMRS auxiliaries. In its 1848 annual report, the AFMRS underscores its members' persistence. Even though the bill initially faced strong opposition, "petitioners have renewed their request from year to year, undaunted by defeat, till not less than one hundred thousand joined in their prayer."[127] AFMRS petition drives in Massachusetts and Ohio had also encouraged those states' legislatures to take up anti-seduction bills, although none passed. New Jersey also considered legislation.

Loopholes and watered-down language made the laws that did pass difficult to enforce and almost symbolic in effect. Nevertheless, moral reformers considered the legislation a victory because it indicated a change in public sentiment, a change brought about in large part by the AFMRS's auxiliaries. Auxiliaries encouraged thousands of citizens to sign their petitions, and they gained the support of many local and city newspapers. In the end, their efforts helped persuade male legislators to broach the subjects of seduction, adultery, abduction, and desertion and, in some instances, declare these male-perpetrated acts crimes. Additionally, the AFMRS's ten-year petition drive further illustrates the mutually beneficial network the AFMRS created.[128]

Altogether, AFMRS auxiliaries helped make the *Advocate of Moral Reform* the era's most widely circulated reform periodical. And at a time when women had limited political means, these auxiliary societies pursued reform through moral suasion and petitioning. Ultimately, auxiliaries became an essential rhetorical tactic as hundreds of AFMRS auxiliaries took to the streets to promote and advocate moral reform. They raised funds, affirmed and encouraged each other amid strong opposition, educated their members about the cause, pursued local efforts, and provided a venue for rhetorical education and advocacy. Auxiliaries also expanded women's webs of interaction and forged bonds based on common concerns and frustrations. Throughout the nineteenth century national women's organizations would follow suit, relying heavily on networks of auxiliary organizations to open the foreign missionary field to women, promote temperance, agitate for women's rights, and campaign for women's suffrage. The AFMRS also turned to its auxiliaries for help when it pursued it next rhetorical tactic—opening an institution.

Chapter 5

Establishing an Institution

Has there *ever* been in any age or portion of the world, a voluntary Female Benevolent Association, existing for twelve years, covering so wide an extent of country as this— composed of so many thousands, and enlisting so much sympathy on the one hand and opposition on the other?

—Advocate of Moral Reform, 1846

Posing this rhetorical question in its twelfth annual report, the American Female Moral Reform Society acknowledged both its success and trials as America's first national women's reform organization. For twelve years, the AFMRS had waged an emphatic public moral reform campaign aimed at awareness, education, and prevention. The unease resulting from the tremendous support and opposition the movement engendered is especially evident in the late 1840s and early 1850s when the society underwent a series of name changes. In 1847 the AFMRS changed its name from the American Female Moral Reform Society to the American Female Reform and Guardian Society, conspicuously dropping the word *moral*. Two years later, when the state legislature allowed charitable institutions to incorporate, the AFMRS incorporated itself simply as the American Female Guardian Society, dropping the word *reform*.[1] In 1847 the AFMRS also changed the name of its periodical from the *Advocate of Moral Reform* to the *Advocate of Moral Reform and Family Guardian*. In 1855 it would drop the words *moral reform* from that title, shortening the periodical's title to the *Advocate and Family Guardian*.

Explaining the periodical's first name change, the *Advocate*'s editor, Sarah Ingraham Bennett, acknowledges the "long standing prejudice against the term 'Moral Reform'" all the while stipulating, "that prejudice is an 'unexamined opinion,' and therefore wrong in itself."[2] Bennett also notes the group's desire to find a title more reflective of the society's work. With regards to the words *family guardian*, she explains how vulnerable, neglected, and needy women and children have come to look at the society as a "GUARDIAN Institution."

The act of naming exerts rhetorical power. It is a means of defining, drawing boundaries, and distinctions.[3] For the AFMRS, these name changes signaled a sea change. In 1846 the AFMRS decided to open an institution, the Home for the Friendless, to provide a refuge and assistance to vulnerable young women and children. Women's benevolent associations had a long history of establishing local institutions—schools, libraries, orphanages, homes for the elderly, employment offices, etc.—to address community needs.[4] However, unlike these institutions, the AFMRS's decision to open a home represents a change in tactics. When it organized in 1834, the AFMRS's first impulse was broad social reform; yet, by the mid-nineteenth century, the era of moral suasion was over. Rather than attempting to redeem society, women's reform groups increasingly pursued social reform through institutions or sought legislative means as "the most effective route to a more limited social transformation." Instead of relying solely on the "authority based on the special morality of female values," they relied on institutions and laws.[5] AFMRS members did not completely abdicate their roles as reformers, but they became far more pragmatic. The AFMRS still sought prevention—dissuading the individuals they encountered and the women and children in their care from immoral behaviors and livelihoods—but its emphasis shifted from awareness and education to direct aid, delivered through the Home for the Friendless. The society continued to warn readers about social problems; however, these increasingly shifted to the plight of street children, the few employment opportunities open to women, and the effect of intemperance on women and children, which were all issues AFMRS volunteers repeatedly encountered while managing the Home for the Friendless.

The AFMRS's decision to open an institution signals the organization's growing expertise. The AFMRS had a far better understanding of the underlying economic and societal factors that forced and enticed young women and girls into prostitution. Their experience visiting poor neighborhoods and operating a Registry Office (employment office), which was the group's first institutional foray, had impressed upon AFMRS members the limited employment opportunities available to the women who continued to flood into the city from rural towns and foreign shores. Moreover, they understood the tenuous situations women faced if their husbands died, deserted them, or were disabled and unable to work.[6] Despite the people it had won over to the cause, the AFMRS recognized its inability to gain broad public support for its prevention campaign, particularly among male business leaders and city officials. In 1844 the AFMRS petitioned New York City's Common Council, asking the city to erect a home to provide a temporary shelter for women who arrived in the city penniless with no place to stay. Yet even though their petition had been favorably received, the city did nothing.[7] So, once again, the AFMRS decided to take matters into its own hands, just as they had done when they assumed the lead role in moral reform. At the same time, by opening a home for vulnerable young women and children, the AFMRS moved into a more accepted space and role, one that aligned with the domestic and benevolent responsibilities traditionally assigned to women. Consequently, this new institutional focus made it easier for the women to ally themselves with prominent ministers and business leaders and to raise the money necessary to build the home they envisioned.

Scholars acknowledge the different rhetorical phases that occur in social movements. In his foundational work, "The Rhetoric of Historical Movements," Leland Griffin proposes a basic framework consisting of inception, rhetorical crisis, and consummation.[8] In the case of the AFMRS, its *inception* phase involved organizing the society and forming a large network of auxiliaries to create a national movement. The AFMRS's decision to open a home represented the second phase, resulting from a *rhetorical crisis* that came about both from the toll of constant opposition and the AFMRS's own evolution. Finally, *consummation* occurred as the AFMRS assumed the role of institutional manager responsible for running the home, which it did well into the twentieth century.

When the AFMRS became an institutional manager, it began to employ its own variation of institutional rhetoric. The women who comprised the AFMRS did not disappear rhetorically when they opened the Home for the Friendless. They continued using the *Advocate*, righteous anger, presence, petitions, and auxiliary societies to varying degrees. At the same time, they began to wield the rhetorical power often associated with institutions. In this chapter, I claim institutional rhetoric as another rhetorical tactic employed by the AFMRS. Discussions of institutional rhetoric in the fields of Rhetoric and Composition and Public Affairs typically focus on the strategic messages churches, government agencies, colleges, businesses, and other institutions convey internally and externally, as well as the methods institutions use to open or limit opportunities for discourse.[9] Similarly, I define institutional rhetoric as the tactical communications the AFMRS uses to support its Home for the Friendless and open discussions about child welfare and women's employment. Additionally, my conception encompasses how the home also served as a material resource providing the AFMRS with numerical, anecdotal, and experiential evidence, as well as how the home operated as a symbol of the AFMRS's public standing.

Fundraising, maintaining backing from auxiliary societies, finding young women employment, placing children in adoptive or foster homes, and supporting social reforms that befitted the home's clients were all tactical communications the AFMRS used to support the home's mission and its day-to-day operations. The Home for the Friendless also became a vital material resource providing an array of evidence for the AFMRS's institutional rhetoric. Krista Ratcliffe suggests that rhetorical material can encompass a rich combination of "bodies of knowledge, bodies of matter (people and things), bodies of evidence, embodied discourses, and a corpus of historically grounded cultural structure."[10] Similarly, Barbara Dickson claims cultural texts are inscribed on human bodies.[11] For the AFMRS, the embodied discourses of the individuals who came to reside in its home as well as the suffering individuals who came to the home in search of assistance alerted and educated society volunteers about economic and social problems. They also provided material evidence for the society. Depictions of these individuals and their circumstances along with the numerical evidence garnered from the home undergirded the AFMRS's communications to supporters and fundraising appeals. This highlights the AFMRS's use of both pathos and logos as meticulous record-keeping became an essential part of its institutional rhetoric. AFMRS volunteers' reactions to the individuals and situations they encountered in the home's reception room also became a rhetorical resource—validating these depictions and both prompting and providing evidence for the AFMRS's appeals and petition drives.

The Home for the Friendless also symbolized the AFMRS's changing role and changing public perceptions about the organization. Scholars have long recognized that both language and objects are imbued with symbolic meaning. In *A Rhetoric of Motives*, Kenneth Burke recognized the power of nonverbal elements to persuade through their symbolic character.[12] Drawing on Henri Lefebvre's *The Production of Space*, Roxanne Mountford similarly notes that certain spaces can move audiences "by suggesting symbolic associations."[13] When the AFMRS opened its Home for the Friendless, the home quickly became the center of the society's operations and the thrust of its institutional rhetoric. The most obvious symbolic association came through its name. Along with its guardianship of young women and children, defining the institution as a home connected the AFMRS to the domestic sphere. This

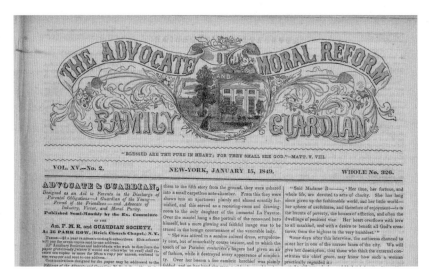

FIGURE 5. In 1849 a woodcut depicting the AFMRS's Home for the Friendless became part of the *Advocate of Moral Reform and Family Guardian*'s masthead. Courtesy of the American Antiquarian Society.

situated AFMRS members in a readily accepted feminine space, and for those in need of the home's services, the name signaled warmth and care. Today, the moniker Home for the Friendless may seem cruel in its assertion that the institutions' occupants have no friends. Yet, it was a common name affixed to orphanages and refuges in the nineteenth century. In the same way that the name could potentially stigmatize the home's occupants, by not concealing or sugarcoating the problem, it could also serve as a clear reminder to communities about those individuals all alone who lack a home.

Ironically, the impressive, three-story, brick-and-mortar edifice did not resemble a home, but it did symbolize importance. In her examination of memorials, Carole Blair explains, "architecture, like natural language use, expresses degrees of significance not just through its symbolic substances but by its very existence." By appearing on the landscape, a structure is deemed "attention worthy."[14] Unlike the AFMRS's ephemeral reform efforts, the Home for the Friendless conveyed permanence and lent credibility. The home was a *place* that writers could describe, a *place* where those in need could seek assistance, a *place* where volunteers could gather, and a *place* where supporters could visit and send material and financial donations. Underscoring the home's importance to the AFMRS's public persona and institutional rhetoric, in 1849 a woodcut of the home became part of the *Advocate*'s masthead.

Indeed, renderings of the AFMRS's Home for the Friendless portray an attention-worthy dwelling that bolstered its presence and helped legitimize the AFMRS's work within and beyond its walls. The *Advocate*, which had been the AFMRS's primary weapon in its moral reform campaign, shifted to become the primary vehicle to support its home's operations. In the remainder of this chapter, I draw on the *Advocate* to show the AFMRS's use of institutional rhetoric in its efforts to establish the Home for the Friendless, manage the home, place children in foster and adoptive homes, and promote social reforms. Ultimately, my examination of institutional rhetoric shows the Home for the Friendless as both the subject of the AFMRS's strategic communication and as a vital resource for that communication—providing both evidence and ethos.

ESTABLISHING A HOUSE OF INDUSTRY AND HOME FOR THE FRIENDLESS

The AFMRS's Home for the Friendless began as a pipe dream. Exasperated by the few options available to shelter those in need, one AFMRS volunteer shared with the businessman Lewis Tappan her wish for a home to provide refuge for women. Tappan suggested that the AFMRS make an appeal in the *Advocate*. The AFMRS executive committee approved the idea and broadened the home's scope to provide a shelter for homeless children as well. Securing refuge for children whose mothers were imprisoned, hospitalized, or deceased was a recurring need the AFMRS encountered. Some members even took children into their own homes until they could find proper living situations for them. Thus, the AFMRS determined that its proposed institution should address both needs. The AFMRS envisioned a House of Industry and Home for the Friendless that would provide refuge and training for young women seeking employment and would also provide guardianship, schooling, and moral education for children who would eventually be adopted or placed in foster homes.[15]

The AFMRS's decision to build and oversee the House of Industry and Home for the Friendless dramatically increased its fundraising responsibility. Indeed, fundraising to establish or maintain an institution is often a major facet of institutional rhetoric. The AFMRS's institutional rhetoric began with a full-page appeal preceding the first issue of the *Advocate* in 1846. Titled "An Appeal for Aid," a subhead stipulates, "$10,000 needed for a specific object." The appeal uses religious pleadings, family titles, and a common benevolent trope—juxtaposing the *haves*—in this case, those who have families and homes, with the *have-nots*—those who are friendless and homeless: "Gentlemen who have hearts, ladies who have homes, mothers, sisters, daughters, fathers, brothers, sons: We beseech you by the mercies of God shown to *you*, to listen to our pleading. We come before in behalf of the orphan, the homeless, and the stranger. . . . There are at this moment many hundred females in this city, from the ages of 14 to 25, who are utterly destitute of food and lodging, except as supplied by the charity of those who having one, are often obliged to beg for the other."[16] The appeal goes on to describe a young woman who recently came to the AFMRS's Registry Office for assistance. The woman was an orphan and immigrant who immigrated to United States in hopes of a better life, but unable to secure regular work, she exhausted her small savings, sold all of her belongings and was about to be thrown out into the street. The young woman explains, she "had rather die than do *bad*, but that when actually starving, and without a place to lie down, in a December night she cannot tell to what she may be tempted." Indeed, the young woman admits that since she came to the city she has seen many women who *have fallen* due to want and homelessness. "'She knows their *faces*, and their *fate*'—and that employment, or even a decent home would have prevented their doom."[17] Here, the AFMRS connects its fundraising appeal to its longstanding objective—prevention. By providing women with temporary shelter, food, and assistance securing respectable employment, donors can prevent women from turning to a life of prostitution.

The appeal specifies that the Home for the Friendless will only serve virtuous, helpless, poor females. In other words, this will not be a home to rescue prostitutes. The New York Female Benevolent Society, discussed in chapter 1, still operated an asylum for prostitutes who sought reclamation. Indeed, one factor that motivated the AFMRS to remove *moral reform* from its name was the fear that individuals would misconstrue the Home for the Friendless as an institution to reform prostitutes, and respectable women would stay away.[18] Conversely, the AFMRS sought to provide a refuge for chaste, unmarried women seeking jobs. Female moral reformers point to this gap in the city's loose confederation of benevolent organizations, noting, "benefits are extended to the orphan, half orphan, colored orphan, and penitent Magdalen; to the deaf and dumb, and blind; the sick and aged. But where is there an asylum for the virtuous poor, who ask only 'the charity of wages?' Where shall the destitute strangers, and *deserted children* of our city find refuge, save in the purlieus of vice, or home of the pauper?"[19] Female moral reformers also point to the large sums sent abroad to assist heathens in foreign missions. While acknowledging the work as commendable, they counter that there are many neglected poor in New York City "verging toward heathenism" who present an immediate need. While it had never attempted to raise funds on the scale of $10,000, the AFMRS was not entirely new to fundraising. Up to this point, its principal expense was publishing the *Advocate of Moral Reform*, which it supported primarily through subscriptions and annual membership dues. In its initial appeal for the Home for the Friendless, the AFMRS also acknowledged the material and monetary donations it had received to provide warm bedding and clothing, food, and coal for poor families, particularly women with children. "But what is most *needed* at the present time," it asserts, "is the means to provide a temporary home for the homeless, and employment for such as cannot obtain it elsewhere."[20]

Throughout its fundraising campaign, the AFMRS stressed the need for a home using an array of tactics that I define as institutional rhetoric. For instance, the AFMRS cited numerical evidence, often from its Registry Office, to stress the tremendous need that existed. Its annual report explained that the project was prompted by "necessities." Later the AFMRS notes that 685 women applied to its Registry Office and the society had obtained employment and homes for almost a third of these, and foster and adoptive homes had been provided for forty-five destitute children.[21] These numbers not only demonstrate the need existing in the city, they lend credibility to the AFMRS by showing its direct understanding of the problem. This numerical evidence also shows how the AFMRS documented needs as it began to perform a precursory social service role. In another article, the AFMRS draws on its knowledge of the city's prisons acquired from its volunteers and missionaries' countless visits. It asserts that many righteous poor are imprisoned because there is nowhere else for them to go. "Of the large number of females now in confinement, 519 are committed for vagrancy, but in fact are either diseased, destitute, or abandoned." The *Advocate* goes on to claim that only one in sixteen imprisoned women were committed for crimes other than vagrancy.[22] In other words, the AFMRS reveals that the city imprisons poor women because no other alternative exists. The AFMRS's Home for the Friendless can be seen as a reaction to the feminization of poverty—"the economic and social consequences of being female that result in higher rates of poverty."[23] In its first twelve years, the AFMRS had learned that women and children were the primary victims of social and economic systems that rigidly assumed a male breadwinner, and with its home it sought to address the problem.

The *Advocate* also frequently uses questions and answers (*hypothora*) to highlight the needs that exist. A report from the AFMRS's Registry Office asks, "Is a House of Industry Needed?" In response, the report notes that since June four hundred women's names have been added to the registry. While jobs were found for fifty, the rest are mostly unemployed, "many of them, at least one hundred, are young, homeless, penniless, and friendless and in danger of starving." A later report shows the number of the women added to the registry has more than doubled to 880 names. In both the cases, the AFMRS uses the numbers it collects as evidence that a home is needed.[24]

Another *Advocate* article asks in a bolded, all-cap title, "IS ATTENTION TO DESTITUTE CHILDREN AN APPROPRIATE WORK FOR THE M. R. SOCIETY?" Addressing this question, posed by one of its auxiliary societies, the AFMRS acknowledges that initially the society had focused primarily on young women and adults; however, its missionaries discovered many children in dire need and vulnerable to corrupting influences. Another article reviews the orphanages in the city and their capacity—providing further evidence of the tremendous need that exists. It concludes "the painful fact still remains, that thousands of the children of poverty, bereavement and degradation, throng our streets and by-ways."[25]

The AFMRS also showed the need that existed by sharing anecdotal evidence of individuals who would be helped by its House of Industry and Home for the Friendless. One article tells the story of a nine-year-old boy who was turned out of the house by his stepfather. The boy came to AFMRS's Registry Office looking for a place to stay, and the women noted that the boy "had marks of abuse," which they suspected the stepfather had inflicted. Another tells the story of young girls, whose widowed mother was forced to give them up because she could not clothe or feed them. Stories such as these humanized the AFMRS's numerical data.[26]

Along with need, prevention was another message the AFMRS used to raise funds, thus reiterating that the AFMRS was still committed to prevention. Like the example of the young woman in its initial appeal, which linked helping young women with preventing their moral ruin, the AFMRS also linked helping children with preventing their moral corruption. The report from its 1846 semiannual meeting, in Clinton, New York, makes a direct call to Christians. Again, using numerical evidence, it asserts: "an average of 1000 unemployed, destitute, deserving women and no place of refuge for them in case of emergency, except the Tombs, the watch-house, or the den of shame, either of which involve disgrace and introduce them to companionship with the vile. Add to this an indefinite number of children of the poor, equally exposed, and similarly cared for—doomed to almost certain ruin, unless Christian hands and hearts open to them a door of safety."[27] Pleas such as these define providing refuge for vulnerable women and children as a soul-saving enterprise. Similarly, another article asserts that at least twenty thousand children in the city attend no school "except a school of vice" and need to be "snatched from contaminating influences before its impression is enstamped indelibly upon the character."[28] The AFMRS also published remarks made by Reverend John Dowling, a prominent Baptist minister in New York, at the

AFMRS's annual meeting. Dowling states, "The object of this 'Home' is not to aid crime, to procure a home for those who have fallen, but to prevent it—to prevent the innocent and unsuspecting from falling into the vile." Dowling adds, "prevention is better than cure."[29] Even the hymn that Lydia Sigourney, a popular poet of the era, penned for the AFMRS's 1846 annual meeting, in New York City, cast prevention as a Christian duty.

> Remember those who reel
> Upon the slippery verge,—
> And snatch from temptation's power,
> And from the whelming surge,—[30]

In addition to calling on Christians to rescue young women and children from the "slippery verge," the emphasis on prevention also added a sense of urgency to the AFMRS's fundraising appeals. While the call for prevention was the same, the AFMRS's institutional rhetoric was asking supporters to help pursue prevention by building a refuge. Unlike a public campaign of moral suasion, it was a less risky enterprise for supporters. A home was also something tangible. It was desperately needed, and Christians could build it.

The AFMRS also bolstered its building campaign with endorsements from prominent New Yorkers and several newspapers. When the AFMRS's executive committee decided to establish a home, it solicited the help of a male advisory committee, which represented a change from its previous women-only approach. Appended to the initial appeal for the Home for the Friendless is a Committee of Reference, which includes the names of sixteen prominent men in the city, including six ministers, two attorneys, two doctors, and former mayor James Harper of Harper and Brothers Publishing. By mid-century many women's organizations added male board members or male advisory boards to gain the support of influential men. While the AFMRS and its auxiliaries had shown that women could go it alone—publishing a paper, operating a Registry Office, employing city missionaries, establishing a vast network of auxiliaries, and orchestrating statewide petition drives—a $10,000 building campaign in 1846 needed substantial financial support and most women either did not work for wages or earned meager incomes. In addition to providing the AFMRS with a broad base of financial support and public influence, this all-male Committee of Reference also assisted the AFMRS in choosing and acquiring a site and designing and constructing the Home for the Friendless.[31]

The tactic appeared to work—the AFMRS received contributions from well-known New Yorkers, including newspaperman Horace Greely, publishers

George Putnam, James Gordon Bennett, and James Lenox, whose extensive library became a foundational part of the New York Public Library. The AFMRS also received contributions from female philanthropists, including Mrs. Cornelius Vanderbilt and Mrs. William E. Dodge. Further highlighting the broad base of support the AFMRS achieved, Reverend George Cheever, editor of the *New York Evangelist*, wrote an editorial in support of the Home for the Friendless and his remarks were published and endorsed in numerous religious and secular papers. Just a decade before, many of these same newspapers and supporters condemned or steered clear of moral reform efforts. Now, they eagerly supported the AFMRS's House of Industry and Home for the Friendless.[32]

The AFMRS also appealed to its most loyal supporters, its auxiliaries, to contribute and help solicit funds. At the AFMRS's 1846 semiannual meeting in Clinton, New York, a member of the Clinton auxiliary proffered the resolution, "That it is the imperative duty and the privilege of this association to prosecute with all diligence the work of collecting funds for the proposed House of Industry until adequate means are obtained to ensure its completion."[33] In the discussion that followed, the women admitted the difficulties of raising such a large sum; they acknowledged, "wearied limbs," "tired lungs," "anxious days," and "sleepless nights." Women were asked to commit to raising $50–$100, and the AFMRS provided books for them to use to record their collections. As I have argued in earlier work, by collecting funds women assumed public advocacy roles.[34] A $50 pledge book encompassing a lengthy list of $.50, $1, and $5 pledges equates to countless hours explaining and advocating a cause. Without the means to pledge large sums, women pledged their time, labor, presence, and passion. Acknowledging women's fundraising prowess, in 1848 the AFMRS hired two women to collect funds.[35]

While auxiliaries had embraced the AFMRS's national moral reform campaign, with its shift to building a Home for the Friendless in New York City, the AFMRS had to explain why individuals living in other areas of the country should support it. In its institutional rhetoric, the AFMRS depicted the home as a national need. In an *Advocate* article, the AFMRS concedes, "It has been suggested, that the *city* should provide this Home; and so it should if those who need its aid were only natives of the city. But this is not so. They represent almost every section of the country."[36] To make this point, as part of its institutional rhetoric, when the Home Committee began publishing reports describing individuals admitted to the Home for the Friendless, it denotes those people from outside of the city.

The list of donors and letters from auxiliaries suggest that contributors generally embrace this message. For instance, the Oberlin, Ohio, auxiliary pledged $50, noting members' support of the home. Another *Advocate* issue lists donations for the home from individuals in Winthrop, Maine; Hadden, Connecticut; Ridgeway, New York; Monson, Massachusetts; and the Moral Reform Society in Meriden, Connecticut. Shifting the *Advocate* to its institutional needs, the AFMRS strategically uses it to recognize donors and track the progress of its building campaign. These contributions serve as endorsements and many become moving appeals in and of themselves. For instance, a group of ladies in Marion, New York, describe it as "a privilege to do something to aid in the benevolent enterprise of establishing a home for the orphan and destitute" and an effort "to love our neighbors as ourselves."[37] Another letter from a woman in Rushford, New York, explains her $5 donation for the home, writing: "One dollar is for myself; the other four is money saved by my little son, Edwin Hatfield Rawson, who died last April. He intended to have bought sheep with his money, and the wool from the sheep, he said, he would have made into clothes for the poor children. I think I cannot appropriate the money more agreeably to his feelings than to the object above named. Although he was but five years and five months old when he died, yet he took a great interest in the cause of Moral Reform."[38] Selecting to publish such a heartrending appeal was certainly intentional. By publishing these letters of support, documenting the need for a home with numerical data and human stories, describing how the home will prevent young women and children from ruin, explaining how the home will serve individuals far beyond New York City, and charting the building campaign's progress, the AFMRS wielded its institutional rhetoric to build its Home for the Friendless.

BECOMING INSTITUTIONAL MANAGERS

The AFMRS's various fundraising appeals proved successful. In May 1848 the building's cornerstone was laid on ground purchased at Thirtieth Street between Fourth and Fifth Avenue, which is just north of what is now Madison Square. Before the Home for the Friendless opened its doors in December 1848, the AFMRS had become so convinced of the urgent need, it began operating a temporary home eighteen months earlier in rented quarters at the corner of First Avenue and Second Street. During its first year of operation, the temporary home provided refuge for 605 individuals (334 adults and 271 children). Most of the adults were successfully placed as domestic servants, seamstresses, and nurses while most of the children were placed in Christian homes through adoption or by a foster arrangement. Generally, the number of individuals housed in the temporary home ranged between thirty and seventy-five. That number increased when the permanent home was completed and opened.[39]

With its temporary home and, later, its permanent home, the AFMRS moved into the complex role of institutional managers and its institutional rhetoric reflects this change. Reporting the home's day-to-day operations demonstrated the need the home was addressing and portrayed the AFMRS as a responsible steward. For ten years the AFMRS had operated its Registry Office, which sought to place women with reputable employers and protect them from unscrupulous intelligence offices. The AFMRS had also organized a Visiting Committee and employed city missionaries, who visited individuals in need and distributed food and clothing. However, when it opened its home for young women and children, the AFMRS assumed a greater social service role that required it to hire staff, and develop admissions requirements, placement procedures, and general modes of operation. The AFMRS formed a Home Committee, which supervised and assisted the home's staff and observed the home's day-to-day operations. The Home Committee's most arduous responsibility was receiving applications in the home's reception room each week.

The Home Committee kept detailed records of individuals who came to the reception room. These records were compiled into a monthly report that was submitted to the board, and excerpts were printed in the *Advocate*. The AFMRS had followed a similar practice of publishing reports from its city missionaries, Visiting Committees, and Registry Office. As the AFMRS's focus shifted to operating the Home for the Friendless, these Home Committee reports served several essential functions in the home's institutional rhetoric. They documented the home's operations and outreach, educated readers about social needs, and solicited support. Thus, they provide a rich source for examining the AFMRS's institutional rhetoric.[40]

Membership on the Home Committee revolved as new members were appointed. Home Committee members took turns writing the reports. In that sense, reports functioned as another form of rhetorical education. The monthly reports, which were published in every other issue of the *Advocate*, follow a general pattern. The title in bold denotes the Report from the Home Committee and the month. The reports begin with a general introduction, which often includes personal remarks from the writer and clarifies that the report's contents are simply a few illustrative cases. These cases are dated, which lends credibility to the reports, and indicates the dates when the reception room was open, usually once a week. The reports conclude with statistics for the home's admission, occupancy, and placement. For instance, the January 1852 report concludes, "Received during the month. Adults 28. Children 6. Total 34. Dismissed [Placed], Adults 18. Children 7. Total 25. Remaining in the Home, Adults 29. Children 68. Total 97."[41] Again, this type of numerical data is a common feature in the AFMRS's institutional rhetoric. The numbers underscore the need and validate the home's operation, which was crucial to maintaining financial support.

The moving accounts of women and children admitted to the Home for the Friendless further illustrate the tremendous need by attaching human stories to the numerical data. The home admitted children who were the victims of abuse and neglect as well as children who had been deserted or orphaned. In 1854 the home admitted many children whose parents died during a cholera outbreak.[42] In one instance, the home admitted two sisters, three and five years old, whose drunken father had murdered their mother. Neighbors described the mother as a kind, caring woman, and when they discovered the crime, they "found the three-year old on the bed by the dead mother, trying to lift the eye-lids and awake her, saying, 'Mamma asleep, mamma asleep.'"[43] Another report shares the story of a sickly father whose wife died a few months before. He had worked to pay the expense of having someone care for his child, but he was too ill to continue. He had no friends able to help him, and did not expect to survive long. The Home Committee member who wrote the report expounds, "The tears fell like rain as he spoke of parting with child, and came forward with trembling steps to sign the legal documents. Our sympathies were moved for him, well knowing by experience the strong yearning of a parent's heart, and the desolateness and suffering that come in the train of illness and bereavement."[44] As these heartrending examples illustrate, the Home Committees' reports extend far beyond documenting cases. By including nonessential details, they functioned as powerful pathetic appeals intended to move readers and show the home's role in providing a vital social safety net. These reports also sought to educate readers. One report writer admits that Home Committee members share their observations of the "shady side of life—with its dark, and sometimes repulsive features" with those who have not encountered them "in the hope of enlisting their sympathies and exertions in the cause of humanity."[45] Like the role Margaret Prior had played as a city missionary, Home Committee members became envoys—making their middle- and upper-class readers aware of the needs and situations they observed.

Home Committee reports also repeatedly emphasize the home's mission by characterizing it as a "protector" for vulnerable women and children. Reports describe young women and children who were brought "under the protection of our roof," "committed to the guardianship and protection of the Home," taken under "this sheltering roof," or "snatched from the destroyer" and "agents of the Spoiler."[46] Supporters of the Home for the Friendless often adopt similar language in their letters and appeals. For instance, in his address before the AFMRS's annual meeting in 1853, the *Advocate* notes that Reverend Taggart "portrayed very beautifully some of the instances of which he had personal knowledge, where the prey had been rescued from the fowler, and the ruin of the innocent prevented, to the multitude who had been sheltered in the Home."[47]

As individuals in need began to fill the home's reception room, which also replaced the AFMRS's Registry Office, Home Committee reports repeatedly stress the AFMRS's efforts to distinguish and assist only the deserving poor. Antebellum white women's societies almost always made this distinction. Hence, Home Committee reports reveal the difficult and problematic role women assumed in judging who was worthy of assistance. Women generally deemed "deserving" the working poor who were unable to find work or unable to work due to illness or injury. Gender was also an important distinction. Antebellum women, especially widows and deserted wives, were usually considered "deserving."[48] AFMRS Home Committee members questioned individuals about their background, family, and what brought them to their current circumstances. They inquired about references and occasionally sent Visiting Committee members to investigate and confirm circumstances. They admit situations where they were deceived and occasionally chide themselves for being suspicious.

All of this was part of the AFMRS's institutional rhetoric, which was intended to assure its donors that the AFMRS was a good steward of their monetary and material donations. To show they were assisting those who were truly in need, they provide details about specific cases. Home Committee reports also repeatedly designate individuals as "worthy," "deserving," and "respectable," and even highlight cases where individuals are poor but proud. For instance, one report tells the story of a girl whose parents were dead. She had lived with a family in Boston that had cheated her out of her wages, so she went to New York hoping to do better, but according to the report, "being a stranger, without means, and having tried in vain to get employment, she felt harassed and discouraged. She said with a look of bitter sorrow, 'This is the first day in my life that I ever had to ask for a meal of victuals.'" After examining her recommendations, the Home Committee admitted her to the Home for the Friendless.[49] In another case, the four children of an alcoholic father and an abusive stepmother were committed to the home, the report explains that Home Committee members had to persuade the two oldest girls, ages twelve and fourteen, to stay at the home. "'They were able to earn their own living,' they said, 'and did not wish to be beholden to anyone for charity.'" It was only after the women assured them that they would help them find respectable and safe working situations that the girls agreed to stay.[50]

Beyond, showing that the AFMRS was assisting individuals who were truly *deserving*, reports also reveal the Home Committee's arduous job as institutional managers. In the mid-nineteenth century, besides poorhouses and prisons, an assortment of benevolent organizations, including the AFMRS's Home for the Friendless, provided the only social safety net for New York City's rapidly expanding population. These institutions were sorely insufficient to meet the overwhelming need. The home's reception room was often full, and AFMRS members faced the difficult task of turning people away. With its Home for the Friendless, the AFMRS sought to provide a temporary refuge for two groups: children under the age of ten who were candidates for adoption and respectable young women who were seeking employment.[51] The AFMRS also tried to assist other individuals, particularly the elderly and widows with children, by providing material items such as warm bedding and clothing. Home Committee members' personal remarks, which often appear in reports, not only acknowledge this daunting administrative task, they also show how personal experience became a rhetorical resource in the AFMRS's institutional rhetoric.

One writer describes Home Committee members' careful balancing act, "To listen patiently to the details of suffering and misfortune, and sometimes gross indiscretion, and then to give advice suited to every case, needs not only much wisdom, but not little tact, for at the same time that we must guard against imposition, we must keep our sympathies fully awake towards the really deserving."[52] Another describes members bracing themselves before entering the reception room. "We never remember having seen our reception room so crowded. Our hearts sunk within us when we saw the formidable array and we instinctively shrank from the investigation of their individual cases. We passed the room once and again, but finally summoned our moral courage and entered."[53] These remarks express the arduous task Home Committee members faced each week when they opened the home's reception room. One report describes the experience of new Home Committee members working in the crowded reception room: "Although not altogether unaccustomed to the different phases which human wretchedness presents, our first day's experience proved a severe ordeal for our nervous system and doomed us to a night of agonizing dreams and soul-harrowing fancies."[54] These frequent personal asides in Home Committee reports underscore both the stress and lingering effect of this work on the women volunteers. Rhetorically, they also lend authenticity and provide a perspective many *Advocate* readers would share.

Reports also attest to committee members' growing expertise and the home's standing as a place of refuge and guidance. Within a few years of opening, the Home for the Friendless received more than one thousand applicants each year, and by 1854 the home was at its capacity with 120 children and 15–25 adults.[55] Even though its admission requirements and limited capacity restricted the number of individuals the AFMRS could admit, committee members became well-versed on other charities and refuges available in the city. Individuals began to come to the home's reception room for counsel as well as assistance. For instance, the Home Committee directed a seaman's widow to the Mariner's Society, they directed a boy beyond their age limit to Friendless Boy's Asylum, and they contacted a Swedish benevolent organization to assist an orphan boy who only spoke Swedish. In another instance, an African American woman forced to give up her children sought the AFMRS's advice. While the Home for the Friendless would admit her children, the Home Committee explained that the children could only stay until they were placed with a family. They noted that the Colored Orphan Asylum would keep children until they were twelve or fourteen and provide schooling up to that point. They also assured her that neither their Home for the Friendless nor the Colored Orphan Asylum would send her children south. Reports also show how the AFMRS had earned a positive reputation in the city. In addition to those in need, police officers, tract visitors, ministers, and other individuals often brought young women and children to the Home for the Friendless. In some instances, people came to the AFMRS instead of the police. For example, when an immigrant girl fell into the hands of an unscrupulous landlord who was holding her few possessions unless she would pay his exorbitant rates, she came to the AFMRS to resolve the problem, which it did. As part of its institutional rhetoric, these stories lent further credibility to the Home Committee. They also show the positive associations tied to the home itself—when people are in need, they go to the AFMRS's Home for the Friendless.[56]

These depictions of individuals in need and the home's role addressing those needs also supported the AFMRS's ongoing fundraising efforts. The *Advocate* continued to serve as an important fundraising tool. In addition to conveying these moving stories, the *Advocate* printed the names of donors, subscribers, and lifetime members. In fact, rather than purchasing lifetime memberships to the AFMRS, individuals became lifetime members for "House of Industry and Home for the Friendless." The *Advocate* also began to ask readers for bequests: an 1852 issue asks, "Have you made your will," and a bequest form was routinely printed on the back page. The Home for the Friendless also relied heavily on an annual day of donation. Usually held around Thanksgiving, the day of donation was an open house during which AFMRS members, Home for the Friendless staff, and residents greeted visitors who came bearing provisions from gardens and fields, clothing, and financial donations. The AFMRS also encouraged pastors to take up special collections for the home at their churches. Additionally, the AFMRS also continued to garner support from its auxiliaries.[57]

Auxiliaries purchased lifetime memberships, distributed the *Advocate*, and sent clothing, bedding, and financial donations to the Home for the Friendless.[58] Under the heading of auxiliary societies, the AFMRS's annual reports acknowledge the receipt of barrels, boxes, and parcels of clothing and provisions throughout the year.[59] The *Advocate* also updated readers on the status of the home's "wardrobe." An 1848 article describes its wardrobe room filled with bed quilts, cradle quilts, warm knit stockings, infant clothing, and "domestic flannels, calicoes, and garments of every kind," all intended for the "deserving poor."[60] Home Committee reports often describe the tenuous circumstances of the elderly, widows with children, and poor families who receive items from the home's wardrobe, and the *Advocate* routinely carried appeals for bedding and warm clothes for its wardrobe prior to winter.

As the AFMRS assumed the role as guardian for children, it also began appealing directly to children for support. Early issues of the *Advocate* encouraged mothers to teach their children about moral behavior and explicitly warn them of dangers that might put their virtue at risk. However, as the AFMRS shifted its focus to the Home for the Friendless, it encouraged *Advocate* subscribers to teach their children about the plight of less fortunate children. The *Advocate* began a children's column, which presented moving stories of poor children, and many auxiliaries formed juvenile societies that sent letters and special gifts for the home's children. The *Advocate* also frequently published excerpts from letters accompanying children's donations, which themselves became appeals. For instance, one child writes:

> Dear Children of the Home,—I am happy to send you something which may contribute a little to your comfort during the cold winter. My mother had told me much about this nice Home for the Friendless and poor Orphan Children, and since she had taken the Advocate, and I have read and learned much more about them, I soon began to feel anxious to do something myself, although but a child. My mother said I could piece a quilt for you. I commenced one which I have completed and send to you. While I have kind parents, a good home, and enough to keep me warm and comfortable, I should not like to think that there are so many little children suffering for the want of that which I enjoy.[61]

Creating a connection between readers' children and the AFMRS's Home for the Friendless was an effective method to both deepen and broaden support for the home. Indeed, the *Advocate* became a family paper, and the ardent and angry tone that had once characterized its pages disappeared.

Even as it employed a variety of fundraising tactics, fundraising remained a constant challenge for the AFMRS. In one article, the women acknowledge the difficulty of continually attracting donations as new charities are established and new asylums for children and the poor are opened. They write, "The 'Home,' which has been long established and where so many hundreds have found refuge, must not be forgotten amid the excitement of building new ones, and opening new fields of labor."[62] Consequently, fundraising was an underlying objective in all of its institutional rhetoric as the AFMRS competed with other benevolent institutions and causes.

In addition to operating the reception room, Home Committee reports provide glimpses of the AFMRS's varied responsibilities as institutional managers. As its official name, House of Industry and Home for the Friendless, implies, the AFMRS initially planned for the home to operate as a house of industry that would take in orders for sewing and other work that the young women staying at the home could complete as part of their training and job preparation. Observing a woman's handiwork would also allow the AFMRS to provide a reference. Some reports note garments made for the home and outside customers, but completing contracted work was sometimes difficult because women were often quickly placed in permanent, wage-paying jobs.[63]

The Home for the Friendless also ran a school for the children in its care. The school fell under the jurisdiction of the County Superintendent of Common Schools, who occasionally visited the home to review the school. Volunteers also provided a Sunday school and held church services at the home, and doctors volunteered their time to care for the children. The home was open to visitors, and the *Advocate* printed observations from visitors who confirmed that the home was well managed.[64] Home Committee reports also indicate the AFMRS's concern for the children under its care. Reports often remark on the children's singing, picnics, field trips, and Thanksgiving and Christmas celebrations. Contemporary readers aware of orphanage abuses might be hesitant to take these anecdotes at face value. However, with oversight by its Home Committee, detailed monthly reports, open doors, and open houses, the AFMRS appears to strive for transparency. Reports also remark on children's health and well-being. For instance, one report notes:

> The little boy whose case had given us so much anxiety, to-day presents a fair prospect of speedy recovery, but we were pained to find the sick bed occupied by one of our most interesting little girls of six years, who is prostrated by disease of the heart. She has been in the Institution nearly eight months, and though one of the most active among our little group, the Matron remarked today that she had never known her to commit an act deserving of the least reproof. This is a commendation not often bestowed upon a child six years of age, and as we have noticed her interesting and amiable traits of character, we have often expressed the hope that she might live to be one of the ornaments of our institution.[65]

Altogether, descriptions from the classroom, outings, and even the sickroom offer evidence of the AFMRS's concern for the children under its care and the close bonds nurtured in the Home for the Friendless. However, the home's goal was not to keep the children, but to place them with foster or adoptive families, which they believed provided a better situation.[66] Descriptions of the home's operations, including numbers of residents and placements, moving stories of the "deserving" individuals assisted, Home Committee member's observations and growing expertise, all became part of the home's institutional rhetoric. These descriptions highlighted needs, the home's role in addressing those needs, and they presented the AFMRS as good stewards, who used funds wisely, and who genuinely cared for the children living in the home.

PLACING CHILDREN

Placing children with adoptive or foster parents was another responsibility in the home's operation and another objective of the home's institutional rhetoric. When the AFMRS expanded its mission to assisting children, it joined numerous city, religious, and benevolent institutions in New York that were trying to assist thousands of orphaned and destitute children in the city. Thus, part of the AFMRS's institutional rhetoric was directed at placing children, which included describing children to its readers, making religious appeals for Christians to foster and adopt children, drawing on its network of supporters, and maintaining detailed placement records. In addition to examining this institutional rhetoric, I will also discuss how the AFMRS's placement of children became part of a larger phenomenon now known as the *orphan trains*. By doing so, I want to both situate the home's efforts within, and contrast them against, this broad migration strategy.

The *Advocate of Moral Reform*, along with the AFMRS's extensive network of auxiliaries and supporters, proved vital in its efforts to place the children admitted to its Home for the Friendless. The *Advocate* frequently included notices on its back page describing children who needed homes. For instance, one notice upholds "a bright healthy boy of six months with blue eyes and winning smiles."[67] The information in these notices was not only intended to depict the children, but also to locate suitable placements. AFMRS Home Committee reports also became pseudo-advertisements, describing children's backgrounds, appearance, and characteristics. One child is described as "healthy," "remarkably active," "possessed of much force of character," and having "fine phrenological developments."[68] In another report, Home Committee members offer a reference attesting: "This little girl is one whom we have long been accustomed to see, in our regular visits to the Home; and we have often thought, that if some of our many friends, who visit the Home, read character as we do, she would not remain thus long unprovided for. She is a laughter-loving child, not delicate, not handsome, but stout well formed, and very healthy looking. She seems fitted for active service in some good cause, if some Christian would only take her and give her the requisite training."[69] As this child's physical description indicates, a family might be persuaded to foster or adopt a child who could assist the household, so an important part of the AFMRS's institutional rhetoric was to show that children were healthy and able to work. In the mid-nineteenth century, children were an essential part of many household economies—particularly on farms, where they might work in the fields or assist with wide-ranging domestic duties. Reports occasionally note the demand for older children, ages eight to twelve.[70]

The AFMRS's use of notices, descriptions, and appeals to place children in adoptive and foster homes may sound odd and even callous today because views of childhood have changed dramatically. Acknowledging these idealized views of childhood, Steven Mintz claims, "We cling to a fantasy that once upon a time childhood and youth were years of carefree adventure, despite the fact that for most young people in the past, growing up was anything but easy. Disease, family disruption, and early entry into the world of work were integral parts of family life." During the nineteenth century, it was common for older children and adolescents in working-class and poor families to search out work in factories and mills or become domestic servants. Mintz stresses that our current conception of a childhood—a long period during which children do not work and focus primarily on education and play—is a fairly recent phenomenon that only became applicable to the majority of American children in the 1950s.[71]

Contrary to adoption demands today, it was also more difficult to place infants, who were considered a drain on household economies. Indeed, the home's nursery was often full. Because it could not make an economic case for young children, the AFMRS shifted its institutional rhetoric—appealing to readers' Christian duty. One back-page notice states, "Homes wanted for Infants—A girl of five months and boy of six months old—both very healthy and promising children, need homes by adoptions—may some vacancy that death has made be soon partially filled by their presence and with it the approving smile of Him who has said, 'Feed my lambs.'"[72] With high infant mortality rates in the nineteenth century, this notice appeals to parents' grief as well as their Christian conscience. In another instance, a Home Committee report describes an infant girl "of a quiet and affectionate disposition," who appears to be frail due to "early neglect and exposure." The article implores that country air and nursing will likely restore this baby, beseeching, "Who will act the part of the good Samaritan to her? What country home is open for her reception, and who will take and cherish her, and do it 'as unto the Lord?'"[73] In *Advocate* articles, writers argue why Christians should not shrink from the duty of taking in orphans and destitute children. Often these appeals to Christian obligation and compassion were bolstered by well-known scriptural passages, including, "Am I my brother's keeper?" and "Suffer little children to come unto me, and forbid them not",[74] thus exhibiting the AFMRS's longstanding Christian commitment, which it believed *Advocate* readers shared.

Even as its Home for the Friendless filled with children, the AFMRS was picky about placing children in what it believed to be good, temperate, Christian homes. In one appeal, the *Advocate* asks its friends and patrons to assist in finding "homes of the right sort," again assuming that its readers will understand *the right sort* means good, Protestant Christian homes.[75] Like many nineteenth-century religious and benevolent organizations, the AFMRS exerted a strong Catholic bias, and it would not place children in Catholic homes even if the children had been raised Catholic. Because of this widespread anti-Catholic sentiment, Catholics established their own child refuges and orphan asylums, which provided their own sectarian religious instruction and sought to place children in Catholic homes. Ultimately, the AFMRS's rhetorical tactics for placing children—making Christian appeals, providing descriptions of children, and offering moving details about children's circumstances—appear to have been effective. Evident from its correspondence, individuals often wrote or came to the Home for the Friendless in search of specific children they had read about, and Home Committee reports reference the placement of children described in previous reports.

The AFMRS especially looked to its auxiliaries to place children in foster and adoptive homes and to locate situations for young women as domestics. In chapter 4 I explain how auxiliaries financially underwrote and geographically expanded the AFMRS's moral reform efforts. When the AFMRS repositioned itself as guardians, it asked its auxiliaries to do the same. In an invitation to its annual meeting, the AFMRS expressed its hope that members would visit its recently opened temporary Home for the Friendless and "transfer some lamb from our fold to a safe country home."[76] During the meeting's proceedings a few women even offered testimony about their experiences adopting children.[77] Whereas moral reformers had previously stressed that no community was immune from immoral behavior, in its efforts to place children, the rural countryside was repeatedly idealized and characterized as a safe refuge and restorative for the city's orphans and street children. An 1854 appeal urges, "Some seventy or eighty little boys, from two years old and upward, are now in our Institution needing permanent homes in the country."[78] In its belief that rural areas provided a better environment for children, and in its efforts to relocate children from the city to the countryside, the AFMRS contributed to a popular pastoral trope and a massive migration effort.

By the 1850s New York and other industrial cities had become home to thousands of vagrant children who assisted their families or supported themselves by stealing, begging, collecting rags, hawking newspapers, or selling handmade flowers. It was estimated that ten thousand vagrant children roamed New York City's streets. Many of these children were rendered destitute due to the loss of one or both parents, which frequently resulted from high maternal mortality rates, cholera or typhoid fever epidemics, unsafe working conditions, unsanitary living conditions, intemperance, or desertion. The Home for the Friendless provides evidence of this growing problem—the number of public and private institutions that cared for destitute children in New York dramatically increased from four in 1825 to more than sixty by 1866. Nonetheless, these institutions were no match for the tremendous need, so many institutions tried to place children and adolescents in adoptive, foster, or employment situations outside of the city. This nineteenth- and early twentieth-century effort to move children from urban eastern cities to rural and western communities is commonly referred to as the orphan trains.[79]

Between 1854 and 1929 it is estimated that two hundred and fifty thousand children were placed out—meaning they were placed in homes outside of the Northeastern urban cities in which they lived.[80] If you search the American Female Guardian Society or its Home for the Friendless, you often find it linked to the orphan trains by individuals researching family genealogy. In fact, a recent genealogical reference on orphan train riders touts that it contains "Entrance Records from the American Female Guardian Society's Home for the Friendless in New York."[81] Consequently, I want to briefly discuss the AFMRS's connection to the orphan trains and contrast its placement efforts with those of the much larger Children's Aid Society.

While more than one hundred hospitals, orphan asylums, refuges, shelters, and benevolent societies, participated in placing out children,[82] the institution most closely associated with the orphan trains is the Children's Aid Society, which was founded by Charles Loring Brace in New York in 1853. Brace promoted the Children's Aid Society's "Emigration Plan" as a revolutionary innovation. However, the AFMRS's placement efforts, which began with its temporary home in 1847, were a forerunner to this massive relocation of children and teenagers. Indeed, there were other precedents, including efforts in Boston, and even the seventeenth- and eighteenth-century indenture system. Indenture, or apprentice, agreements placed children in situations where they would provide labor usually until the age of twenty-one in exchange for being trained in a craft or trade as well as receiving food, shelter, clothing, and a basic education. In Great Britain and the United States, indenture agreements were occasionally used to remove "undesirable or potentially criminal children." In its efforts to remove vagrant children, the orphan train operated under a similar motivation.

The Children's Aid Society followed a model much like indenture agreements. Many of the children under its charge were provided with food, shelter, clothing, and a basic education in exchange for their work as farmhands or domestic workers. Some older boys were even paid wages. However, unlike indentured individuals, these children were not bound to these families. Unless adopted, the children's birth parents or the Children's Aid Society retained guardianship, and the children or families could end the relationship at any time. At least in theory. The Children's Aid Society's oversight of the children it placed was tenuous at best. Generally, the children were pretty much on their own.[83]

Numerous factors combined to the drive the orphan train phenomenon, including the overwhelming number of vagrant children in eastern cities, worries about civil unrest, the belief that children could be saved if they were placed in the proper environment, the need for population and labor in western communities, and the expansion of railroads. Brace and other reformers, including Jacob Riis and Kate Douglas Wiggin argued that the scores of poor children in urban centers could become "productive citizens if removed from their environment of poverty and squalor."[84] Like the AFMRS, these reformers reflected a pervasive optimism that virtuous country life held restorative powers. Thus, sending children to rural and western regions to undertake wholesome work on farms not only addressed the problem of vagrant children but also addressed concerns about future unrest because it was believed that relocation would make these children upstanding citizens. Of course, these designs rested on ill-informed and romanticized notions of farm life, which had its own share of hardship and struggle. They also overlooked the toll from the trauma and abuse many of these children had experienced. At the same time, the need for agricultural labor was real. With cheap land and expanding western boundaries, the demand for farm laborers and domestic help continued throughout the nineteenth century. And the rapidly expanding railroads, which helped create this need, helped address it by efficiently conveying groups of poor urban children westward at discounted rates.[85]

The AFMRS's placing out of children was motivated by the same factors and romanticized beliefs, but it differed from the Children's Aid Society's approach in some distinct ways. First, it differed in terms of scale. Whereas the Children's Aid Society placed approximately 105,000 children between 1853 and the 1930s, in 1934 the AFMRS reported that it had placed 6,452 children. By this time, the Home for the Friendless was also operating as a permanent foster home for children. Clearly, this difference in scale influenced the distinct ways these two institutions handled child placements. For instance, the AFMRS saw its role as a guardian organization. While it sought employment situations for young women, it usually sought permanent placement in adoptive or foster homes for children. For that reason, the AFMRS required parents to relinquish their guardian rights if they placed their children in the Home for the Friendless.[86] Conversely, the Children's Aid Society, which touted adoptions, also provided a means for poor city children to obtain jobs without requiring their parents to give them up for adoption. Frequently, older children chose to leave their families in search of employment opportunities. One analysis of the Children's Aid Society's first year of operation found that about 20 percent of placements resulted in adoptions, another 24 percent resulted in satisfactory work situations in which children remained throughout the term of their agreement (usually adulthood), and 56 percent of the placements were terminated either by the children or their employers. Some children ran away or sought other jobs while others returned home or were retrieved by family members. Other analyses suggest the number of successful placements, where children remained for the full term of their agreement, rose to as high as 60 percent, although there is no indication as to how many of these children were adopted. There are no similar analyses of the AFMRS's placement success. However, reports in the *Advocate* show how the AFMRS handled the placement of the young women and children in its home differently.[87]

As I described earlier, the AFMRS sought individual placement for children using the *Advocate of Moral Reform* and appealing to its network of supporters. It invested tremendous rhetorical effort in trying to locate suitable situations. The Children's Aid Society, on the other hand, typically sent a group of children along with a chaperone to communities. O'Connor explains, "Sending these children out west in groups and letting interested men and women simply pick out the boy or girl they liked best was enormously cheaper and faster than placing each child individually." Brace chose this approach, recognizing the multitudes of poor children in the city and the few funds available to most children rescue organizations. Other organizations employed different placement methods. For instance, the New York Foundling Hospital, founded by the Sisters of Charity of Saint Vincent de Paul in 1869, relied on its nationwide network of priests to place children with Catholic parishioners in their communities.[88]

Surprisingly, many of the institutions that placed children kept scant records, including the Children's Aid Society. This may be because of the number of children it placed and a reluctance to allocate funds for record keeping, or the Children's Aid Society simply may not have perceived its role as a guardian organization like the AFMRS.[89] In contrast, the AFMRS kept detailed records, further highlighting its rhetorical work. The AFMRS claims: "The children placed in homes abroad are never forgotten at the Home. The record of each has been faithfully kept from the first; so that we possess a brief but complete history of each child from its introduction into the Home until its majority is attained. The standing rule of the Society that a communication shall be received from each one at least once a year brings regularly the "welfare letters," from which our records are built up."[90] The AFMRS goes onto state that it dispatched agents if personal supervision was required and a visiting secretary position was established to visit children and oversee the children's interests.[91] A letter from a volunteer published in an 1853 issue of the *Advocate* further illustrates some of the AFMRS's placement and follow-up efforts. The female volunteer escorted ten children and two young women by train out west to place them in previously arranged homes throughout Ohio. The woman both describes and assesses the families who take the children. For instance, at one stop, she writes, "Mrs. H. is a feeble, but I should judge an excellent woman . . . I was much pleased with the parties at A—, and think the children will find parental care." In another instance, she noted that a woman at one of the homes was a longtime *Advocate* subscriber and "everything relating to this family was very pleasing." Nonetheless, when she began to leave, the little boy from the Home for the Friendless began to weep and ran after her, and the volunteer admits, "this distributing of children tears the heart strings."[92]

Along her trip, the volunteer also checked on children from the Home for the Friendless who had previously been placed with families in these communities. She talks to the children, notes their health, appearance, demeanor, and school attendance. One boy was described as "indolent, but improving"; another "very industrious," but with a nervous condition that made it difficult for him to attend school, and a girl was described as "sprightly," boasting that "she had not missed school a single day" during the year.[93] Other visitors made follow-up visits to the children and the families with whom they had been placed. Visitors' reflections, which were published in the *Advocate*, typically recorded the child's health, appearance, dress, and observations of the child's interaction with the family. For instance, one visitor reports, "In the same town, we saw the 'wee baby' we took there to be adopted a year since—but Oh, how changed! She had grown finely, and was perfectly well; we recognized her, only, when she smiled. She lisped 'papa' and 'mama' so sweetly, and seemed so happy when in her papa's arms."[94] With these rudimentary screening and follow-up efforts, AFMRS volunteers acted as precursors to professional social workers. They also provide a distinct contrast to the Children's Aid Society's approach to placing children.

Letters from children or their new families were also frequently published in the *Advocate* and the AFMRS's annual reports. In one issue of the *Advocate*, two letters sharing the joy of their adopted children appear under the headline "Testimony from Foster-Parents."[95] Occasionally, Home Committee reports also share visits to the Home for the Friendless from children and young women who were former residents. One report noted a couple who had adopted a child and returned to the home to adopt another.[96] As part of its institutional rhetoric, these efforts to follow up with former Home for the Friendless residents and stories of successful placements contribute to the AFMRS's institutional ethos, provide evidence that the home is successfully carrying out its mission, and they lend persuasive power to would-be contributors and adoptive parents. However, other institutions, which similarly placed out children, including the Children's Aid Society, made similar use of letters, reports, and positive anecdotes.

Even though it was operating on a smaller scale, sought individual placements, kept detailed records, and attempted regular follow-up, the AFMRS was still complicit in the orphan trains. It was addressing the same crisis and pursuing the same solution as the Children's Aid Society. Studies of the Children's Aid Society ultimately show that judging the orphan trains is difficult. O'Connor explains:

> Some of these children were abused by their new families in all the ways that we are familiar with from present-day news reports about the tragedies of foster care, and some were just as happy as the literature of their placement agencies said they were. Two boys placed by the CAS [Children's Aid Society] became governors, one became a Supreme Court justice, and several others became mayors, congressmen, or local representatives. Many children grew up to become drifters and thieves, and at least one became a murderer. The vast majority led lives of absolutely ordinary accomplishment and satisfaction. And many, perhaps also a majority (because there is nothing extraordinary about unhappiness), saw no end to the misery into which they had been born.[97]

In the nineteenth century, few social safety nets existed, and those available were poorly funded and unable to handle the demand. There simply were no good solutions for the thousands of orphaned, poor, and vagrant children in America's eastern cities. By assuming the role as guardians, and by trying to locate homes for the children outside of the city, AFMRS volunteers believed they were acting in the children's best interest, which is reflected in its institutional rhetoric.

PURSUING SOCIAL REFORMS

While the women in the AFMRS increasingly assumed roles as guardians, focusing most of their energy and rhetoric on operating the Home for the Friendless and placing its residents, they did not entirely relinquish their former roles as activists and social reformers. Volunteers' reactions to the situations women encountered in the home's reception room prompted the AFMRS to advocate more employment opportunities for women, protection for street children, and temperance. Again, these appeals show how their observations and reactions became powerful rhetorical resources in their institutional rhetoric, and how their position as institutional managers lent credence to their claims. Consequently, I view these calls for reform as another facet of the AFMRS's institutional rhetoric

Advocating Better Pay and More Occupations for Women

Even today, many female-headed households linger near the poverty line. In nineteenth-century New York this was almost always the case; the city's new urban economy was a patriarchal economy predicated on a woman's dependence on a man's income. According to the feminist scholar Christine Stansell, "to be a widow, deserted wife, or orphaned daughter of a laboring man, even a prosperous artisan, was to be poor," because the few avenues for female employment such as domestic service, sewing, and washing, paid little, "female self-support was synonymous with indigence."[98] The AFMRS not only encountered innumerable poor women, it frequently saw women whose indigence forced them to give up their children. Because the Home for the Friendless sought foster homes and adoptive homes for children outside of the city, parents who brought their children to the home had to sign documents relinquishing their parental rights. The AFMRS often provided families with items from its wardrobe and other assistance to help sustain them. However, if the situation was too dire, the Home Committee assumed the difficult role of counseling a parent to give up a child, although the AFMRS had no authority to remove children from harmful situations.[99]

Many women with children often sought employment situations, but these were difficult to find. One Home Committee report notes, "Applications were numerous from mothers, with small children, willing to do almost anything for an honest livelihood, if they could only keep their little ones. Our hearts were often sorely grieved at the pressing wants of this numerous class."[100] Another tells the story of a woman who came to the Home for the Friendless in search of a position that would allow her to keep her youngest child. This mother had already been forced to give up two older children because she was unable to provide for them. With no prospects, the woman was about to fill out the paperwork to surrender her remaining child, when the home learned of a situation in the country that would accept a mother and child. "We rejoice with her that it was in her power to keep a little longer her heart's treasure as her own without suffering," wrote the Home Committee. Then adding, "For just as hard is it to the poor mother to give up her treasured ones as it would be to the rich, and did not actual want stare her in the face, she could not be induced to do it."[101] Here, the AFMRS is emphasizing the universality of a mother's love. Just because poor women were forced to give up their children, a circumstance likely unimaginable to many *Advocate* readers, the AFMRS stresses that it is poverty that forced her hand. Poor women do not love their children any less was the clear message as the AFMRS voiced respect for poor mothers. Indeed, through this shared value of motherhood, the AFMRS sought to connect women regardless of class and circumstance.

Reports often acknowledge mothers who put their children's need for food and shelter above the agony of letting a child go. Even in instances of severe want and suffering, Home Committee members rarely saw mothers give away children "as if happily relived of a burden . . . more generally we see in the mother an evidence of self-sacrifice, which marks a devotion to the interests and advantage of the child, so expressive of moral principles, that while we pity, we cannot but admire."[102] For instance, a woman, whose husband had left for California two years prior and had not been heard from, was struggling to support herself and her infant son on her income of five dollars a month. According to the report, when she learned that admitting her son to the Home for the Friendless required her to relinquish her parental rights, "the big tear told us the mother's heart was there struggling with its necessities. 'Yes,' she said, 'it is better to give him away than to see him destroyed.'"[103] Home Committee reports are filled with heartrending stories of these separations. In some instances, fathers who have lost their wives and have no one to care for their children will bring them to the home, but most of these separations are women forced to give up their children due to their inability to earn sufficient income or because of poor health.

One story describes a "worthy" widow with six children who had tried to support her family and keep them together, but had finally decided to give up three of her children—two girls, seven and five years old, and a three-year-old boy. According to the Home Committee report: "They were as bright and happy as could be till the parting scene came; their mother left about noon; and their cries and tears had not ceased when we took our departure at half-past five. Everything that could be devised to cheer and comfort them was entirely unavailing; sorrow seemed to have taken entire possession of their being; there they stood, hand in hand, sending forth their piteous lamentations, enough to melt a heart of stone."[104] Here, the report writer's description renders a powerful emotional appeal. Another report tells the story of a German widow in failing health who brought her seven-year-old daughter to the Home for the Friendless. After the woman had toured the home and remarked on the schoolroom, the report notes, she "said repeatedly, as if to calm her own feelings, *'She'll be well off here, yes she will.'*" Parting with her daughter, the report describes the woman in tears trembling with emotion and asserts, "We pitied her much."[105]

More than 160 years removed, these heartrending accounts of women relinquishing their children are agonizing to read, and I contend that this effect was a deliberate part of the AFMRS's institutional rhetoric. As pathetic appeals, these narratives would have drawn sympathy for these children, of good parents, who needed foster and adoptive homes, and support for the home's mission. Moreover, I believe these accounts reflect growing resentment by AFMRS members. In a society that viewed a mother's role as sacrosanct, forcing women to give up their children was untenable, particularly in cases where women could not earn sufficient income to support them no matter how hard they worked. Moved by the scenes they observed in the home's reception room, the AFMRS repeatedly showed readers the plight of poor women who could not earn enough to keep their children.

Even if women could find work, the few avenues of employment open to them barely paid subsistence wages. For decades, domestic service and sewing had been women's primary avenues for employment. The fact that these continued throughout the Industrial Revolution underscored the new patriarchal economy in which men monopolized gainful employment. While women were allowed into certain light industries such as bookbinding or weaving, they were precluded from so-called skilled trades, which paid higher wages. In the 1830s seamstresses were paid 6 to 12.5 cents per shirt, thus even working from sunrise to sunset, a shirtmaker would struggle to earn much more than a dollar a week with the cost of living averaging $1.50 to $1.75 a week. These wages saw little if any increase over the next three decades with tides of female immigrants and, later, with the invention of the modern sewing machine. In addition to long, tedious hours, distorted posture and poor eyesight were common ailments associated with sewing trades. Domestic service was one of the other limited options available to women, but this field was seldom open to women with children. Acknowledging the few employment options available to women, Virginia Penny dedicated her 1863 book, *The Employments of Women: A Cyclopedia of Woman's Work*, to "worthy and industrious women in the United States, striving to earn a livelihood." In it, Penny decries, "The false opinion that exists in regard to the occupations suitable for women must be changed where women have free access to all those in which they may engage . . . I would love to see thrown open to women the door of every trade and profession in which they are capable of working."[106]

The AFMRS's institutional rhetoric similarly took up this charge evident in numerous *Advocate* articles with titles such as: "Women Can't Live by Plain Sewing in New York," "Young Women Wanting Employment," "New Employment for Women," "Women's Wages," and "Useful & Remunerative Employment for Women."[107] Frustrated by the plight of poor women they saw, Home Committee reports also argued for better wages and more employment opportunities for women. One report describes the AFMRS's efforts to assist "two widows with their infants in their arms, who were struggling to sustain themselves at *starvation wages*." The report then avows, "we trust the day is at hand when every needle-woman will receive a fair compensation for her labor."[108]

Advocate articles particularly took aim at the low wages paid for sewing, one of the few occupations that allowed a woman to work at home and keep her children. Other articles point to the irony of business owners *willing* to contribute to charities, but *unwilling* to pay the "charity of wages."[109] Another outlines the paltry sums paid to needlewomen for everything from cotton shirts to fine linen shirts to overalls and trousers, asserting, "the seamstress who is fortunate enough to get steady work, earns from 75 cents to $2 a week."[110] Decrying businesses that grow rich on the labor of poorly compensated women, one article argues: "The workwoman has indeed no rights of her own. She can be oppressed, cheated, trampled upon, until the joyous life within her becomes a dead and poisonous impulse that drives her through the world eager for the grave, or stings her into desperation and revenge. But how revenge her wrongs? She has not redress, neither in those laws she did not sanction, nor in the public opinion she cannot influence, and which regards her not."[111] This article, which connects the dots between women's oppression and her lack of legal rights and political power, belies a growing feminist consciousness in the AFMRS. The women grew increasingly frustrated by the situations they saw. Years earlier, female moral reformers were angry that poor wages often forced women into prostitution as a matter of survival. Here, they see low wages make it impossible for many women to care for and keep their children. While the AFMRS could not raise women's wages, it did look to its own reception room to fill staff vacancies and it hired female editors, bookkeepers, fundraisers, agents, and missionaries.[112]

The AFMRS also used the *Advocate of Moral Reform* to promote more occupations for women. One article advised women to turn their needles to making gaiter boots because they are far more profitable than shirts or trousers. The same article holds up as an example Mr. Stimson, proprietor of Day

Book, who has trained girls to set type for which they are compensated a dollar a day. According to the article, Stimson's "experience satisfies him that the poor sewing girls might be taught to set type and earn, at the usual prices paid to men, from five to ten dollars a week."[113] One writer asserts that it is so obvious that a woman could more properly fill the position of store clerk that it scarcely requires argument. Another writer describes a hat- and bonnet-pressing machine invented by Mrs. C. C. Dow of New York, which was displayed in New York's Crystal Palace during the Exhibition of the Industry of All Nations. Because the invention requires, "tact rather than strength," the writer claims that it opens this field of labor to women. The article also calls on men to vacate departments that are appropriate to women. Specifically, it notes that women should be employed in shops, especially where bonnets, ribbons, and lace are sold, and as clerks, copyists, and typesetters. The article even argues that women should be admitted to design schools.[114] Carroll Smith Rosenberg notes that the AFMRS even tried to help open the medical profession to women. When Elizabeth Blackwell received a medical degree, the first woman to do so in the United States, the "*Advocate* featured a story dramatizing Dr. Blackwell's struggles. The door was now open for other women, the editors urge; medicine was a peculiarly appropriate profession for sensitive and sympathetic womankind." The AFMRS even offered to assist women gain admission to medical school.[115]

The authors of these articles often anticipate male opposition, primarily the fear that women would push men out of jobs. In response, one writer wryly asks why no one considers the welfare of women shut out of almost all opportunities for employment. "Is it not time to remember that women cannot live on air, or even on compliments; and that both justice and policy demand their admission into walks of usefulness suited to their powers, and yielding the means of decent livelihood."[116] Both the number and tenor of these articles published in the *Advocate* show the AFMRS's growing frustration with an economy that prevents women from earning a living wage. AFMRS volunteers had repeatedly witnessed the plight of widows and women abandoned by their husbands; without a male breadwinner, most women were unable to earn a living. Moreover, mothers were often forced to do the unimaginable—give up their children. AFMRS members knew the notion that men will take care of women was erroneous, so they used the *Advocate* to lobby for better pay and more occupations for women.

Advocating Children's Welfare

Beyond providing a refuge for children, the AFMRS also used its institutional rhetoric to advocate for children's welfare. Again, it pressured the state legislature with a petition drive. Because of its depictions of the dire situations in the city's poor neighborhoods, the AFMRS had little difficulty marshaling its New York auxiliaries to sign and circulate petitions in support of New York's truancy law. In part, the petition read: "Whereas there are many children in the large town and cities of our State, familiarly known as 'street children,' whose parents being intemperate, or idle and profligate, permit them to run at large, receiving only such education and training as will fit them to become a curse to society, and in the result fill our prisons and houses of correction. And whereas no adequate provision can be made for such children legally, except a law shall be enacted to meet their case."[117] The truancy law, which passed in 1853, authorized the police to arrest vagrant children ages four to fourteen. If they were orphans, the children were made wards of the state and placed in city institutions such as the House of Refuge and New York Juvenile Asylum. If the children had parents, their parents were required to send them to school unless the children were regularly employed. These stipulations became a condition for receiving any family relief. If parents still failed to keep their children off the streets, authorities were authorized to remove the children "and place them under better influences, till the claim of the parent shall be re-established by continued sobriety, industry and general good conduct."[118] Like the orphan trains, truancy laws were another attempt to address the thousands of children on New York City's streets. In fact, children placed in city institutions were often placed out through the orphan trains.[119]

Truancy laws also reflected the belief that schools were a source of both education and moral instruction. Beyond child welfare, the laws addressed anxiety about crime, disorder, and morality, particularly among poor and immigrant populations. Such laws were problematic in the sense that they imposed middle- and upper-class mores about families and children on the poor without providing any assistance. Admittedly, private, charitable institutions, including the Home for the Friendless, routinely used this same middle-class purview. After it passed, the AFMRS continued to support the truancy law by presenting it as a safeguard for children. An 1854 *Advocate* editorial acknowledges the belief that children should not be taken from their parents, but counters, asserting, "A self-abandoned parent, who leaves his offspring to suffer hunger, cold and nakedness, and the greater moral wrong of ignorance of all that is good and lovely and desirable in the paths of knowledge, who loves to indulge his appetite for strong drink, more than he loves the bodies or souls of his children, forfeits his legal and moral claim to retain them in his possession."[120]

While the AFMRS empathized with poor mothers forced to give up their children, it had no patience with parents it deemed irresponsible. The

AFMRS's institutional rhetoric is also evident in depictions that show children who were saved by the new truancy law. The AFMRS's twentieth annual report presents three such cases to readers, including the story of a twelve-year-old girl who had attended one of the society's industrial schools and was then admitted to the Home for the Friendless. According to the annual report:

> Shortly after her intemperate mother, learning where she was, called, and used every entreaty to induce her [daughter] to leave, promising to be kind to her in future. The child replied, 'You have said so before, and when I went home you would beat me and my step father would curse me every time I took a bit of bread in my mouth, and put me out of the house' . . . She would cling to whatever object she was near, apparently in an agony of fear lest her cruel mother should take her by force. It appears from statements elicited that she had been driven out from the drunkard's home on the most inclement nights of the winter, and made to suffer almost beyond endurance. The new law justified the protection given to this desolate child, and she is now with kind friends in a pleasant Christian family in the country.[121]

Evident in this story and others, the AFMRS believed it was saving children by removing them from families and circumstances that relegated them to street vagrants. It was also showing members and supporters the importance of their petitioning efforts. However, the truancy law ultimately proved unsuccessful in assisting the city's vagrant children. The city-run House of Refuge and the New York Juvenile Asylum, which received many of these children, primarily assumed a custodial function that closely resembled prisons, and with the law's harsh terms police officers were reluctant to make arrests. The truancy law further underscores the difficulty in addressing the city's multitudes of vagrant children.[122]

Temperance

The AFMRS had long used its institutional rhetoric to condemn intemperance. Alcohol abuse posed a major social problem in New York and much of nineteenth-century America. By the mid-1820s the growth of western grain production, new distilling technologies, and cheap transportation made cheap liquor widely available to New York City residents. During the first third of the nineteenth century, American adult males drank more distilled liquor than at any other time in the country's history. Cultural mores, which tended to curb women's alcohol consumption, made intemperance primarily a male problem; however, women and children often suffered its harshest effects. Because men were the principle wage earners, alcohol abuse could lay ruin to a family with men becoming violent, imbibing rent and food dollars, debilitating themselves for work, or going to jail. Moreover, women had few legal rights, which made it almost impossible to protect themselves, their children, or their possessions. Through the mid-nineteenth century, traditional coverture laws—which viewed married women, their possessions, and their children as property of the husband—persisted. Consequently, women's efforts to promote temperance were closely connected to the protection of women and children.[123]

These connections are evident in the AFMRS's institutional rhetoric. Home Committee reports repeatedly describe cases where drunkenness rendered parents unfit and often abusive. One report describes a young girl, now residing in the Home for the Friendless, who was forced to appeal to police for protection from her inebriate and abusive mother.[124] Another describes three young girls turned out onto the street by their drunken father.[125] One Home Committee report describing two little girls residing at the Home for the Friendless, states, "the father, who should have been their earthly protector, was given to use the intoxicating cup."[126] Numerous reports also show women and children in dire need because of intemperate husbands. One report describes a number of desperate women with small children crowded into the home's reception room in search of work. It concludes, "Many there are with intemperate husbands."[127] With this last line, the AFMRS's institutional rhetoric accentuates the root problem. A husband's alcoholism might force a mother to give up her children in order to protect or provide for them.

Underscoring the seriousness with which the AFMRS viewed intemperance, it would not release children to the care of inebriate parents unless legally forced. In one instance, they even refuse to allow a family that tended bar to foster children. Occasionally they went to court to protect children from drunken fathers, but there was little legal recourse available at the time.[128] A father, no matter how unfit, retained custody of his children. Even in instances where fathers abused or refused to support their children, the Home for the Friendless, which did not operate as a refuge, but sought to place children with families, was legally restrained from accepting the children without the father's consent. In one especially moving case where a mother tries to rescue her two young boys from an intemperate and abusive father by bringing them to the Home for the Friendless, the Home Committee report bemoans, "Oh, how crushing and almost maddening is the reflection that the law, in such a case provides no redress; but the poor victims of a father's in humanity and brutality must suffer on, till death closes the scene."[129] As this example demonstrates, women's temperance efforts revealed custody and property laws that left women and children vulnerable to drunken and abusive men. Consequently, women's temperance efforts and the pursuit of women's rights were commingled. Indeed, many well-known women's rights activists were also active in the temperance movement.[130]

At mid-century, the same time when AFMRS was inveighing intemperance in the *Advocate*, New York City was a hotbed for temperance and women's rights activism.[131] AFMRS members were likely influenced by these temperance efforts; some probably belonged to temperance societies and attended the temperance conventions held in the city. They were also influenced by what they observed. Witnessing the devastation wrought by rampant alcoholism, the AFMRS moved beyond promoting temperance to promoting legal restrictions. In 1850 Maine passed a law that banned the manufacture of alcohol and restricted its sale. The AFMRS's institutional rhetoric repeatedly calls attention to Maine's law. Pointing to Maine as an example of what could happen if New York passed a similar law, the *Advocate* reprints an article by the editor of a national temperance periodical who visited Portland, Maine, and describes the positive results of the law, including the restoration of an entire neighborhood that was previously a "collection of miserable hovels."[132]

An 1854 editorial urges women to use their influence to help pass a law similar to the Maine law in New York. It argues, "In the one case, the rich may lose their gains from a vile traffic; but, in the other, the poor and helpless, who by this traffic have suffered the loss of all things most valuable, will be universally benefitted."[133] Here, the AFMRS is calling out business owners who profit from alcohol in the same manner it called out business owners who profited from the subsistence wages they paid women. Along with its support for a law banning the manufacture of alcohol and restricting its sale, arguing against liquor trafficking becomes a popular refrain in the *Advocate*. Concluding one of its reports, the Home Committee asserts, "Almost every case of destitution and suffering which comes under our notice of late, has resulted either directly or indirectly from the liquor traffic."[134] These calls for temperance and regulation of liquor sales offer further evidence of the AFMRS's activism on behalf of women and children—the primary victims of drunkenness. The AFMRS's frustration with widespread alcoholism also foreshadow both the Woman's Crusade of 1873–1874, during which women turned out en mass to demonstrate and hold prayer vigils in front of saloons, and the formation of the powerful Women's Christian Temperance Union in 1873, which would become the largest women's reform movement of the century, and play an instrumental role in passing Prohibition.

CONCLUSION

By 1854, the AFMRS's twentieth anniversary, members had fully embraced
their role as guardians and institutional managers. While members continued to promote reform in their institutional rhetoric, these efforts were
closely tied to their work in the Home for the Friendless. Women's experience
working in the home also inspired new efforts and institutions. For instance,
the AFMRS began to open industrial schools as another way to help the city's
poor children. Like its home, these schools show the impulse to pursue social
reform through institutions. The society explained in its twentieth annual
report that it opened an industrial school in a location where many children
were found engaged as street beggars, bone pickers, street sweepers, and
wood gatherers. The AFMRS hired a teacher, who in the morning instructed
the children in basic subjects as well as Christianity, and after lunch, the society's corps of volunteers instructed the girls in sewing. The children were
also provided with new clothes, some sewn with their own needles and others
from the home's wardrobe. The AFMRS even placed some of the girls from
the school in families with adoptive or foster parents.[135] However, the primary
object of the school was to provide "proper inducements to them to forsake
an idle, vagrant, life, and aspire to something higher and better."[136] In that
sense, the schools were imparting the AFMRS's moral and religious ideology
as well.

Echoing its earlier moral reform work, the women believed the school protected these girls from the evils, temptations, and dangers of street life. In
other words, they believed the school provided a "saving moral influence."[137]
In its first year, the school registered 105 girls with daily attendance averaging
between 50 and 60. Nonetheless, the society acknowledged the difficulty inherent in teaching children who had grown up with little to no guidance amid
extreme poverty, misery, and crime, but "the result was unexpectedly encouraging both as to the improvement in the morals and manners of the children
and as to their learning to read and write and do rudimentary school work."[138]

The AFMRS took pride in its industrial school pupils, and they invited
them to the Home for the Friendless to share Christmas dinner with residents.
They even gave these girls warm hoods and scarves as Christmas gifts. Indeed, the initial school's success heartened the society to open a second school
in 1857, a third school in 1858, and a fourth school in 1861. Other benevolent organizations, including the Children's Aid Society, also opened industrial schools as another means to address the city's large number of vagrant
children. The AFMRS was a leader in this effort. Eventually it opened twelve
schools in various parts of the city, serving close to five thousand children.

Some of these schools were for boys or girls; others were co-ed. The industrial schools supplemented children's basic education with instruction in manual work such as basket weaving, carpentry, chair caning, cobbling, sewing, and cooking. Even after public school became compulsory for all children in the city, the AFMRS believed its industrial schools were still necessary. Initially, there were not enough public schools to serve all the city's children. Moreover, the AFMRS claims that for many of these poor children, "Their lack of suitable clothing, and the necessity which often requires their assistance at home, or in some method of self-support during the early morning hours, precludes them from attendance at the public school, where the rules are strict and unbending. In the industrial schools, these points are waived for the good of the children." However, the AFMRS maintains the system of instruction is the same, and often students do move from the industrial schools to public schools, and some even moved on to a normal college. Much like modern alternative schools, industrial schools also provided a second chance for students expelled from public schools. In fact, the AFMRS ran industrial schools up until the 1930s, at which time the number of public schools had increased, and their facilities far exceeded those of the AFMRS's industrial schools.[139]

The Home for the Friendless itself remained open for 128 years. In 1856 the AFMRS purchased an adjoining lot on Twenty-Ninth Street. The building they erected was referred to as the Home Chapel because it included a chapel as well as schoolrooms, infirmaries, a large hall or playroom, and printing offices in the basement, which produced the semimonthly *Advocate and Family Guardian*, which at that time had a circulation of forty-eight thousand. In 1878 a donor gave the society a home in Oceanport, New Jersey, which it initially used as a summer retreat for its home children. Later it was used as an overflow for older children when the Home for the Friendless became full, and eventually the grounds and quarters expanded until the site operated like a camp. At the turn of the century, the AFMRS built the Home for the Friendless Woody Crest Home in the Bronx. The home received government funding and gradually transitioned to a permanent or foster home where children could stay until they completed high school. Eventually the society became the Woodycrest Youth Service, helping children from broken homes, and in 1974 the home merged with another social service organization and moved to Rockland County.[140]

When the AFMRS celebrated its hundredth anniversary in 1934, the Home for the Friendless reported that it had placed 6,452 children. It also included stories of former home children, who went on to become ministers, teachers, lawyers, nurses, soldiers, and doctors, who later reconnected with the home as adults. One of these is the story of Dr. Mary Glenton.

About 1880 her mother, overburdened and struggling to earn a living, placed her child with us. She made her way into the hearts of her caretaker and the Secretary by her sterling uprightness, her eager desire to learn, and her wonderful memory. When the mother three years later came for her she was urged not to put her out to service, as she planned, but to make every effort to give her an education. Finally, our Secretary paved the way for the young girl to attend the Twelfth Street Public School, then the best in the city. She filled two or three positions after leaving school, and sometime later the Home staff received invitations to attend her graduation as a nurse in Chicago. She went as a missionary nurse to Alaska, then, feeling she could do better work as a physician, entered a medical school. When she graduated she was sent to China as a medical missionary by the Episcopal Board of Missions in 1898. She was the senior physician in a hospital in Wuchang for twenty years when illness necessitated her return to America, where she served a hospital in North Carolina. She died in 1923.[141]

It seems fitting to conclude *Reforming Women* with Dr. Glenton's story. Imagine how gratified AFMRS members, who had argued for more employment opportunities for women, would have been to see a girl who, with the assistance of their Home for the Friendless, later became a doctor and medical missionary. Even as the AFMRS's mission and rhetorical tactics changed its members continually sought to bolster and empower women. It encouraged women to voice their outrage, demand a single moral standard for men and women, organize auxiliaries, circulate petitions, raise funds, educate themselves, protect other women, visit and assist the poor, open employment offices, provide a refuge for young women and children, volunteer in the home's reception room, locate jobs and promote more employment opportunities for women, open industrial schools for street children, advocate legal reforms and women's rights and, in the case of Dr. Glenton, pave the way for a young girl to receive an education and eventually become a doctor.

Epilogue

Unresolved

Resolved, That the same amount of virtue, delicacy, and refinement of behavior, that is required of woman in the social state, should also be required of man, and the same transgressions should be visited with equal severity on both man and woman.

—Declaration of Sentiments and Resolutions, 1848

I began *Reforming Women* with this sixth resolution of the *Declaration of Sentiments and Resolutions* ratified at the Seneca Falls Convention in 1848 in order to show the influence antebellum female moral reformers had on women in their own era. To conclude, I return to this sixth resolution to underscore how these women and their concerns still speak to us today, especially after witnessing the power of the #MeToo movement. When I teach undergraduate courses in women's rhetoric, I usually begin by reading and analyzing the *Declaration of Sentiments and Resolutions*. In this document, early women's rights activists demanded "immediate admission to all the rights and privileges which belong to them as citizens of the United States." As part of my class discussion, I divide my students into groups and ask them to review the list of twelve resolutions and rank them in order—from those that have been achieved to those that are furthest from being achieved. Ironically, the ninth resolution, demanding women's right to vote, which was the most controversial resolution in 1848, has been achieved. As they rank other resolutions, my students acknowledge that in addition to suffrage women in this country have gained access to education, public forums from which to speak, and most professions. Women have the right to financial independence, even as the gender wage gap continues. Equal rights legislation provides women legal avenues to address gender discrimination. Yet, inevitably as we work down their lists, students acknowledge that different codes of moral conduct for men and women persist. In other words, *the sixth resolution remains unresolved.*

Students have discussed how assertiveness is often viewed negatively in women, but positively in men. We have talked about the "boys will be boys" mindset that excuses certain behaviors in boys and men, but not girls and women. One student shared how her parents applied different curfews and rules of conduct to her and her brother. Students have pointed to different expectations for sororities and fraternities. And others note the stigma they have seen attached to pregnant high school girls while those girls' boyfriends receive relatively little attention. Ultimately, my classes draw the same conclusion as antebellum female moral reformers: changing deeply engrained values, ideologies, and gender constructions is a long, arduous struggle.

Some of these differing expectations enforce traditional gender stereotypes or limit women's opportunities by discouraging certain behaviors. Others put women at greater personal risk than men. For instance, girls who take the lead or tell others what to do are often called bossy, but boys who exhibit the same behavior are seldom described the same way because that behavior is expected and even reinforced in boys.[1] Similarly, in the workplace, female managers are expected to be nurturing and sensitive; yet those same behaviors are not expected in male managers.[2] The same holds true for female instructors in the academy.

With regards to sexual behavior, women's virginity is still treated differently from men's. Losing one's virginity is something a young man often celebrates and something a young woman often hides because she feels shame or fears being judged negatively. Clear distinctions also emerge in patterns of violence. One in seven women are severely injured by intimate partners during their lifetimes compared to one in eighteen men.[3] One in five women are sexually assaulted while attending college compared to one in sixteen men, and 90 percent of sexual assault victims on college campuses do not report the assault.[4] In part, this is because victims often blame themselves. Sadly, our society contributes to this self-blame through the messages we convey to victims. In her essay "We Should All Be Feminists," the author Chimamanda Ngozi Adichie illustrates the different expectations we have for men's and women's moral conduct and behavior. She asserts:

> Recently a young woman was gang-raped in a university in Nigeria, and the response of many Nigerians, both male and female, was something like this: "Yes, rape is wrong, but what is a girl doing in a room with four boys?" Let us, if we can,

forget the horrible inhumanity of that response. These Nigerians have been raised to think of women as inherently guilty. And they have been raised to expect so little of men that the idea of men as savage beings with no self-control is somehow acceptable.[5]

Adichie draws her example from Nigeria, but my own university in the United States, like many others, has been the site of highly publicized sexual assault cases, including gang rapes. I have also repeatedly heard: "She shouldn't have been out so late," "she shouldn't have been at the party," "she shouldn't have been at that bar" "she shouldn't have been drinking," "she shouldn't have been with those guys," "she shouldn't have gone to his apartment," etc. What message do these comments send? According to one of my first-year female students, "Girls are responsible for holding boys accountable rather than boys holding themselves accountable." Do we expect so little of men that the majority of our efforts to prevent sexual assault and rape are directed at potential victims?

In the same way that antebellum society blamed "fallen" women, our society tends to look primarily at young women to prevent sexual assault and rape or implies their culpability when a sexual assault occurs. Similarly, the #MeToo movement has not only demonstrated the scourge of sexual assault and harassment in America's workplaces, but women's reluctance, until recently, to make public claims. In most cases, these women feared retribution and blame, or they assumed no one would believe them. Not surprisingly, they collectively found courage to act. Making direct comparisons between the contexts and challenges antebellum female moral reformers faced with those facing twenty-first-century society is impossible and even problematic. Nonetheless, I believe antebellum female moral reformers can still inspire and speak to us today— urging us to resolve the sixth resolution. These early female reformers recognized double standards in moral conduct and behavior as forms of inequality, and they fought to change them. The AFMRS used the rhetorical tactics available to them to create awareness, to reveal libertines, to organize, to hold elected officials accountable, and to establish institutions when needs were not being met. They encouraged parents to raise their daughters and sons with the same moral standards. They demanded that society hold individuals accountable for their behavior regardless of their sex, and that blame be shifted away from victims to their perpetrators. While much has changed in our society, these demands remain the same. How can we use our behaviors, our influence, and all the rhetorical tactics available to us to demand change? Like the authors of the Seneca Falls resolutions and members of the AFMRS, we must recognize that eliminating double standards in moral conduct and behavior remains a matter of securing the equal rights and privileges that we all deserve.

Notes

INTRODUCTION: RESONATING RHETORIC

Epigraph: Stanton, Anthony, and Gage, *History of Woman Suffrage*, vol. 1, 72.

1. The New York Female Moral Reform Society changed its name as its scope and mission changed. In 1839 it became the American Female Moral Reform Society; in 1847 it changed its name to the American Female Reform and Guardian Society; and in 1849 it incorporated as the American Female Guardian Society. To avoid confusion, I refer to the group as the American Female Moral Reform Society (AFMRS) throughout this manuscript.

2. Whiteaker, *Seduction, Prostitution, and Moral Reform*, x.

3. Whiteaker, xiv.

4. *AMR*, 1835: 1–2. When referencing the *Advocate of Moral Reform* (1835–1846), the *Advocate of Moral Reform and Family Guardian* (1847–1854), and the *Advocate and Family Guardian* (1855), I use the abbreviation *AMR* followed by the year of publication and page number. The eight-page semimonthly *AMR* used continuous pagination for each yearly volume.

5. Luke 12:2.

6. *AMR*, 1835: 2.

7. Whiteaker, *Seduction, Prostitution, and Moral Reform*, 124; *AMR*, 1840: 82.

8. Fletcher, *History of Oberlin College*, 302–3.

9. Sánchez, *Reforming the World*, 124.

10. Cohen, *Murder of Helen Jewett*, 310; Wright, "*First of Causes to Our Sex*," 1; Rosenberg, "Beauty, the Beast, and the Militant Woman," 584.

11. Mattingly, *Well-Tempered Women*.

12. Sharer, *Voice and Vote*, 5–8.

13. Scott, *Natural Allies*, 37.

14. See Mattingly, *Well-Tempered Women*; Gere, *Intimate Practices*; Logan, *Liberating Language*; Zaeske, *Signatures of Citizenship*.

15. Buchanan, *Regendering Delivery*, 77–80.

16. de Certeau, *Practice of Everyday Life*, 37–38.

17. Scott, *Natural Allies*, 2.

18. See my discussion of the AFMRS's auxiliary societies in chapter 4.

19. With the availability afforded by digital archives, periodicals are increasingly recognized and examined as important cultural artifacts representative of the social and political contexts in which they were produced. See Latham and Scholes, "Rise of Periodical Studies."

20. Stearns, "Reform Periodicals and Female Reformers," 678. Italics are mine.

21. Royster and Kirsch, *Feminist Rhetorical Practices*, 23; 156n5.

22. Boylan, "Women in Groups," 500.

23. Carlson, "Creative Casuistry and Feminist Consciousness," 18.

CHAPTER 1: GENDERING MORAL REFORM

Epigraph: AMR, 1835: 1–2.

1. Enoch, "Releasing Hold," 68.

2. Buchanan, *Regendering Delivery*, 1–2.

3. Mattingly, *Well-Tempered Women*, 40.

4. Johnson, *Gender and Rhetorical Space in American Life*, 119–21; Buchanan, *Regendering Delivery*, 118–21.

5. Quoted in Gilfoyle, *City of Eros*, 29.

6. Gilfoyle, *City of Eros*, 31.

7. Hill, *Their Sisters' Keepers*, 16, 52, 184–94; Burrows and Wallace, *Gotham*, 435–36; Richardson, *New York Police*, 25–26; Cohen, *Murder of Helen Jewett*, 70–71.

8. Ellington, *Women of New York*, 196.

9. Both male and transsexual prostitution also existed in this brothel subculture. See Gilfoyle, *City of Eros*, 136–38.

10. Hill, *Their Sisters' Keepers*, 180.

11. Whitman, *New York Dissected*, 121.

12. Hill, *Their Sisters' Keepers*, 180.

13. The full title is *Prostitution Exposed; or, a Moral Reform Directory, Laying Bare the Lives, Histories, Residences, Seductions, &e. of the Most Celebrated Courtezans and Ladies of Pleasure of the City of New-York, Together with a Description of the Crime and its Effects, as also, of the Houses of Prostitutions and their Keepers, Houses of Assignation, Their Charges and Conveniences, and other Particulars Interesting to the Public*.

14. Whitman, *New York Dissected*, 96.

15. Quoted in Gilfoyle, *City of Eros*, 18. Gilfoyle also includes a description of Berrian's public confession, 17–20.

16. Gilfoyle, 112–15; Cohen, *Murder of Helen Jewett*, 69.

17. Hill, *Their Sisters' Keepers*, 109–19; Cohen, *Murder of Helen Jewett*, 74.

18. Hill, 126–31; Gilfoyle, *City of Eros*, 87.

19. Quoted in Hill, *Their Sisters' Keepers*, 139.

20. Whiteaker, *Seduction, Prostitution, and Moral Reform*, 27–28.

21. Whiteaker, 29–30.

22. Sanger, *History of Prostitution*, 450–549.

23. Hill, *Their Sisters' Keepers*, 55–58. Hill also notes that many black women did support brothels by working as servants and sometimes acting as assistants to madams.

24. Sanger, *History of Prostitution*, 473–76.

25. Sanger, 475.

26. Sanger, 483.

27. Hobson, *Uneasy Virtue*, 93.

28. Sanger, *History of Prostitution*, 488; Cohen, *Murder of Helen Jewett*, 71, 73, 85; Hill, *Their Sisters' Keepers*, 87.

29. Quoted in Hill, 87.

30. Hill, 103; Gilfoyle, *City of Eros*, 69–74. Gilfoyle also notes that while male laborers and tradesmen were earning $250 and $600 annually on the eve of the Civil War, a successful brothel could earn an annual income in excess of $26,000.

31. Sanger, *History of Prostitution*, 455–56.

32. Hill, *Their Sisters' Keepers*, 60–61.

33. Whiteaker, *Seduction, Prostitution, and Moral Reform*, 4–5; 25.

34. Ely, *Visits of Mercy*, 27.

35. Ely, 62.

36. Ely, 63.

37. Ely, 88.

38. Ely, 89.

39. Many institutions and societies serving prostitutes and unwed mothers were named for the biblical Mary Magdalen, one of Christ's most devout followers, who has often been portrayed in Christian tradition as a reformed prostitute.

40. Ely, *Visits of Mercy*, 158.

41. Teeters, "Early Days of the Magdalen Society of Philadelphia," 158–59.

42. Magdalen Society of New York, *Constitution and By-Laws*; Whiteaker, *Seduction, Prostitution, and Moral Reform*, 12.

43. Magdalen Society of New York, 8.

44. See Becker, "Isabella Graham and Joanna Bethune." Isabella Graham was one of the most influential philanthropic women in New York. In 1797 she founded the Society for the Relief of Poor Widows. Joanna Graham Bethune, whose husband, merchant Divie Bethune, was on the board of the Magdalen Society, founded the Orphan Asylum Society in New York in 1806, and opened the first free infant school in the city in 1827.

45. Magdalen Society of New York, *First Annual Report*, 5.

46. Magdalen Society of New York, *Second Annual Report*, 4.

47. Magdalen Society of New York, *Third Annual Report*, 10.

48. Magdalen Society of New York, *Second Annual Report*, 5.

49. Later, reformers would acknowledge that the paltry wages paid in the sewing trades drove some women to prostitution.

50. Ely, *Visits of Mercy*, 56–57.

51. See Magdalen Society of New York, *First Annual Report*, 6; Magdalen Society of New York, *Second Annual Report*, 7; Magdalen Society of New York, *Third Annual Report*, 6. By the second year, over 100 had become life members of the society with a donation of $25 or more, and an additional 222 people had paid the annual $5 membership dues.

52. Gilfoyle, *City of Eros*, 64–65.

53. Boylan, "Women in Groups," 501.

54. Hill, *Their Sisters' Keepers*, 16.

55. *Magdalen Report*, 5.

56. Whiteaker, *Seduction, Prostitution, and Moral Reform*, 50–55.

57. McDowall, *Memoir and Select Remains*, 194; Burrows and Wallace, *Gotham*, 534.

58. Whiteaker, *Seduction, Prostitution, and Moral Reform*, 57–58.

59. *Magdalen Report*, 13.

60. Whiteaker, *Seduction, Prostitution, and Moral Reform*, 59.

61. See Cohen, *Murder of Helen Jewett*, 71. This equated to one in every seven women between the ages of fifteen and forty-five in the city.

62. *Magdalen Report*, 8.

63. Burrows and Wallace, *Gotham*, 535.

64. Quoted in Hill, *Their Sisters' Keepers*, 18.

65. Hill, 18.

66. Gilfoyle, *City of Eros*, 59.

67. Hill, *Their Sisters' Keepers*, 18.

68. See Whiteaker, *Seduction, Prostitution, and Moral Reform*, 26. Ely had charged that there were seven thousand prostitutes, which was 10 percent of the city's population at the time.

69. *Magdalen Report*, 9.

70. Whiteaker, *Seduction, Prostitution, and Moral Reform*, 60. Elijah Pierson kept the asylum open at his own expense until he was forced to close it in April 1832 because of financial difficulties.

71. Whiteaker, *Seduction, Prostitution, and Moral Reform*, 86, 94–95.

72. Whiteaker, 62–63. The FBS is sometimes referred to as the New York Female Benevolent Society.

73. Female Benevolent Society of the City of New York, *First Annual Report*, 1.

74. Whiteaker, *Seduction, Prostitution, and Moral Reform*, 69.·

75. Whiteaker, 67–73.

76. Whiteaker, 72.

77. Richmond, *New York and Its Institutions,* 320.

78. Whiteaker, *Seduction, Prostitution, and Moral Reform*, 85.

79. Boylan, "Women in Groups," 502.

80. While its objectives have changed, amazingly the organization that began as the FBS in 1832 continues today. In 1851 the FBS incorporated as the New York Magdalen Benevolent Society, changed its name to New York Magdalen House in 1913 and, later, to Inwood House when it moved to the northern tip of Manhattan. It shifted its focus to address evolving needs, including providing an asylum for unwed mothers, helping women gain custody of their children, providing career education, opening New York City's first clinic to treat gonorrhea and syphilis, and providing sex education. Today Inwood House's mission is empowering New York teens to escape the cycle of poverty.

81. Wright, *"The First of Causes to Our Sex,"* 17.

82. Whiteaker, *Seduction, Prostitution, and Moral Reform*, 87; 92–93.

83. See Whiteaker, 100–101. In its second year of publication, circulation for *McDowall's Journal* rose to fourteen thousand. Half of this number went to subscribers and half were handed out as tracts. The journal extended beyond New York into New England and even Ohio.

84. Quoted in Whiteaker, *Seduction, Prostitution, and Moral Reform*, 101.

85. Whiteaker, 109–18.

86. Northup, *Record of a Century*, 15–16.

87. Initially, the AFMRS did sponsor a parallel effort focused on converting and reforming prostitutes, but this failed effort was short-lived as the group determined a national moral reform crusade was its principle focus. See Rosenberg, "Beauty, the Beast, and the Militant Woman," 568–70.

88. Whiteaker, *Seduction, Prostitution, and Moral Reform*, xii.

89. Boylan, "Women in Groups," 514.

90. Wright, *"The First of Causes to Our Sex,"* 1–2.

91. Wright, 1.

92. Wright, 16; Cott, *Bonds of Womanhood,* 140; Rosenberg, "Beauty, the Beast, and the Militant Woman," 567; Stansell, *City of Women,* 69.

93. Women's efforts were especially directed at women, and as they visited women in the city's prisons, they increasingly came into contact with streetwalkers and slum prostitutes. See Whiteaker, *Seduction, Prostitution, and Moral Reform,* 47.

CHAPTER 2: RADIATING RIGHTEOUS ANGER IN THE *ADVOCATE OF MORAL REFORM*

Epigraph: AMR, 1835: 10.

1. *AMR,* 1835: 10.

2. Hardesty, *Women Called to Witness,* 140.

3. Quoted in Whiteaker, *Seduction, Prostitution, and Moral Reform, 101.*

4. Rosenberg, "Beauty, the Beast, and the Militant Woman," 562.

5. Bebbington, *Dominance of Evangelicalism,* 22.

6. Hardesty, *Women Called to Witness,* 10.

7. Quoted in Fletcher, *History of Oberlin College,* 298.

8. Lorde, "The Uses of Anger," 127.

9. Deming, "On Anger," 213.

10. Grasso, *The Artistry of Anger,* 4. Italics are mine.

11. Grasso, 14–15.

12. Quoted in Ceplair, *Public Years of Sarah and Angelina* Grimké, 211. Italics are mine.

13. Grasso, *The Artistry of Anger,* 124.

14. Grasso, 51.

15. Alcott, *Little Women,* 79.

16. Grasso, *The Artistry of Anger,* 5.

17. Welter, "Cult of True Womanhood."

18. "Reflection on the State of Marriage," 104.

19. "Parental Influence," 196.

20. Child, *Mother's Book,* chapter 1.

21. Child, chapter 4.

22. Grasso, *The Artistry of Anger,* 41.

23. Walker, "Enthymemes of Anger," 359.

24. Walker, 360.

25. Grasso, *The Artistry of Anger,* 12.

26. Scheman, "Anger and the Politics of Naming," 177.

27. Walker, "Enthymemes of Anger," 364.

28. Trebbel and Zuckerman, *Magazine in America*, 8; Mott, *History of American Magazines*, vol. 1, 342.

29. Trebbel and Zuckerman, *Magazine in America*, 1.

30. Mott, *History of American Magazines*, vol. 1, 342.

31. Mott, *History of American Magazines*, vol. 2, 140–41; Trebbel and Zuckerman, *Magazine in America*, 17.

32. Mott, *History of American Magazines*, vol. 1, 165.

33. Logan, *Liberating Language*, 97; Okker, *Our Sister Editors*, 4, 9.

34. Stearns, "Reform Periodicals and Female Reformers," 678.

35. Northup, *Record of a Century*, 15.

36. Northup, 15.

37. *AMR*, 1840: 82; Rosenberg, "Beauty, the Beast, and the Militant Woman," 570.

38. Ginzberg, *Women and the Work of Benevolence*, 129–30.

39. Stearns, "Reform Periodicals and Female Reformers," 683–84. In 1841 Smith became Sarah Towne Smith Martyn after marrying her late sister's husband, Reverend Job H. Martyn. In 1845 the AFMRS's treasurer failed to record a payment. After a dispute, the treasurer was expelled, and Martyn and a few other members withdrew from the society. Sarah R. Ingraham (later Bennett) followed her as editor and the direction of the periodical changed. As I explain in chapter 5, changes in the *Advocate* also reflected the AFMRS's changing mission and methods.

40. Harris, "Women Editors in the Nineteenth Century," xxv. Harris notes that women editors "cast doubts on constructions of women's limited roles in society" and "moved woman into the realm of public commentator."

41. *AMR*, 1837: 266.

42. Harris, "Women Editors in the Nineteenth Century," xxviii.

43. Harris, xxvii.

44. *AMR*, 1837: 210.

45. *AMR*, 1840: 39.

46. Gries, *Still Life with Rhetoric*, 15.

47. Rosenberg, "Beauty, the Beast, and the Militant Woman," 578.

48. Berg, *Remembered Gate*, 201.

49. *AMR*, 1835: 1.

50. *AMR*, 1835: 1.

51. Cohen, *Murder of Helen Jewett*, 312.

52. Ritchie and Ronald, "Introduction," xxvii.

53. *AMR*, 1836: 162.

54. *AMR*, 1838: 125–26.

55. *AMR*, 1837: 253.

56. *AMR*, 1835: 3. Italics are mine.

57. Ryan, "Power of Women's Networks," 79.

58. Mattingly, *Well-Tempered Women*, 28–29.

59. Whiteaker, *Seduction, Prostitution, and Moral Reform*, 41–42.

60. Carlson, "Creative Casuistry and Feminist Consciousness," 20.

61. *AMR*, 1835: 11.

62. Quoted in Stearns, "Reform Periodicals and Female Reformers," 681.

63. *AMR*, 1836: 99–100.

64. *AMR*, 1837: 198.

65. *AMR*, 1837: 251.

66. *AMR*, 1837: 285.

67. *AMR*, 1838: 41.

68. *AMR*, 1835: 8.

69. *AMR*, 1837: 341.

70. *AMR*, 1838: 126, 138; 1837: 291.

71. *AMR*, 1836: 98.

72. *AMR*, 1835: 1.

73. *AMR*, 1837: 198.

74. Ginzberg, *Women and the Work of Benevolence*, 27.

75. Scott, *Natural Allies*, 39.

76. *AMR*, 1837: 211.

77. *AMR*, 1840: 84.

78. Campbell, *Man Cannot Speak for Her*, vol. 1, 37–48.

79. Ehrlich, *Regulating Desire*, 7.

80. Rosenberg, "Beauty, the Beast, and the Militant Woman," 564.

81. *AMR*, 1835: 2.

82. *AMR*, 1836: 98.

83. *AMR*, 1838: 16.

84. *AMR*, 1835: 13.

85. Sánchez, *Reforming the World*, 97.

86. Sánchez, 93, 116; Cohen, *Murder of Helen Jewett*, 405.

87. Samuel Richardson wrote *Pamela* (1740), Susanna Rowson wrote *Charlotte Temple* (1791), and Hannah Webster Foster wrote *The Coquette* (1797).

88. *AMR*, 1838: 145.

89. *AMR*, 1838: 145.

90. *AMR*, 1838: 146.

91. *AMR*, 1840: 78.

92. *AMR*, 1838: 62.

93. Lefkowtiz, *Rereading Sex*, 153.

94. *AMR*, 1840: 76.

95. *AMR*, 1837: 213.

96. *AMR*, 1838: 54.

97. Whiteaker, *Seduction, Prostitution, and Moral Reform*, 128.

98. *AMR*, 1837: 293.

99. *AMR*, 1840: 129.

100. *AMR*, 1837: 308.

101. *AMR*, 1837: 215.

102. *AMR*, 1837: 215.

103. *AMR*, 1840: 127.

104. *AMR*, 1840: 32.

CHAPTER 3: BEING PRESENT

Epigraph: Prior, *Walks of Usefulness*, 101.

1. Prior, *Walks of Usefulness*, 102.

2. Crowley and Hawhee, *Ancient Rhetorics for Contemporary Students*, 198.

3. de Certeau, *The Practice of Everyday Life*, 98–99, 104.

4. DeLuca, "Unruly Arguments," 9–21.

5. Stansell, *City of Women*, 69.

6. Boylan, *Origins of Women's Activism*, 21, 28; Woloch, *Women and the American Experience*, 168–70; Scott, *Natural Allies*, 14; Berg, *Remembered Gate*, 162; Ginzberg, *Women and the Work of Benevolence*, 41; Ryan, "The Power of Women's Networks" 75.

7. Lewis, "'Lectures or a Little Charity,'" 248; Donawerth, *Conversational Rhetoric*, 11.

8. Westerkamp, *Women and Religion in Early America*, 155–56; Ginzberg, *Women and the Work of Benevolence*, 43.

9. Berg, *Remembered Gate*, 166.

10. Scott, *Natural Allies*, 15; Berg, *Remembered Gate*, 170; Woloch, *Women and the American Experience*, 168–71.

11. Reynolds, "Ethos as Location," 333.

12. Hawhee, *Bodily Arts*, 16.

13. Halloran, "Aristotle's Concept of Ethos," 60.

14. LeFevre, *Invention as a Social Act*, 45.

15. Applegarth, "Genre, Location, and Mary Austin's Ethos," 43.

16. Mountford, *Gendered Pulpit*, 17.

17. Reynolds, "Ethos and Location," 325–26.

18. Prior, *Walks of Usefulness*, 46–47.

19. The New York Orphan Asylum Society was founded in 1806 by Joanna Graham Bethune and women who had been active in the Society for the Relief of Poor Widows, an organization Bethune's mother, Isabella Graham, had helped found in 1797.

Bethune and others became concerned about the plight of the children when their mothers died. See Ginzberg, *Women and the Work of Benevolence*, 39.

20. Benson, "Prior, Margaret Barrett Allen."

21. Enoch, *Refiguring Rhetorical Education*, 10.

22. Gold and Hobbs, "Introduction," 3–4.

23. Prior, *Walks of Usefulness*, 32.

24. *Anti-Slavery Convention, of American Women, 1837*; *Anti-Slavery Convention, of American Women, 1838*.

25. *Anti-Slavery Convention, of American Women, 1838*, 5–6. The 1838 convention's proceedings explained that Prior also agreed "slaveholders and their apologists are guilty before God," but she believed there was still "moral power sufficient in the church, if rightly applied, to purify it."

26. Burton, *Spiritual Literacy in John Wesley's Methodism*, 2, 9–10.

27. Prior, *Walks of Usefulness*, 15, 37, 60–61.

28. Lobody, "'That Language Might be Given Me,'" 136.

29. Lyerly, *Methodism and the Southern Mind, 1770–1810*, 103.

30. Lobody, "'That Language Might be Given Me,'" 136.

31. Lyerly, *Methodism and the Southern Mind*, 103.

32. Prior, *Walks of Usefulness*, 42. Her memoir acknowledges the benefit of this past experience traveling house-to-house in her tract districts.

33. Nord, *Faith in Reading*, 52.

34. Nord, 114; Brown, *The Word in the World*, 51.

35. "Guide to the Systematic Monthly Tract Distribution."

36. "New Instructions for Christian Efforts, in Connection with Monthly Tract Distribution."

37. "New Instructions for Christian Efforts, in Connection with Monthly Tract Distribution."

38. Whiteaker, *Seduction, Prostitution, and Moral Reform*, 128; Ginzberg, *Women and the Work of Benevolence*, 39.

39. Prior, *Walks of Usefulness*, 43; Buchanan, *Regendering Delivery*, 136. Ingraham later married and became Sarah Bennett. See *Our Golden Jubilee*, 50–51.

40. Prior, 43.

41. Benson, "Prior, Margaret Barrett Allen."

42. *AMR*, 1838: 142.

43. *AMR*, 1839: 80; 96; 191.

44. *AMR*, 1840: 83.

45. *AMR*, 1853: 31.

46. *AMR*, 1854: 166.

47. Prior, *Walks of Usefulness*, 47, 49.

48. Prior, 55–56.

49. Prior, 221.

50. Prior, 120.

51. Prior, 114.

52. Robert, *American Women in Mission*, xviii.

53. See my discussion of the AFMRS's reception room and the wardrobe it maintained in its Home for the Friendless, chapter 5.

54. Prior, *Walks of Usefulness*, 299.

55. Prior, 60.

56. Prior, 206.

57. Ginzberg, *Women and the Work of Benevolence*, 15.

58. Prior, *Walks of Usefulness*, 142–43.

59. Prior, 65.

60. Prior, 76–77.

61. Prior, 242.

62. Prior, 203.

63. Prior, 279.

64. Applegarth, "Genre, Location, and Mary Austin's Ethos," 55.

65. Prior, *Walks of Usefulness*, 107–08.

66. Prior, 206.

67. Ingraham's collaborative assistance is evident here.

68. Prior, *Walks of Usefulness*, 94–95.

69. Prior, 144,

70. Prior, *Walks of Usefulness*, 144–46.

71. Lewis, "'Lectures or a Little Charity,'" 248–49.

72. Prior, *Walks of Usefulness*, 52.

73. Mountford, *Gendered Pulpit*, 130.

74. Prior, *Walks of Usefulness*, 253.

75. Prior, 127.

76. Prior, 51.

77. Prior, 115.

78. Perelman, *The Realm of Rhetoric*, 36–37.

79. Prior, *Walks of Usefulness*, 215.

80. Bizzell, "Frances Willard, Phoebe Palmer, and the Ethos of the Methodist Woman Preacher," 396.

81. de Certeau, *The Practice of Everyday Life*, 98.

82. Stansell, *City of Women*, 2–18.

83. Prior, *Walks of Usefulness*, 162.

84. Prior, 162.

85. Lindley, *"You Have Stept out of Your Place,"* 66.

86. Applegarth, "Genre, Location, and Mary Austin's Ethos," 49.

87. DePalma, Ringer, and Webber, "(Re)Charting the (Dis)Courses of Faith and Politics," 331.

CHAPTER 4: IGNITING AUXILIARY POWER

Epigraph: *AMR*, 1839: 32.

1. Wright, *"The First of Causes to Our Sex,"* 109–18, 124.

2. See Scott, *Natural Allies*; Ginzberg, *Women and the Work of Benevolence*, and Boylan, *The Origins of Women's Activism*.

3. OED Online.

4. Nord, *Faith in Reading*, 61–88.

5. Wright, *"The First of Causes to Our Sex,"* 3.

6. McNeill and McNeill, "Webs of Interaction in Human History," 11.

7. Scott, *Natural Allies*, 12–13; n193.

8. Ginzberg, *Women and the Work of Benevolence*, 37; Boylan *Origins of Women's Activism*, 28.

9. Recognizing women's important role as moral agents, the American Anti-Slavery Society encouraged the formation of female societies. See Beth A. Salerno, *Sister Societies*, 28.

10. Woloch, *Women and the American Experience*, 169.

11. Hardesty, *Women Called to Witness*, 21.

12. Ginzberg, *Women and the Work of Benevolence*, 36; Boylan, "Women in Groups," 507.

13. *AMR*, 1837: 266.

14. *AMR*, 1838: 118.

15. *AMR*, 1838: 56.

16. Ginzberg, *Women and the Work of Benevolence*, 39–40.

17. Lindley, *"You Have Stept out of Your Place,"* 98–99; Scott, *Natural Allies*, 45.

18. Salerno, *Sister Societies*, 26.

19. Free-produce societies encouraged boycotting goods produced by slave labor.

20. Salerno, *Sister Societies*, 26–28; Scott, *Natural Allies*, 46.

21. Salerno, 24–25, 30, 35–37; Scott, 48.

22. Fletcher, *History of Oberlin College*, 290–315. Fletcher draws from the Oberlin Female Moral Reform Society's meeting minutes, which were kept from 1835 to 1859.

23. Fletcher, 302–3. Lucy Stone later gained prominence as an abolitionist and women's rights activist. Antoinette Brown Blackwell became the first American woman ordained as a minister. She was also an abolitionist and women's rights activist.

24. Daniel Wright notes the Young Ladies Domestic Seminary in Clinton, New York, and the Huron Institute in Milan, Ohio. See Wright, *"The First Causes to Our Sex,"* 62.

25. Fletcher, *History of Oberlin College*, 300.

26. In 1845 the AFMRS's treasurer failed to record a payment. After a dispute, the treasurer was expelled, and the *Advocate*'s editor, Sarah Towne Smith (Martyn), and a few other members withdrew from the society. See Stearns, "Reform Periodicals and Female Reformers," 683; *AMR*, 1846: 20.

27. Fletcher, *History of Oberlin College*, 312.

28. Quoted in Northup, *Record of a Century*, 16.

29. Quoted in Northup, 16.

30. *AMR*, 1835: 2.

31. For a more detailed geographical breakdown, see Wright, *"The First Causes to Our Sex,"* 63–70.

32. Boylan, *Origins of Women's Activism*, 214.

33. See Cohen, *Murder of Helen Jewett*, 20–25.

34. American Female Guardian Society and Home for the Friendless, *An Appeal, to the Wives, Mothers and Daughters of Our Land*, 9.

35. *AMR*, 1837: 268.

36. Ginzberg, *Women and the Work of Benevolence*, 39–40; Northup, *Record of a Century*, 22.

37. Salerno, *Sister Societies*, 15.

38. *AMR*, 1838: 6.

39. *AMR*, 1839: 32.

40. Scott, *Natural Allies*, 25.

41. *AMR*, 1839: 16.

42. *AMR*, 1839: 7.

43. *AMR*, 1837: 287.

44. *AMR*, 1837: 343.

45. *AMR*, 1840: 23.

46. Female Moral Reform Society of the City of New York, *First Annual Report*.

47. *AMR*, 1837: 295.

48. *AMR*, 1838: 7.

49. *AMR*, 1838: 143.

50. *AMR*, 1838: 151.

51. *AMR*, 1837: 270.

52. Here, I am drawing on Benedict Anderson's concept of imagined communities, whereby a widely distributed periodical can create a sense of community as individuals imagine each other reading the same text. See Anderson, *Imagined Communities*, 5.

53. *AMR*, 1839: 54.

54. *AMR*, 1839: 64.

55. *AMR*, 1837: 194. Italics are mine.

56. *AMR*, 1838: 39.

57. *AMR*, 1840: 39.

58. *AMR*, 1839: 16.

59. *AMR*, 1838: 11.

60. *AMR*, 1840: 31.

61. *AMR*, 1839: 7.

62. *AMR*, 1839: 136.

63. *AMR*, 1840: 112.

64. *AMR*, 1836: 103; 1837: 255, 280.

65. *AMR*, 1837: 346.

66. *AMR*, 1837: 266; 1840: 83; Wright, *"The First of Causes to Our Sex,"* 64.

67. *AMR*, 1837: 326.

68. *AMR*, 1837: 294, 331.

69. *AMR*, 1837: 270.

70. *AMR*, 1840: 151.

71. *AMR*, 1836: 103.

72. Wright, *"The First of Causes to Our Sex,"* 61–63; Hewitt, *Women's Activism and Social Change*, 59; *AMR*, 1837: 255, 343, 347; 1838: 22. "Mother in Israel," a traditional title of respect taken from the characterization of Deborah in the Old Testament, was used to refer to a woman considered a strong spiritual leader.

73. *AMR*, 1838: 85; 1839: 55, 95.

74. *AMR*, 1837: 343.

75. *AMR,* 1837: 255.

76. *AMR*, 1840, 15.

77. *AMR*, 1836: 103; 1837: 204; 1840: 12.

78. *AMR*, 1839: 46.

79. *AMR*, 1838: 151.

80. *AMR*, 1838: 151.

81. Scott, *Natural Allies*, 43.

82. *AMR*, 1838: 143; 1839: 110; 1840: 127.

83. *AMR*, 1838: 29.

84. *AMR*, 1838: 172–73.

85. Wright, *"The First of Causes to Our Sex,"* 64.

86. American Equal Rights Association (1866), National Woman Suffrage Association (1869), American Woman Suffrage Association (1869), National Woman Suffrage Association (1890).

87. *AMR*, 1836: 164.

88. *AMR*, 1837: 207.

89. *AMR*, 1838: 28.

90. *AMR*, 1837: 194.

91. *AMR*, 1838: 39.

92. *AMR*, 1837: 295.

93. McDowall's memoir, published in 1838, was titled *Memoir and Select Remains of the Late Rev. John R. M'Dowall: The Martyr of the Seventh Commandment, in the Nineteenth Century*. Auxiliaries in West Stockbridge, Massachusetts, and Torringford, Connecticut, for example, purchased copies of McDowall's memoirs to circulate among their members. See *AMR*, 1839: 16; 1840: 134.

94. *AMR*, 1839: 95.

95. *AMR*, 1837: 319.

96. *AMR*, 1838: 142.

97. *AMR*, 1838: 55.

98. See Buchanan, *Regendering Delivery*, 41–76; Wright, "God Sees Me," 116–33.

99. Logan, *Liberating Language*, 65.

100. *AMR*, 1838: 11; 1839: 47, 191.

101. *AMR*, 1838, 11.

102. *AMR*, 1838: 22.

103. *AMR*, 1838: 166.

104. *AMR*, 1837: 327; 1838: 28; 1840: 15.

105. *AMR*, 1840: 15.

106. *AMR*, 1837: 343.

107. Mrs. John Fuller, Boston; Miss Mary Parker, Boston; Miss Sarah G. Buffum, Fall River, Massachusetts; Mrs. Storrs, Utica, New York; Mrs. Margaret Dye, New York; and Mrs. Margaret Prior, New York. See *AMR*, 1838: 85; *Anti-Slavery Convention of American Women*, Proceedings, 1837.

108. Salerno, *Sister Societies*, 50–54.

109. *AMR*, 1838: 36.

110. Wright, "*The First of Causes to Our Sex*," 14.

111. *AMR*, 1838: 85.

112. *AMR*, 1840: 176.

113. *AMR*, 1838: 184.

114. Salerno, *Sister Societies*, 54–57.

115. *AMR*, 1840: 141; Wright, "*The First of Causes to Our Sex*," 64–65.

116. *AMR*, 1838: 86; 1839: 53. The invitation to the 1839 convention made a plea for delegates to come to convention to learn the most practical methods of petitioning.

117. Zaeske, "Signatures of Citizenship," 155.

118. *AMR*, 1840: 168.

119. Zaeske, "Signatures of Citizenship," 152, 155–56.

120. Salerno, *Sister Societies*, 22–23; Zaeske, "Signatures of Citizenship."

121. *AMR*, 1841: 156.

122. *AMR*, 1839: 159.

123. *AMR*, 1839: 159.

124. *AMR*, 1839: 63; 1840: 83.

125. *AMR*, 1840: 83.

126. *AMR*, 1838: 173.

127. *AMR*, 1848: 83.

128. *AMR*, 1848: 53; Wright, *"The First of Causes to Our Sex,"* 150, 154–55; White-aker, *Seduction, Prostitution, and Moral Reform*, 143–44. The laws in Pennsylvania and Michigan appear to have passed without any concerted petition drives by AFMRS auxiliaries.

CHAPTER 5: ESTABLISHING AN INSTITUTION

Epigraph: *AMR*, 1846: 83.

1. Northup, *Record of a Century*, 32–33.

2. *AMR*, 1846: 189.

3. Ann Berthoff describes the "lively" dialectic involved in naming and defining, and Sharon Crowley asserts that naming, which is a way of drawing distinctions and boundaries, is "never disinterested." See Berthoff, *Forming, Thinking, Writing*, 63–70; Crowley, "Afterword," 363.

4. Scott, *Natural Allies*, 25.

5. Ginzberg, *Women and the Work of Benevolence*, 101, 124.

6. *AMR*, 1848: 81.

7. Northup, *Record of a Century*, 28–29.

8. Griffin, "The Rhetoric of Historical Movements," 186.

9. See Lynch, "Institution and Imprimatur"; Bean, "'A Complicated and Frustrating Dance'"; Ianetta, "If Aristotle Ran the Writing Center."

10. Ratcliffe, "Review," 613–14.

11. Dickson, "Reading Maternity Materially," 298.

12. Burke, *Rhetoric of Motives*, 172.

13. Mountford, "On Gender and Rhetorical Space," 49.

14. Blair, "Contemporary U.S. Memorial Sites," 34–36.

15. Northup, *Record of a Century*, 28; *Our Golden Jubilee*, 22–25.

16. *AMR*, 1846: i.

17. *AMR*, 1846: i. Italics in the original.

18. Northup, *Record of a Century*, 32–33.

19. *AMR*, 1846: 6. Italics in the original.

20. *AMR*, 1846: 6. Italics are mine.

21. *AMR*, 1846: 81–82.

22. *AMR*, 1846: 37.

23. Pearce, "Feminization of Poverty," 28.

24. *AMR*, 1846: 116, 155.

25. *AMR*, 1846: 62, 69–70.

26. *AMR*, 1846: 70, 115.

27. *AMR*, 1846: 155.

28. *AMR*, 1846: 62.

29. *AMR*, 1846: 85.

30. *AMR*, 1846: 86.

31. *AMR*, 1846: i; Ginzberg, *Women and the Work of Benevolence*, 127.

32. Northup, *Record of a Century*, 31; *AMR*, 1846: 81.

33. *AMR*, 1846: 155.

34. See Shaver, *Beyond the Pulpit*, 76.

35. *AMR*, 1848: 81.

36. *AMR*, 1846: 155.

37. *AMR*, 1848: 23.

38. *AMR*, 1846: 183.

39. *AMR*, 1848: 81–82; Northup, *Record of a Century*, 30–35.

40. *AMR*, 1848: 98.

41. *AMR*, 1852: 31. Dismissed generally means placed. However, individuals could leave the home voluntarily, or they could be dismissed if they do not abide by the rules, but these appear to be infrequent occurrences.

42. *AMR*, 1852: 111; 1853: 47, 63, 95; 1854: 143.

43. *AMR*, 1848: 109.

44. *AMR*, 1852: 111.

45. *AMR*, 1853: 190.

46. *AMR*, 1848: 52, 60; 1852: 30; 1853: 126; 1854: 94.

47. *AMR*, 1853: 85.

48. See Scott, *Natural Allies*, 14; Gilman, "From Widowhood to Wickedness"; Ryan, *The Grammar of Good Intentions*, 21.

49. *AMR*, 1848: 182.

50. *AMR*, 1852: 140.

51. *AMR*, 1852: 6.

52. *AMR*, 1852: 131.

53. *AMR*, 1854: 174.

54. *AMR*, 1854: 174.

55. *AMR*, 1852: 81; 1854: 119.

56. *AMR*, 1848: 86; 1852: 94; 1854: 46, 47.

57. *AMR*, 1852: 111, 173; 1853: 112, 189; 1854: 191.

58. *AMR*, 1852: 7.

59. *AMR*, 1852: 81; 1853: 81.

60. *AMR*, 1848: 27.

61. *AMR*, 1854: 31.

62. *AMR*, 1853: 173.

63. *AMR*, 1848: 82; 189; 1852: 82.

64. *AMR*, 1852: 82; 1854: 79.

65. *AMR*, 1852: 71.

66. The home did become a permanent foster home much later.

67. *AMR*, 1853: 48.

68. *AMR*, 1852: 141.

69. *AMR*, 1852: 175.

70. *AMR*, 1852: 174–175; 1853: 143.

71. Mintz, *Huck's Raft*, 2–3.

72. *AMR*, 1852: 8.

73. *AMR*, 1852: 140.

74. *AMR*, 1854: 70–71.

75. *AMR*, 1854: 125.

76. *AMR*, 1848: 61.

77. *AMR*, 1848: 87.

78. *AMR*, 1854: 125.

79. Holt, *The Orphan Trains*, 21–23.

80. While this is the most commonly cited number, this is little more than a guess. See O'Connor, *Orphan Trains*, 149.

81. Riley, *Orphan Train Riders*.

82. In what is referred to as a partial list, Connie DiPasquale lists ninety-seven New York City–area institutions that sent orphans west on orphan trains. See DiPasquale, "A Partial List of Institutions that Orphan Train Children Came From."

83. O'Connor, *Orphan Trains*, 94–96.

84. Holt, *The Orphan Trains*, 26.

85. For a discussion of factors that contributed to the orphan trains, see Holt, 9–40.

86. This requirement is dropped later in the nineteenth century when the home began to operate as a foster home.

87. O'Connor, *Orphan Trains*, 149–51; Northup, *Record of a Century*, 93.

88. O'Connor, 103; 171–73.

89. O'Connor, 140.

90. *Our Golden Jubilee*, 55.

91. *Our Golden Jubilee*, 55.

92. *AMR*, 1853: 175.

93. *AMR*, 1853: 175.

94. *AMR*, 1854: 6.

95. *AMR*, 1854: 12.

96. *AMR*, 1854: 30.

97. O'Connor, *Orphan Trains*, xvii.

98. Stansell, "Women, Children, and the Uses of the Streets," 321.

99. *AMR*, 1853: 127; 1852: 188; 1854: 47.

100. *AMR*, 1854: 14.

101. *AMR*, 1854: 190.

102. *AMR*, 1848: 174.

103. *AMR*, 1854: 46.

104. *AMR*, 1853: 95.

105. *AMR*, 1853: 111.

106. Hobson, *Uneasy Virtue*, 94–95; Hill, *Their Sisters' Keepers*, 82; Gilfoyle, *City of Eros*, 59; Penny, *The Employments of Women*.

107. *AMR*, 1848: 21; 1852: 141; 1853: 75, 174.

108. *AMR*, 1853: 63. Italics are mine.

109. *AMR*, 1848: 21; 1852: 135. Italics are mine.

110. *AMR*, 1848: 166.

111. *AMR*, 1848: 166.

112. *AMR*, 1853: 159.

113. *AMR*, 1854: 20.

114. *AMR*, 1852: 77; 1853: 174.

115. Rosenberg, "Beauty, the Beast, and the Militant Woman," 581; *AMR*, 1850: 10.

116. *AMR*, 1852: 77.

117. *AMR*, 1854: 82.

118. Burrows and Wallace, *Gotham*, 780.

119. The New York–area institutions that sent orphans west on orphan trains include the New York House of Refuge and the New York Juvenile Asylum. See DiPasquale, "A Partial List of Institutions."

120. *AMR*, 1854: 21.

121. *AMR*, 1854: 83.

122. Burrows and Wallace, *Gotham*, 780.

123. Burrows and Wallace, 532; Rorabaugh, *The Alcoholic Republic*, 17; Mattingly, *Well-Tempered Women*, 11, 14; Fletcher, *A History of Oberlin College*, 14.

124. *AMR*, 1848: 14.

125. *AMR*, 1854: 4.

126. *AMR*, 1853: 30.

127. *AMR*, 1854: 14.

128. *AMR*, 1848: 99, 174–75; 1852: 141.

129. *AMR*, 1853: 191.

130. Amelia Bloomer became widely known through her temperance periodical, the *Lily* (1849). Susan B. Anthony got her activist start within the Daughters of Temperance. Antoinette Brown Blackwell, Elizabeth Cady Stanton, Mary C. Vaughn,

Lucy Stone, and Francis Dana Gage were all active in antebellum women's temperance organizations. Additionally, Amelia Bloomer, Lydia F. Fowler, and Clarina Howard Nichols were prominent temperance lecturers who also persuasively advocated equal rights for women. See Mattingly, *Well-Tempered Women*, 23.

131. Mattingly, 23–38.

132. *AMR*, 1854: 144.

133. *AMR*, 1854: 45.

134. *AMR*, 1854: 79.

135. *AMR*, 1854: 93.

136. *AMR*, 1854: 83.

137. *AMR*, 1854: 45, 47.

138. Northup, *Record of a Century*, 37.

139. Northup, 38; *Our Golden Jubilee*, 47–48. Normal colleges provided a two-year program that trained high school graduates to be teachers, usually for primary schools.

140. "Our City Charities"; *Our Golden Jubilee*, 36, 50–56; Northup, *Record of a Century*, 83; Rosenberg, "Beauty, the Beast, and the Militant Woman," 562–63, n1.

141. Northup, 96.

EPILOGUE: UNRESOLVED

Epigraph: Stanton, Anthony, and Gage, *History of Woman Suffrage*, 72.

1. Sandberg, *Lean In*, 19. Sandberg later helped launch a Ban Bossy campaign to make people aware of how characterizations such as these can damage girls' confidence and dissuade girls from assuming leadership roles.

2. Heilman and Okimoto, "Why Are Women Penalized for Success at Male Tasks?" 81–92.

3. "Facts about Domestic Violence and Physical Abuse."

4. "Statistics about Sexual Violence."

5. Adichie, *We Should All Be Feminists*, 32–33.

Bibliography

Adichie, Chimamanda Ngozi. *We Should All Be Feminists*. New York: Anchor Books, 2015.

Advocate of Moral Reform, 1835–1846. New York: American Female Moral Reform Society.

Advocate of Moral Reform and Family Guardian, 1847–1854. New York: American Female Guardian Society.

Advocate and Family Guardian, 1855–1941. New York: American Female Guardian Society.

Alcott, Louisa May. *Little Women*. New York: Penguin, [1868] 1989.

American Female Guardian Society and Home for the Friendless. New York. *An Appeal, to the Wives, Mothers and Daughters of Our Land, in the City and the Country, Earnestly and Affectionately Presented, by the Ladies of the New York Female Moral Reform Society*. New York: H. R. Piercy, 1836. Nineteenth Century Collections Online. Accessed September 18, 2017. http://tinyurl.galegroup.com/tinyurl/5CjYi3.

Anti-Slavery Convention, of American Women, held in the City of New-York, May 9th, 10th, 11th, and 12th, 1837. Proceedings. New York: William S. Dorr, 1837.

Anti-Slavery Convention, of American Women, held in the City of Philadelphia, May 15th, 16th, 17th and 18th, 1838. Proceedings. Philadelphia: Merrihew and Gunn, 1838.

Anderson, Benedict. *Imagined Communities: Reflections on the Origin and Spread of Nationalism*. London: Verso, 1991.

Applegarth, Risa. "Genre, Location, and Mary Austin's Ethos." *Rhetoric Society Quarterly* 41, no. 1 (2011): 41–63.

Bean, Hamilton. "'A Complicated and Frustrating Dance': National Security Reform, the Limits of 'Parrhesia,' and the Case of the 9/11 Families." *Rhetoric and Public Affairs* 12, no. 3 (2009): 429–59.

Bebbington, David W. *The Dominance of Evangelicalism: The Age of Spurgeon and Moody.* Downers Grove, IL: InterVarsity Press, 2005.

Becker, Dorothy G. "Isabella Graham and Joanna Bethune: Trailblazers of Organized Women's Benevolence." *Social Service Review* 61, no. 2 (1987): 319–36.

Benson, Mary Sumner. "Prior, Margaret Barrett Allen (1771–Apr. 7, 1842)." In *Notable American Women: 1607–1950.* Cambridge, MA: Harvard University Press, 1971.

Berg, Barbara. *The Remembered Gate Origins of American Feminism: The Woman and the City 1800–1860.* Oxford: Oxford University Press, 1978.

Berthoff, Ann E. *Forming, Thinking, Writing: The Composing Imagination.* Montclair, NJ: Boynton/Cook, 1982.

Bizzell, Patricia. "Frances Willard, Phoebe Palmer, and the Ethos of the Methodist Woman Preacher." *Rhetoric Society Quarterly* 36, no. 4 (2006): 377–98.

Blair, Carole. "Contemporary U.S. Memorial Sites as Examples of Rhetoric's Materiality." In *Rhetorical Bodies*, edited by Jack Selzer and Sharon Crowley, 16–57. Madison: University of Wisconsin Press, 1999.

Boylan, Anne M. *The Origins of Women's Activism: New York and Boston, 1797–1840.* Chapel Hill: University of North Carolina Press, 2002.

Boylan, Anne M. "Women in Groups: An Analysis of Women's Benevolent Organizations in New York and Boston, 1797–1840." *Journal of American History* 71, no. 3 (1984): 497–523.

Brown, Candy Gunther. *The Word in the World: Evangelical Writing, Publishing, and Reading in America, 1789–1880.* Chapel Hill: University of North Carolina Press, 2004.

Buchanan, Lindal. *Regendering Delivery: The Fifth Canon and Antebellum Women Rhetors.* Carbondale: Southern Illinois University Press, 2005.

Burke, Kenneth. *A Rhetoric of Motives.* Berkeley: University of California Press, 1969.

Burrows, Edwin G., and Mike Wallace. *Gotham: A History of New York City to 1898.* New York: Oxford University Press, 1999.

Burton, Vicki Tolar. *Spiritual Literacy in John Wesley's Methodism: Reading, Writing, and Speaking to Believe.* Waco, TX: Baylor University Press, 2008.

Campbell, Karlyn Kohrs, ed. *Man Cannot Speak for Her.* Vol. 1. New York: Greenwood, 1989.

Carlson, A. Cheree. "Creative Casuistry and Feminist Consciousness: The Rhetoric of Moral Reform." *Quarterly Journal of Speech* 78, no. 1 (1992): 16–32.

Ceplair, Larry. *The Public Years of Sarah and Angelina Grimké: Selected Writings, 1835–1839.* New York: Columbia University Press, 1989.

Child, Lydia Maria, *The Mother's Book*, 2nd ed. Boston: Carter and Hendee, 1831. Nineteenth Century Collections Online: Women's Transnational Networks.

Christian Advocate (New York), 1826–1832. American Periodical Series II, reels 1749–1750. Ann Arbor, MI: University Microfilm.

Cohen, Patricia Cline. *The Murder of Helen Jewett: The Life and Death of a Prostitute in Nineteenth-Century New York.* New York: Vintage, 1999.

Cott, Nancy F. *The Bonds of Womanhood: "Woman's Sphere" in New England, 1780–1835.* New Haven, CT: Yale University Press, 1977.

Crowley, Sharon. "Afterword: The Material of Rhetoric." In *Rhetorical Bodies*, edited by Jack Selzer and Sharon Crowley, 357–66. Madison: University of Wisconsin Press, 1999.

Crowley, Sharon, and Debra Hawhee. *Ancient Rhetorics for Contemporary Students*, 2nd ed. Boston: Allyn and Bacon, 1999.

de Certeau, Michel. *The Practice of Everyday Life*. Translated by Steven Rendall. Berkeley: University of California Press, 1984.

DeLuca, Kevin Michael. "Unruly Arguments: The Body Rhetoric of Earth First!" *Argumentation and Advocacy* 36, no. 1 (1999) 9–21.

Deming, Barbara. "On Anger." In *We are All Part of One Another: A Barbara Deming Reader*, edited by Jane Meyerding with a foreword by Barbara Smith, 207–17. Philadelphia: New Society Publishers, 1984.

DePalma, Michael-John, Jeffrey M. Ringer, and Jim Webber. "(Re)Charting the (Dis)Courses of Faith and Politics, or Rhetoric and Democracy in the Burkean Barnyard." *Rhetoric Society Quarterly* 38, no. 3 (2008): 311–34.

Dickson, Barbara. "Reading Maternity Materially: The Case of Demi Moore." In *Rhetorical Bodies*, edited by Jack Selzer and Sharon Crowley, 297–313. University of Wisconsin Press, 1999.

DiPasquale, Connie. "A Partial List of Institutions that Orphan Train Children Came From," The Kansas Collection. Accessed September 26, 2016. http://www.kancoll.org/articles/orphans/or_homes.htm.

Donawerth, Jane. *Conversational Rhetoric: The Rise and Fall of a Women's Tradition, 1600–1900*. Carbondale: Southern Illinois University Press, 2012.

Eastman, Carolyn. "'A Vapour Which Appears but for a Moment'": Oratory and Elocution for Girls during the Early American Republic." In *Rhetoric, History, and Women's Rhetorical Education: American Women Learn to Speak*, edited by David Gold and Catherine L. Hobbs, 38–59. New York: Routledge, 2013.

Ehrlich, J. Shoshanna. *Regulating Desire: From the Virtuous Maiden to the Purity Princess*. Albany: State University of New York Press, 2014.

Eldred, Janet Carey, and Peter Mortensen. "'A Few Patchwork Opinions': Piecing Together Narratives of U.S. Girls' Early National Schooling." In *Girls and Literacy in America: Historical Perspectives to the Present*, edited by Jane Greer, 23–50. Santa Barbara, CA: ABC CLIO, 2003.

Ellington, George. *The Women of New York or the Under-world of the Great City*. New York: Arno, [1869] 1972.

Ely, E. S. *Visits of Mercy Being the Journal of the Stated Preacher to the Hospital and Almshouse, in the City of New-York, 1811*. London: William and Son, 1813.

Enoch, Jessica. *Refiguring Rhetorical Education: Women Teaching African American, Native American, and Chicano/a Students, 1865–1911*. Carbondale: Southern Illinois University Press, 2008.

Enoch, Jessica. "Releasing Hold: Feminist Historiography without the Tradition." In *Theorizing Histories of Rhetoric*, edited by Michelle Ballif, 58–73. Carbondale: Southern Illinois University Press, 2013.

"Facts about Domestic Violence and Physical Abuse." NCADV. 2015. www.ncadv.org.

Female Benevolent Society of the City of New York. *First Annual Report of the Female Benevolent Society of the City of New York*. New York: West and Trow, 1834.

Female Moral Reform Society of the City of New York. *First Annual Report of the Female Moral Reform Society of New York with Constitution, List of Officers, Names of Auxiliaries, &c.*, 1835. Darlington Library Texts. Accessed March 6, 2014. http://digital library.pitt.edu.

Fletcher, Holly Berkley. *Gender and the American Temperance Movement of the Nineteenth Century.* New York: Routledge, 2008.

Fletcher, Robert Samuel. *A History of Oberlin College: From its Foundation through the Civil War.* Vol. 1. Oberlin, OH: Oberlin College, 1943.

Gere, Anne Ruggles. *Intimate Practices: Literacy and Cultural Work in U.S. Women's Clubs, 1880–1920.* Urbana: University of Illinois Press, 1997.

Gilfoyle, Timothy J. *City of Eros: New York City, Prostitution, and the Commercialization of Sex, 1790–1920.* New York: W. W. Norton, 1992.

Gilman, Amy. "From Widowhood to Wickedness: The Politics of Class and Gender in New York City Private Charity, 1799–1860." *History of Education Quarterly* 24, no. 1 (1984): 59–74.

Ginzberg, Lori D. *Women and the Work of Benevolence: Morality, Politics, and Class in the Nineteenth-Century United States.* New Haven, CT: Yale University Press, 1990.

Gold, David and Catherine L. Hobbs. "Introduction: American Women Learn to Speak—New Forms of Inquiry into Women's Rhetorics." In *Rhetoric, History, and Women's Rhetorical Education: American Women Learn to Speak*, edited by David Gold and Catherine L. Hobbs, 1–18. New York: Routledge, 2013.

Grasso, Linda M. *The Artistry of Anger: Black and White Women's Literature in America, 1820–1860.* Chapel Hill: University of North Carolina Press, 2002.

Gries, Laurie E. *Still Life with Rhetoric: A New Materialist Approach for Visual Rhetorics.* Boulder: University Press of Colorado, 2015.

Griffin, Leland M. "The Rhetoric of Historical Movements." *Quarterly Journal of Speech* 38, no. 2 (1952): 184–88.

"Guide to the Systematic Monthly Tract Distribution." *Religious Intelligencer*, December 25, 1830, 15.

Halloran, Michael. "Aristotle's Concept of Ethos, Or If Not His Somebody Else's." *Rhetoric Review* 1, no. 1 (1982): 58–63.

Hardesty, Nancy A. *Women Called to Witness: Evangelical Feminism in the Nineteenth Century.* 2nd ed. Knoxville: University of Tennessee Press, 1999.

Harris, Sharon. "Women Editors in the Nineteenth Century." In *Blue Pencils Hidden Hands: Women Editing Periodicals, 1830–1910*, edited by Sharon M. Harris, xxv–xxxvi. Boston: Northeastern University Press, 2004.

Hawhee, Debra. *Bodily Arts: Rhetoric and Athletics in Ancient Greece.* Austin: University of Texas Press, 2004.

Heilman, Madeline E., and Tyler G. Okimoto. "Why Are Women Penalized for Success at Male Tasks?: The Implied Communality Deficit." *Journal of Applied Psychology* 92, no. 1 (2007): 81–92.

Hewitt, Nancy A. *Women's Activism and Social Change.* Ithaca, NY: Cornell University Press, 1984.

Hill, Marilynn Wood. *Their Sisters' Keepers: Prostitution in New York City, 1830–1870.* Berkeley: University of California Press, 1993.

Hobson, Barbara Meil. *Uneasy Virtue: The Politics of Prostitution and the American Reform Tradition.* New York: Basic Books, 1987.

Holt, Marilyn Irvin. *The Orphan Trains: Placing Out in America.* Lincoln: University of Nebraska Press, 1992.

Horowitz, Helen Lefkowitz. *Rereading Sex: Battles over Sexual Knowledge and Suppression in Nineteenth-Century America.* New York: Knopf, 2002.

Ianetta, Melissa. "If Aristotle Ran the Writing Center: Classical Rhetoric and Writing Center Administration." *Writing Center Journal* 24, no. 2 (2004): 37–59.

Johnson, Nan. *Gender and Rhetorical Space in American Life, 1866–1910.* Carbondale: Southern Illinois University Press, 2002.

Latham, Sean and Robert Scholes, "The Rise of Periodical Studies," *PMLA* 121, no. 2 (2006): 517–31.

LeFevre, Karen Burke. *Invention as a Social Act.* Carbondale: Southern Illinois University Press, 1987.

Lewis, Paul. "'Lectures or a Little Charity': Poor Visits in Antebellum Literature and Culture." *New England Quarterly* 7, no. 2 (2000): 246–73.

Lindley, Susan Hill. *"You Have Stept out of Your Place": A History of Women and Religion in America.* Louisville: Westminster, 1996.

Lobody, Diane H. "'That Language Might Be Given Me': Women's Experience in Early Methodism." In *Perspectives on American Methodism: Interpretive Essays,* edited by Russell E. Richey, Kenneth E. Rowe, and Jean Miller Schmidt, 127–44. New York: Abingdon, 1993.

Logan, Shirley Wilson. *Liberating Language: Sites of Rhetorical Education in Nineteenth-Century Black America.* Carbondale: Southern Illinois University Press, 2008.

Logan, Shirley Wilson. *"We Are Coming": The Persuasive Discourse of Nineteenth-Century Black Women.* Carbondale: Southern Illinois University Press, 1995.

Lorde, Audre. "The Uses of Anger: Women Responding to Racism." In *Sister Outsider: Essays and Speeches,* 124–33. Trumansburg, NY: Crossing Press, 1984.

Lyerly, Cynthia Lynn. *Methodism and the Southern Mind, 1770–1810.* New York: Oxford University Press, 1998.

Lynch, John. "Institution and Imprimatur: Institutional Rhetoric and the Failure of the Catholic Church's Pastoral Letter on Homosexuality." *Rhetoric and Public Affairs* 8, no. 3 (2005): 383–403.

MacHaffie, Barbara J. *Her Story: Women in Christian Tradition,* 2nd ed. Minneapolis: Fortress Press, 2006.

Magdalen Report, First Annual Report of the Executive Committee of the N.Y. Magdalen Society, Instituted January 1, 1830. New York: s.n., 1831.

Magdalen Society of New York. *Constitution and By Laws.* New York: J. Seymour, 1812.

Magdalen Society of New York. *First Annual Report of the Magdalen Society of New York.* New York: J. Seymour, 1813.

Magdalen Society of New York. *Second Annual Report of the Magdalen Society of New York.* New York: J. Seymour, 1814.

Magdalen Society of New York. *Third Annual Report of the Magdalen Society of New-York.* New York: s.n., 1815.

Mattingly, Carol. *Well-Tempered Women: Nineteenth-Century Temperance Rhetoric.* Carbondale: Southern Illinois University Press, 1998.

McDowall, John Robert. *Magdalen Facts.* New York: s.n., 1832.

McDowall, John Robert. *Memoir and Select Remains of the Late Rev. John R. M'Dowall: The Martyr of the Seventh Commandment, in the Nineteenth Century*. New York: Leavitt, Lord, 1838.

McDowall's Journal. John R. McDowall, New York, 1833–1834.

McNeill, J. R., and William H. McNeill. "Webs of Interaction in Human History." *Historically Speaking* 4, no. 2 (2002): 11–12.

Mintz, Steven. *Huck's Raft: A History of American Childhood*. Cambridge, MA: Belknap Press, 2004.

Mott, Frank Luther. *A History of American Magazines*, 5 vols. Cambridge, MA: Harvard University Press, 1938–68.

Mountford, Roxanne. "On Gender and Rhetorical Space." *Rhetoric Society Quarterly* 31, no. 1 (2001): 41–71.

Mountford, Roxanne. *The Gendered Pulpit: Preaching in American Protestant Spaces*. Carbondale: Southern Illinois University Press, 2003.

"New Instructions for Christian Efforts, in Connection with Monthly Tract Distribution." *New York Observer and Chronicle*, January 12, 1833, 11. American Periodicals Online.

Nord, David Paul. *Faith in Reading: Religious Publishing and the Birth of Mass Media in America*. Oxford: Oxford University Press, 2004.

Northup, Flora L. *The Record of a Century: 1834–1934*. New York: American Female Guardian Society and Home for the Friendless, 1934.

O'Connor, Stephen. *Orphan Trains: The Story of Charles Loring Brace and the Children He Saved and Failed*. Chicago: University of Chicago Press, 2001.

OED Online, "Auxiliary, Adj. and N." Accessed August 28, 2013. http://www.oed.com.

Okker, Patricia. *Our Sister Editors: Sarah J. Hale and the Tradition of Nineteenth-Century American Women Editors*. Athens: University of Georgia Press, 1995.

"Our City Charities: The Home for the Friendless." *New York Times*, July 20, 1860.

Our Golden Jubilee: A Retrospect of the American Female Guardian Society and Home for the Friendless from 1834 to 1884. New York: American Female Guardian Society, 1884.

"Parental Influence." *Christian Advocate*, August 5, 1831, Parent's Department.

Pearce, Diane. "The Feminization of Poverty: Women, Work, and Welfare." *Urban and Social Change Review* 11, no. 1/2 (1978): 28–36.

Penny, Virginia. *The Employments of Women: A Cyclopedia of Woman's Work*. Boston: Walker, Wise and Company, 1863.

Perelman, Chaim. *The Realm of Rhetoric*. Translated by William Kluback. Notre Dame, IN: University of Notre Dame Press, 1982.

Prior, Margaret. *Walks of Usefulness, Or Reminiscences of Mrs. Margaret Prior*. Edited by Sarah R. Ingraham. New York: Garland, [1843] 1987.

Ratcliffe, Krista. "Review: Material Matters: Bodies and Rhetoric." *College English* 64, no. 5 (2002): 613–23.

"Reflection on the State of Marriage." *Christian Advocate*, March 3, 1827.

Reynolds, Nedra. "Ethos as Location: New Sites for Understanding Discursive Authority." *Rhetoric Review* 11, no. 2 (1993): 325–38.

Richardson, James F. *The New York Police; Colonial Times to 1901*. Oxford: Oxford University Press, 1970.

Richmond, J. F. *New York and Its Institutions, 1609–1872*. New York: E. B. Treat, 1872.

Riley, Tom. *Orphan Train Riders: A Brief History of the Orphan Trail Era (1854–1929) with Entrance Records from the American Female Guardian Society's Home for the Friendless in New York*. Vol. 1. Berwyn Heights, MD: Heritage, 2014.

Ritchie, Joy, and Kate Ronald. "Introduction: A Gathering of Rhetorics." In *Available Means: An Anthology of Women's Rhetoric(s)*, edited by Joy Ritchie and Kate Ronald, xv–xxxi. Pittsburgh: University of Pittsburgh Press, 2001.

Robert, Dana L. *American Women in Mission: A Social History of Their Thought and Practice*. Macon, GA: Mercer University Press, 1996.

Rorabaugh, W. J. *The Alcoholic Republic: An American Tradition*. New York: Oxford University Press, 1979.

Rosenberg, Carroll Smith. "Beauty, the Beast, and the Militant Woman: A Case Study in Sex Roles and Social Stress in Jacksonian America." *American Quarterly* 23, no. 4 (1971): 562–84.

Royster, Jacqueline Jones, and Gesa E. Kirsch. *Feminist Rhetorical Practices: New Horizons for Rhetoric, Composition, and Literacy Studies*. Carbondale: Southern Illinois University Press, 2012.

Royster, Jacqueline Jones. *Traces of a Stream: Literacy and Social Change among African American Women*. Pittsburgh: University of Pittsburgh Press, 2000.

Ryan, Mary P. "The Power of Women's Networks: A Case Study of Female Moral Reform in Antebellum America." *Feminist Studies* 5, no. 1 (1979): 66–85.

Ryan, Susan M. *The Grammar of Good Intentions: Race and the Antebellum Culture of Benevolence*. Ithaca, NY: Cornell University Press, 2005.

Salerno, Beth A. *Sister Societies: Women's Antislavery Organizations in Antebellum America*. DeKalb: North Illinois University Press, 2005.

Sánchez, María Carla. *Reforming the World: Social Activism and the Problem of Fiction in Nineteenth-Century America*. Iowa City: University of Iowa Press, 2009.

Sandberg, Sheryl. *Lean In: Women, Work, and the Will to Lead*. New York: Knopf, 2013.

Sanger, William W. *The History of Prostitution*. New York: Arno, [1859] 1972.

Scheman, Naomi. "Anger and the Politics of Naming." In *Women and Language in Literature and Society*, edited by Sally McConnell-Ginet, Ruth Borker, and Nelly Furman, 174–87. New York: Praeger, 1980.

Scott, Anne Firor. *Natural Allies: Women's Associations in American History*. Chicago: University of Illinois Press, 1991.

Selzer, Jack, and Sharon Crowley, eds. *Rhetorical Bodies*. Madison: University of Wisconsin Press, 1999.

Sharer, Wendy B. *Voice and Vote: Women's Organizations and Political Literacy, 1915–1930*. Carbondale: Southern Illinois University Press, 2004.

Shaver, Lisa J. *Beyond the Pulpit: Women's Rhetorical Roles in the Antebellum Religious Press*. Pittsburgh: University of Pittsburgh Press, 2012.

Stansell, Christine. *City of Women: Sex and Class in New York, 1789–1860*. New York: Knopf, 1986.

Stansell, Christine. "Women, Children, and the Uses of the Streets: Class and Gender Conflict in New York City, 1850–1860." *Feminist Studies* 8, no. 2 (1982): 309–35.

Stanton, Elizabeth Cady, Susan B. Anthony, and Matilda Joslyn Gage, eds. *History of Woman Suffrage*. Vol. 1, 1848–1861. New York: Fowler and Wells, 1881.

"Statistics about Sexual Violence," National Sexual Violence Resource Center. Accessed December 14, 2016. http://www.nsvrc.org/sites/default/files/publications_nsvrc_factsheet_media -packet_statistics-about-sexual-violence_0.pdf.

Stearns, Bertha-Monica. "Reform Periodicals and Female Reformers, 1830–1860." *American Historical Review* 37, no. 4 (1932): 678–99.

Teeters, Negley K. "The Early Days of the Magdalen Society of Philadelphia." *Social Service Review* 30, no. 2 (1956): 158–67.

"Tract Distribution." *Christian Advocate*, April 29, 1836, 10, 36.

Trebbel, John, and Mary Ellen Zuckerman. *The Magazine in America, 1741–1990*. New York: Oxford University Press, 1991.

Walker, Jeffrey. "Enthymemes of Anger in Cicero and Thomas Payne." In *Constructing Rhetorical Education*, edited by Marie Secor and Davida Charney, 357–81. Carbondale: Southern Illinois University Press, 1992.

Welter, Barbara. "The Cult of True Womanhood: 1820–1860." *American Quarterly* 18, no. 2 (1966): 151–74.

Westerkamp, Marilyn J. *Women and Religion in Early America, 1600–1850*. London: Routledge, 1999.

Woloch, Nancy. *Women and the American Experience*. 4th ed. Boston: McGraw-Hill, 2006.

Whiteaker, Larry. *Seduction, Prostitution, and Moral Reform in New York, 1830–1860*. New York: Garland, 1997.

Whitman, Walt. *New York Dissected: A Sheaf of Recently Discovered Newspaper Articles by the Author of Leaves of Grass*. Folcroft: Folcroft, [1936] 1972.

Wright, Daniel S. *"The First of Causes to Our Sex": The Female Moral Reform Movement in the Antebellum Northeast, 1834–1848*. New York: Routledge, 2006.

Wright, Elizabethada. "'God Sees Me'; Surveillance and Oratorical Training at Nineteenth-Century St. Mary-of-the-Woods in Indiana." In *Rhetoric, History, and Women's Oratorical Education: American Women Learn to Speak*, edited by David Gold and Catherine L. Hobbs, 116–33. New York: Routledge, 2013.

Zaeske, Susan. *Signatures of Citizenship: Petitioning, Antislavery, and Women's Political Identity*. Chapel Hill: University of North Carolina Press, 2003.

Zaeske, Susan. "Signatures of Citizenship: The Rhetoric of Women's Antislavery Petitions." *Quarterly Journal of Speech* 88, no. 2 (2002): 147–68.

Index